Understanding The Japanese Mind

June 26th 1935
WIEN IX., BERGGASSE 19

Dear Mr. Ohtski

I do get your Journal regularly and received your book, the title of which you translate as "Psychyanalytische Miszellaneen", Idealized in both cases by the impossibility of making out what ought to be a very interesting content.

What you write about the resistance in your country is no surprise to me; it is just as we may have expected, but I am sure you have, given psychoanalysis a solid foundation in Japan, which is not likely to be swept away.

I am sorry I am so old and invalid now, or I would have grasped an opportunity to come over and have a nice talk with all of my dear friends in Japan.

With kind regards
yours sincerely
Freud

LETTER FROM DOCTOR FREUD TO JAPANESE
PSYCHOANALYST MR. KENJI OHTSKI

UNDERSTANDING THE JAPANESE MIND

BY

JAMES CLARK MOLONEY,

GREENWOOD PRESS, PUBLISHERS
NEW YORK   1968

This book is
affectionately dedicated
to
Margaret
James
and
Sue Ann

It does not seem as if man could be brought by any sort of influence to change his nature into that of the ants; he will always, one imagines, defend his claim to individual freedom against the will of the multitude.

> — Sigmund Freud: *Civilization and Its Discontents*

PREFACE

It is the natural tendency, and probably the right, of every profession to regard the world through its own particular set of binoculars. Accordingly, each calling's evaluation of what it sees is apt to be regarded by the others as limited by the range of the viewer's lenses—much as the sighted onlooker would evaluate the description of the elephant made by the blind men. Yet, with the world in its present chaotic state, it behooves the serious thinker to consider well the interpretations of all commentators upon the scene.

My curiosity about the unique qualities of the Japanese was whetted by two visits I made to their islands in the 1940's; it began at the point of my acquaintance with some of my professional counterparts in Japan, but has gradually broadened and deepened to include an interest in the whole people. It would be quite understandable and justifiable for the lay reader to accuse a psychoanalyst like myself of snap-judgments, were I to have arrived at my conclusions about Japan "out-of-context." For this reason, I have endeavored to support my deductions by borrowing freely from recorded disciplines other than my own: anthropology, history, sociology, and religion.

My principal departure from the thinking of many previous writers on Japan is my conviction that its people are neither "mysterious," "inscrutable," nor "unpredictable"; but that they are, in fact, entirely reasonable, understandable, and predictable when one fully understands the restrictions which have been placed upon their behavior, individual and collective, by the traditions of the ages.

The significance of such predictability to the nations of the world today—to the United States most of all, concerned as we are with the revamping of the governmental and social systems of Japan, and even with the behavior and attitudes of the Japanese people—should be evident. Not only can one readily foresee the result of each step taken by this nation in the administrative handling of Japan through the period of the Occupation; it is also evident what must surely befall if the Japanese government should revert to its own pre-war militarist pattern, or if it should become an independent, but only partially-trained, democracy, or if, unhappily it should fall under communist domination. To be able to predict with certainty the response of the Japanese should mean that the course of policy of other nations toward Japan should be equally possible to plot.

Other professional observers are coming to regard the situation in Japan as not so simple and clear-cut as some of the early investigators into the Occupation's apparent effects have believed it to be. Closely paralleling my own conclusions are the views of such men as New York Times correspondent Lindesay Parrott, whose article, "Japan at Her Time of Decision," in the *New York Times Magazine*, April 15, 1951, should help to discourage the skeptical layman from believing that my ideas are those of a hasty viewer or an arm-chair theorist.

INTRODUCTION

"Let Mikado's empire stand
Till a thousand years, ten thousand years shall roll,
Till the sand in the brooklets grow to stone,
And the moss these pebbles emeralds make."*

Kenji Ohtski, a lay psychoanalyst, who practices psychoanalysis in Tokyo, Japan, contributed to the *Tokyo Journal for Psychoanalysis,* July, 1952, an article entitled, "Three Types of Japanese Characters." In this article Ohtski said:

". . . he (Nobunaga Oda) was, indeed, the original inventor of tactics of sudden attack. His battle at Okehasama (1500) [1560] against Imagawa was a prototype of that at Pearl Harbour. The tactics were very relevant, rational, and daring, when the less force should stand against the larger. After that there have been given so many imitations. So if one should know well of Japanese history, the Pearl Harbour attack might have been inferentially expected. Some one maintains, indeed, that it was really expected, and the Japanese air forces fell ensnared in the trick. I know not, of course, if it is true or not; nor if there has ever been prototype of atomic assault at Hiroshima in the American History."

This is a puzzling statement. In fact, it is a startling statement. But it suddenly dawned on me my reason

* Japanese National Anthem, "Kimi Ga Up Wa," *The Americana Encyclopedia.* Edition 1922.

for being startled. Ohtski, in his paper, "Three Types of Japanese Characters," is delivering a communication that is of grave significance to the United States. I sincerely suspected that he voiced a message within a message, and that the key to this riddle would be found in an analysis of certain features of the socio-politic history of Sixteenth Century Japan.

During that Century and during the early days of Nobunaga Oda, the Shogun resided at Kyoto. Without going into all of the intricate details that would establish the difference in rank between the Shogun and the Emperor or Mikado, it is enough for the purpose of this narrative to say that the Shogun was theoretically, at least, the Emperor's administrative officer.

Despite the fact that the Shogun symbolized the temporal power of Japan and despite the fact that his physical character rather than his spiritual character seemed to outweigh the influence of the Mikado during these days that prefaced the prestige of Nobunaga Oda, he was nevertheless not particularly cogent. There were many feudal lords who were intrinsically more powerful. Many of these feudatories were more talented military-wise and more ingenious.

And these feudal lords were jealous of each other. Border incidents were numerous. Each lord lived in a state of intolerable suspense. Often they attempted to reduce this suspense by political marriages, and by other types of intrigue. For political reasons, but executed strictly in accordance with their institutions, mores, and codes, betrayal was frequent. Treachery toward and assassinations of men in power added to the unrest. In these riotous times a solution, for reasons that will be detailed later, would not only afford unity to Japan, but it would also position in official power the feudal lord or aggregate of lords able to accomplish this coup.

In 1540 A.D., four central and eastern chiefs were interested in solving their political differences. They were Uyesugi in Echigo, the most northern and western of the involved provinces; Daimyo Hojo of Odawara in the Kwanto; Imagawa in Totomi; Mikawa and Suruga and Takeda in Kai. Takeda was the most accomplished and talented of them all.

These Daimyos understood very well that to resolve their difficulties the proper formula must include one essential ingredient. This ingredient was the "peaceful" coercion of the Shogun, at Kyoto. It is to be emphasized that this coercion idea did not entail a plan to attack the forces of the Shogun nor to do violence to his person. The plan in its entirety was dependent upon the realization that the Shogun would be and must be "persuaded" by a show of force.

However, it was not until 1560 that any one of the competing feudatories was ready for the march upon Kyoto. Then the Daimyo Imagawa levied men from his three provinces and trekked westward on his way to the Shogun's stronghold. Scarcely had he passed the western frontiers of his own area when he was pounced upon by the numerically inferior forces of Nobunaga Oda. The men of Imagawa were annihilated and Imagawa himself was slain.

Though Nobunaga previously had repelled a threat from the Province of Ise, and though he was selected by Hideyoshi as being the most talented leader in Japan, still at the time that he routed the superior forces of Imagawa he was referred to as, "Baka-dono" or "Lord Fool." The rout of Imagawa is recorded in history as the famous battle of Okehazama—the "Okehasama" mentioned by Ohtski!

Ethnocentric occidentals might wonder about the actual fashion of the feudatory approach to the quest for Japanese power. The western world has always been mystified by the jejune, rigid, and compulsive methods employed by the feudal antagonists. Naive politicos of Europe and America were puzzled by the indirection. Why couldn't the Shogun be assassinated or why didn't the Daimyos ignore the Shogun and fight it out between themselves?

As a matter of fact, the fourteenth Shogun of the Ashikaga family was assassinated by his ministers, Miyoshi and Matsunaga. But this did little to alter the frame of reference subsuming the official concept and the official operations of the Shogun. Yoshiaki, a younger brother of the assassinated Ashikaga Yoshiteru, set about dethroning the puppet supported by Miyoshi and Matsunaga.

What is important in all this is the fact that the warring feudal Daimyos, steeped in internecine conflict, felt compelled to wage war against each other in a precise fashion subscribed to by their mores and institutions. They felt compelled to march upon Kyoto for the express purpose of establishing influence over the Shogun—the administrative, the temporal officer for the Mikado. Even the whisper of a rebellious act must not be levelled against the Mikado.

"The history of the family [Taira] had so far been full of honor, a record of distinguished service to the Emperor; but Masakado, the grandson of the founder of the Taira, was destined to earn an unenviable notoriety in history as a rebel, the only personage in all the long history of Japan who dared to raise sacrilegious eyes to the throne."*

This item of information is teased out of context from the main corpus of Japanese history for the purpose of illustrating a characteristic feature that expresses the Japanese principle of coevality. It is almost unbelievable that the imperial succession could exist for so many centuries with but one single rebel aspirant to the throne. But this is Japan!

According to their mores, a Daimyo given over to the idea of control of Japan by weight of arms did not dare direct his attack against the person of the Mikado. In fact as it has already been discussed, any conquering activity must be manipulated in a manner that would bring about the coercion of the Shogun. The Daimyo that accomplished this coercion would gain the Shogun's approbation of the Daimyo's military activities. Further, his future conquests then could be made officially in the name of the Shogun. Also, by his influence over the Shogun, he could expunge his past military record from evidences of disloyalty.

Nobunaga was the first of these self-appointed catalysts and guardians of Japanese integrity conceived and formulated on a national level. But to my mind it was not only the suddenness and the daring of the surprise attack upon Imagawa at Okehazama executed by Nobunaga and his captain, Hideyoshi, for the synthesis of Japan, that preoccupied Ohtski in his article, "Three Types of Japanese Characters." In my opinion Ohtski, not in the spirit of a threat, but in a veiled warning was referring to the cardinal principles of the national entity

* Joseph H. Longford, *The Story of Old Japan* (New York: Longmans. Green, and Co., 1910), 86.

of Japan. The Japanese believe in and have repetitiously and compulsively experienced the concept of coevality. In brief, to the Japanese, Japan always was and always will be. Because of their compulsivity significant accidental happenings to Japan either from the inside or from the outside are repeated over and over again. They become a part of the Japanese ritual executed on a national scale. Even during the last war, during the struggle with the United States, the Japanese continued to celebrate Matthew Perry Day (the day, April 10, 1853, that Commodore Matthew Perry, USN, invaded Japan, in the name of the President of the United States). It was a sad day for the Japanese when Perry set foot upon Japanese soil. Yet so much enslaved by their compulsive customs, the day was honored despite the new outbreak and current hostilities with Perry's government.

Perry's enterprises, I am sure, entered into Ohtski's calculations about the predictability of the Japanese attack upon the United States. Perry, not knowing that the Shogun was not the Emperor, forced the unprotected Shogun on March 31, 1854 to conclude a trade treaty with the United States. Perry's objective was the same as was the objective of Hojo, Imagawa, and Takeda in Nobunaga's time. It was Perry's intent to force the capitulation of the Shogun, and he did.

It might be said that Perry's attack not only was a daring but a surprise attack upon Japan. But just as daring and just as surprising was the sudden appearance of Townsend Harris upon the Japanese horizon in the year of 1856.

Harris, after suddenly appearing in Japan, blandly announced that he was there to represent the United States as an accredited consul. The Japanese were thunderstruck. They knew of no such arrangement with

Perry nor with the United States. They thought that consuls were to be exchanged between the two countries only if *each country* desired consular representation. When the Japanese repaired to reread their copy of the treaty, which was written in Dutch, they were amazed to find that the actual wording of the treaty said if *either country* requested consular representation, a consular exchange was to be effected.

In this contingency, the Japanese were without Japanese precedent. Not knowing the proper protocol, the proper procedure, they attempted delaying actions to give them time to meet this undesirable denouement. But Harris was not only arrogant, he was persistent, tenacious, insistent. Peculiar as it may seem he, too, did not know that the Shogun was not the Emperor, and he, like Perry, believed that the Shogun was the undisputed ruler of Japan. Accordingly, he demanded to see the Shogun. But despite his insistence, the Japanese, by delaying tactics, successfully obstructed the meeting for many months.

Eventually, however, Harris with cajolery and finally with threats, holding over the heads of the uninformed Japanese the mystical information possessed by himself that the piratical blood thirstiness of the British and Russian fleets was about to be let loose on Japan, forced an audience with the Shogun.

That audience took place on December 7, 1857!

It was on December 7, 1941 that the Japanese after the fashion of Perry, Harris, and Nobunaga executed their surprise attack upon Pearl Harbor.

I know Ohtski to be a courageous man, not given to threats. But I also know that he is aware of certain peculiarities in the Japanese makeup, peculiarities which I have tried to explain and to cover in this book, that fit them as a nation into the psychiatric formula known as the "repetition compulsion."

When Ohtski casually inquires about an American prototype for the atomic bombing of Hiroshima, we all know immediately that there is no American prototype for the atom bombing of Hiroshima. The attack upon Hiroshima by the atom bomb, was the first atom bomb attack ever made by one warring nation upon another warring nation.

But now, unfortunately, the atom bomb attack upon Hiroshima has established a precedent in Japan, a precedent analogous to the precedent established by Perry's sudden attack and coercion of the Shogun, and Harris' sudden declaration and execution of his intent to overwhelm the Shogun! Both acts were conducted in the name of the President of the United States.

In answer to Ohtski's inquiry as to whether the United States had a prototype for the atom bomb attack upon Hiroshima, I would venture to say that there is a much more important subject involved than an immediate and direct answer to Ohtski's question.

If the Perry-Harris sneak attack upon Japan led to Pearl Harbor, what might we eventually expect in return from the desolation of Hiroshima by our first atom bomb?

THE AUTHOR

CONTENTS

1

AMERICAN INDIVIDUALISM, JAPANESE CONFORMITY, AND PSYCHOANALYSIS

IT is unfortunate that when an individual has been accustomed to policing during infancy, life in a liberal environment where policing does not exist produces anxiety in him; he is like a fish out of water. Conscious cooperation with society is one thing and unconscious self-policing is another, even though, to unsosophisticated eyes, they may appear the same.

On rare occasions, poets have sensed that their striving for liberty is directed against unhealthy restrictions to which they were subjected during infancy.* As adults they seek liberty because the infantile restrictions are unconsciously represented and continue to bind them for the remainder of their lives. One poet, Michael Chazarian Nalbandian, while in a Russian prison, identified and associated the lack of national liberty with the lack of liberty occasioned by swaddling the new-born infant:

"Wrapped round with many swaddling bands,
    all night I did not cease to weep,
And in the cradle, restless still,
    My cries disturbed my mother's sleep.

1

"O Mother! in my heart I prayed,
Unbind my arms and leave me free!
And even from that hour I vowed
To love thee ever, Liberty!"[1]

Is there mental health in liberty itself, or merely in slavishly conforming to the established cultural institutions, or to authority?

There appear to be two distinct and diametrically opposed cultural concepts affecting both the individual and national culture of peoples. Borrowing from Hamlet's famous quandary,[2] I have christened these the "to be free" concept and the "not to be free" concept. The Japanese insist upon the *insignificance of the individual,* the "not to be free" concept; while American political theory stresses individualism, the "to be free" idea. The Japanese psychiatrist, Tsuneo Muramatsu, drawing upon his knowledge of the Tokugawa era, described the traditional difference between the development of American and Japanese national goals and the difference between the character structure of the Japanese adult and the American adult: "Americans were emphasizing *individuality,** spontaneity, efficiency, progressivism, rationalism and mutual cooperation in a 'gesellschaftlich'** or 'contractual' relationship between individuals. In contrast the Japanese were still stressing the concept of society as a unit under the direction of a single authority uniformity, in each defined status, the *insignificance of the individual,** with conservatism, conventionalism, traditionalism and loyalty in a 'gemeinschaftlich'*** or 'family' relationship between individuals."[3]

One should realize, however, that American individualism, the "to be free" idea, has largely degenerated into an American myth. Holly Whyte, (in an article entitled "The Class of '49")[4] assembled pertinent information regarding the students graduated by American colleges and universities in that year. Whyte's findings were, I think, a reflection of our modern culture, and give evidence of the type of individual it is producing.

"The Class of '49" wants material security, first and foremost. For that reason, the majority ignores the possibilities of independent business and looks toward a position with a large, "safe" company which is representative of this type of security. Economic depression, an integer of our complicated economic system, has molded these young people into "security-conscious" individuals. The field of personnel in large industry is a very popular vocational interest of the "Class of '49." Claiming a desire to be helpful to other people, they are, in fact, rationalizing their drive for material and even spiritual security.

We are producing a highly efficient type of business man, geared to large industry, who, in his search for material security, is losing interest in the cultivation of the arts, and, most important of all, allocates less time to his family. We are becoming, therefore, a culture of one-parent families. From the "Class of '49," and from the classes immediately preceding and following it, we find that security-consciousness has been molded by economic depression and war. We may expect opposition to any suggestion of change in our present "highly efficient" system, and the more we talk about these changes, the more rebellion will arise against them.

The principle of "rugged individualism," celebrated as being characteristically American, is actually quite clearly structured, i.e., specifically organized. "Rugged individualism" provides a cultural medium for the adolescent striving of American youth. Yet the fashion in which an American becomes an "individualist" is precise and patternized; the degree of individualism is circumscribed and established by custom. Some categories of citizen are permitted more individualism than others: poets or artists are allowed irregular and unconventional modes of behavior; but a banker, even if a pioneer in some banking venture, is expected to operate within the framework of a pattern previously blueprinted for banking activities. Even when acceptance is accorded the individualist, there is never complete American permissiveness. The artist pays for his individualism; he is dubbed "eccentric." Criminals codify criminal behavior —"There is honor among thieves." The conduct of an onlooker at a Negro card game is structured: any nonparticipant seeing a player cheating is expected to maintain silence.[5] At times, "crime" is an evidence of moral behavior—the pattern of the criminal performance being structured by a Fagan-style superego. Bettelheim and Sylvester described this point of view in a paper entitled "Delinquency and Morality."[6]

While the American, by virtue of his democratic institutions, lays claim to the right "to be free," in actual practice American rugged individualism is virtually non-existent, and what passes for individualism is often a consistently rigid anti-social gesture. Even neurotic nonconformism, or American autonomy, performs in a most predictable fashion. Yet only a person grown to the limits of his constitutionally-determined developmental potential, from a dynamic point of view, achieves maturity.

By freeing the individual, the psychoanalyst* attempts to re-create a rugged individualist, the American prototype. American analysts hope to turn out a product theoretically free from abnormal compulsiveness.

4

Included in the criteria for a complete psychoanalytic cure, by American standards, are: integration with the reality situation; adequate capacity for concentration and sustained effort; adequate capacity for sharing; flexibility; spontaneity; sense of time and space; ability to relate oneself to other people without employing intervening ghosts or inanimate systems for people; possession of a correct evaluation of one's worth; a correct evaluation of the worth of others; an objectively correct body image; a reduction to a controlled minimum of escape from difficult reality situations (through tangentiality or day-dreaming); and noncompulsive creativity.

Even after considerable thought and study, and a careful examination of the contrasts evident in individualism and submissiveness, one is still in the throes: "To be or not to be free?" Should the American and the Japanese psychoanalytic therapist encourage individualism or should they insist upon insensible and unconscious submissive conformity to the existing culture?*

This question of aims is not easily answered. Freudian psychoanalysis is practiced, for the most part, in cultures quite similar to that of its origin; Japan and India constitute two possible exceptions, cross-cultural studies of which would prove exceedingly informative. It is astonishing that very little occidental interest has been accorded to activities of psychoanalysis as practiced in Japan. In fact, it seems to me incredible that psychoanalysis exists at all under the Meiji (authoritarian) type of oligarchy, and my amazement is increased when I consider the wealth of material describing the character traits of the Japanese. Dr. Muramatsu says of his people that: "While Western peoples were seeking for—and establishing—national independence and individual freedom, and while Protestant pioneers colonized and organized America, the Japanese were still living in a medieval, feudal, hierarchal family system and society. This condition persisted until the Meiji 'Revolution' of 80 years ago. During the Tokugawa Era, for about two and a half centuries preceding the Meiji Restoration, an extremely rigid, stratified type of society and family were characteristic of Japan."[7]

Muramatsu points out that a child's status in the family and in society is determined at birth. "One was educated and trained from early childhood," he says, "to adjust to the prescribed and appropriate way of life in an authoritarian atmosphere. To the extent that the individual was obedient and faithful to his allotted position, and was content with his lot in family and society, he could have personal security."[8]

He speaks of the strict stratification of Japanese life according to the class of the person in question—the kind, color, size, and type of house, the kind of language, the rules for time and manner of bowing, and general behavior, and notes that: "All these were prescribed for [the *bun*] the status in society, which was calculated on such criteria as the individual's position in the family, economic condition, occupation, age, sex, and marital status." Violation of these unwritten codes of behavior, morality and custom exposed one to "ridicule (*waraware mono*) or even exile from the community or family."[9]

Of the importance of the family in Japanese life, Muramatsu says: "The family or [*ie*] 'house' was the most important symbol in life. Preservation of the family line and its dignity was regarded as the most important duty to the ancestors. Consequently, a wife who could not bear children was sometimes divorced and dishonored. Members who disgraced the family were often

6

expelled. Loyalty to the house [*ie*], and, if necessary sacrifice in the interest of the family [*ie*], were demanded as a matter of routine. The status of the family, [*ie gara*], was determined by the community. Ordinarily, the first son of the head of the main family, was the heir [*honke*]. In place of direct inheritance, the other sons were established as branch houses, [*bunke*], with subordinate positions."[10]

These statements are not merely a matter of a single man's opinion. John C. Pelzel, writing for the *American Sociological Review,* points up some of the ways in which the Japanese societal structure is antithetic to the more modern aims of Freudian psychoanalysis. "Formalism and stratifying mechanisms," he writes, "are strong in non-family relations. . . . Other relations tend to be structured in terms of family. Ethical guides to conduct at home become standards for behavior outside. . . ."[11] He also delineates the strict dimensions of the Japanese caste systems: "Before the beginning of Meiji, a legal social-class system partitioned the population among several classes and castes from which the individual had little chance of escape. There were a number of dimensions to this system, and it was reasonably close to a total social-class system. It was occupational. It was also the arbiter of standard of living. Farmers might not eat white rice or wear silks. Merchants must live in houses of mean exterior. Outcasts were not allowed any other floor in their houses than the bare dirt. Perhaps the most critical basis for classification, however, was possession of the political and military power of the State. On this dimension, all classes fell into two fairly clear divisions—those who controlled and those who were controlled."[12]

Speaking of the effect upon the individual of such

7

a system, Pelzel writes: "The social class system before Meiji was supported by a powerful and explicit ideology of social class. This ideology stressed family and counseled subordination of the individual to the group. . . . It is difficult to advance one's own head above those of the others with whom one is bound except as part of a general advance of the group and along somewhat narrowly circumscribed lines."[13]

Pelzel says that the pre- and post-Meiji eras have certain least common denominators which, to my mind, would appear inimical to psychoanalysis. "It urged cooperation, rather than self-interest," he says, "as a motivation for relations with the members of one's community, one's own class and superior and inferior classes. At the same time, it taught subordination to superiors and leadership over inferiors and placed high evaluations upon the control of other men, especially through the channels of State organizations."[14] He points out that the same patterns are marked in Japanese life today. "It is difficult," says Pelzel, "to rationalize self-interest. Mobility is, to a considerable extent, thought of not so much as mobility of the individual, but as that of a group of which the individual is one part, and this group is typically the family or, to a lesser extent, the simulated family."[15]

This Japanese system, stressing, as it does, organizational patterns, rather than emphasizing the rights of the individual, has not changed to any great extent throughout the ages. In 1841, Dr. Von Siebold, then with the Dutch factory of "Dezima," observed: "It is held to be the duty of every individual to remain through life in the class in which he was born, unless exalted by some very peculiar and extraordinary circumstance. To endeavour to rise above his station is some-

8

what discreditable; to sink below it, utterly so. These classes are eight."[16]

Of his reception when he went from Nagasaki to Yedo, Von Siebold records the unchanging mode of behavior of the Japanese: "This is the whole of the ceremonial now practiced at the court of Yedo, in the reception of foreigners, as given by writers of the present century. It differs not much from the forms described by Kaempfer, as observed nearly 150 years ago; but the modern relations want the second part of the earlier narrative."[17] Other observers, going back hundreds of years, have cited the rigidity of the Japanese cultural patterns. A Swedish physician wrote, in 1796: "Dress in Japan deserves, more than anywhere else in the world, the name of national; as it not only differs from that of every other nation, but at the same time is uniform from the monarch down to the most inferior subject, similar in both sexes, and (which almost surpasses all belief), has been unchanged for the space of two-thousand five-hundred years. It consists everywhere of long and wide night-gowns, one or more of which are worn by people of every age and condition in life."[18]

There are many evidences that the culture of the Japanese has not changed since medieval times, and in some aspects not since long before that era. "Upon the first symptoms of pregnancy, a girdle of braided red crape is bound round the future mother's body, immediately below the bosom. This is performed in great ceremony, with religious rites appointed for the occasion; and the selection of the person who presents the girdle is a point of extreme importance and dignity. This singular custom is, by learned Japanese, said to be practiced in honour of the widow of a *mikado*, who, some sixteen centuries ago, upon her husband's death,

9

being then in an advanced state of pregnancy, thus girding herself, took his vacant place at the head of his army, and completed the conquest of [Korea] Corea."[19]

There is even a record of Japanese unwillingness to change their food habits: "As early as the seventh century we find notices of official efforts to encourage alternative or subsidiary crops such as wheat, barley, millet, buckwheat, beans, and peas, but both growers and consumers stubbornly kept to rice, despite constant famines."[20]

Townsend Harris took note of Japanese rigidity: "The Japanese have *fixed days* for their change of clothing. The *law* settles the matter beforehand, and no inclemency of weather can postpone the change. The following are the periods and changes of their dress for our year 1857: On the first day of the fourth month, April 24, they threw off their wadded clothes and put on unwadded ones, but of thick materials. On the fifth day of the fifth month, May 23, they will put on their summer clothing. On the first day of the ninth month, October 18, they will resume the same clothing as that put on on the 24th of April. On the ninth day of the ninth month, October 26, they will put on their winter clothing. This is made of the same material as the previous change, only it is thickly *wadded* with cotton or silk wadding."[21] Modern Japan is ancient Japan attired in borrowed clothing.

* * *

"It may be stated with reason," says Nyozekan Hasegawa, "that the history of no other country in the world mirrors the past and present-day character of the nation with as much clarity and precision as that of Japan. This unique feature arises from the fact that few nations in the world have succeeded in maintaining,

10

unbroken and almost unaltered, since prehistoric times up to the present, the essence, character, and form of the racial group in the way the Japanese have done. Japan stands perhaps without parallel either in the East or the West in this respect. Here is a racial group which has succeeded for a period of thousands of years, within the same area and under the same line of rulers, in perpetuating without any revolutionary changes and in developing without interruption a civilization that has remained steadfastly the same in essence as in origin."[22] This has left its impress in the nationalistic writings of the twentieth century: "That our Imperial Throne is coeval with heaven and earth means indeed that the past and the future are united in one in the 'now,' that our nation possesses everlasting life, and that it flourishes endlessly. Our history is an evolution of the eternal 'now,' and at the root of our history there always runs a stream of eternal 'now.' "[23]

Talcott Parsons writes: "Japan . . . made the transition to modernization with minimum immediate disturbance of her preindustrial social structure. The peasant base remained essentially intact. The old upper classes faced greatly altered conditions, but on the whole as a group remained in the top positions of prestige, wealth, and power. The military values and code of the samurai had an opportunity for a new field of expression in the form of the armed forces of a modern nation, supported by a nationalistically tinged system of universal education.

"With these older patterns and values there also remained intact the Japanese family system with its rigid system of obligations subordinating all individual interests to those of family units. Through long centuries of conditioning by a hierarchical social system, these patterns of subordination of the individual to his larger family, of the young to the old, of women to men, shaded almost imperceptibly into a subordination of people of lower to those of higher status in a highly crystallized class system, and of general predisposition to accept legitimate authority. The imperial institution —master symbol of this highly hierarchized and integrated system—not only remained intact but was also exalted to a new position of prestige which was exploited systematically by the new ruling group."[24]

"Superficial, verbalistic imitations of democracy, and imitations of American fashion and mass-cultural elements, are to be found everywhere . . ." writes Muramatsu. "On the other hand, the old *oyabun-kobun* organizations remain prominent. Even a street girl cannot pursue her trade unless she gets permission from the boss of one of these guild-like groups.

"In families, traditions like the *on* of parents, the *giri* between individuals, and the *sekentei* (face, or appearance before the world) seem to remain very important. Such deeply rooted ways of thinking cannot be expected to vanish overnight."[25] And again, it is said of the modern Japanese that the police " . . . have meticulously 'supervised the thoughts' of all Japanese subjects. Someone in power evidently distrusted the popular devotion to Kodo and feared imminent revolt."[26]

A Japanese sizes up the conflict between the rights of the individuals and the rights of bureaucracy saying that "in organization and in power the Japanese administration is very strong and effective, and in fact may be termed bureaucratic. On the other hand, the legislature is still in its infancy, and the security for individual rights as against acts of government is still inadequate."[27]

12

The Japanese jingoists would never be satisfied with this watered-down expression of an earlier Japanese authoritarian organization. *Kokutai No Hongi* states: "An individual is an existence belonging to a State and her history which form the basis of his origin, and is fundamentally one body with it. However, even if one were to think of a nation contrariwise and also to set up a morality by separating the individual alone from this one body, with this separated individual as the basis, one would only end in a so-called abstract argument that has lost its basis."[28]

"When people determinedly count themselves as masters and assert their egos," *Kokutai No Hongi* says, "there is nothing but contradictions and the setting of one against the other; and harmony is not begotten. . . . The society of individualism is clashes between a people and a people, and history may be all looked upon as that of class wars. Social structure and political systems in such a society, and the theories of sociology, political science, statecraft, etc., which are their logical manifestations, are essentially different from those of our country which makes harmony its fundamental Way. Herein indeed lies the reason why the ideologies of our nation are different from those of the nations of the West."[29]

Under such vigorous and time-honored rigidities, the social and political demands of the Meiji, what could be the criteria for psychoanalytic cure in Japan? The government insists upon disindividualization; at birth a person is expected to become nothing at all (*mimpi*). He is directed to respect authority (*kanzan*). He is trained to obligate himself obsequiously to the father (*ko*)* or to any father or parent substitute (*oya bun*), or to the emperor (*chu*),** or the emperor's way (*kodo*). He is required to become a god (*kami*), or to fulfill the

13

way of the gods *(shinto)*. As a Japanese, he is respectful of his own level in society and of that of his associates *(enryo)* and obedient to his guild *(shokunin katagi)*. He must lose his individuality to save face *(sekentei)*. He ceases to be an individual, performing *giri* (an elaborate institution requiring him to behave in a prescribed fashion expressive of his nationalism) to his empire and doing that which is expected of him *(jicho)*.

On first inspection, *jicho* seems to be in the interest of the self-system (self-respect), but, according to Ruth Benedict, it is also structured. She writes: "An employee says, 'I must respect myself (jicho),' and it means, not that he must stand on his own rights, but that he must say nothing to his employers that will get him into trouble. 'You must respect yourself' had the same meaning, too, in political usage. It meant that a 'person of weight' could not respect himself if he indulged in anything so rash as 'dangerous thoughts.' It had no implication, as it would in the United States, that even if thoughts are dangerous, a man's self-respect requires that he think according to his own lights and his own conscience."[30] He must discharge his duty to his work *(nimmu)*. His fullest debt in certain obligations *(kochu)* cannot be erased by payment or by the passage of time *(gimu)*. As passive recipient of a favor, he is obliged through the strict application of a cultural institution to repay that favor. He might receive from or need to be obligated to the emperor *(ko on)*, his parents *(oya on)*, his lord *(nushi no on)*, or his teacher *(shi no on)*.

Nitobe, writing at the beginning of the twentieth century, describes another one of these Japanese cultural requirements, *bushido*: "Bu-shi-do means literally Military-Knight-Ways—the ways which fighting nobles should observe in their daily life as well as in their vocation;

in a word, the 'Precepts of Knighthood,' the *noblesse oblige* of the warrior class."[31]

* * *

Under these politico-cultural demands, should Japanese psychoanalysis suppress and repress and sublimate the alleged "constitutional ferocities" of mankind, thereby effecting an adaptation to the Japanese cultural expectation, or should it advance the rights of the individual? In psychiatric circles, in contradistinction to psychoanalytic circles, psychotherapy is employed in Japan with the aim of adjusting within the individual his *ninjo* (human emotion) requirements to the demands of *giri* (obligation to the Japanese institutions and mores). Thus, the Japanese would seek out a self-determined individual and attempt to "cure" him. A liberalizing therapeutic goal, if practiced at all in Japan, most certainly would oppose the ideology of the Meiji, their Zaibatsu, their Diet, their military organizations, their institution of *kanzan*.

An army ant behaves practically the same in South America as in South Africa; but the Japanese behave differently from all other human beings. LaBarre, some 40 years after Nitobe (q.v., above), observes some of the same sort of structuring. Even the *Nisei* (second-generation Japanese Americans) differ in personality makeup from the *Isei* (first generation) Japanese.[32] My quest for the normal mind, to settle once and for all the problem "to be or not to be free," sensitized me to the possibilities of elucidation contained in this particular oriental society which, at least theoretically, is antithetic to American culture. I was determined to discover, if at all possible, what characterized a cure in the Japanese version of the psychoanalytic process.

By doing some quiet investigation on my own, I

learned the absolute truth of the statement by Muramatsu that the "intense emphasis on in-group characteristics in feudal Japan resulted in exclusiveness, cliquism, and hostility toward outsiders." For example, the
samurai (warrior) was set against *samurai* of other *daimyos* (lords); "the villager against strangers; and family
members against persons outside of the family. Elaborate
rules were set up to govern necessary out-group relations. From these developed those elaborate patterns of
etiquette which are often regarded as characteristically
Japanese."[33]

One of the most clearly elucidated reasons for ques-
tioning whether the occidental type of psychoanalysis
can be practiced in a frame of reference that proscribes
individual decision has been expounded by Fred N.
Kerlinger, of the University of Michigan: "The Morals
(*Shushin*) textbooks which were used throughout the
Japanese school system as a guide to the 'good' Japanese
life, stressed the necessity for subjugating the individual
to the group. Since, in Japan, the individual is de-em-
phasized, it follows that individual decisions must be
proscribed. And so they are. In fact, when faced with
the necessity of making an outright decision that may
lead to a positive course of action, a Japanese shrinks
and may go to what seem fantastic lengths to avoid making the decision. Even if he should commit himself
verbally to a course of action, he will frequently end
by doing nothing. He lacks a sense of personal responsibility. . . ."[34]

2

CHILD TRAINING AND JAPANESE CONFORMITY

NOTHING in psychology is more exciting nor more important to liberty and to world peace than the dynamics behind such slavish "ingroup-outgroup" combinations as that of Japan: the ingroup antagonism toward the outgroup stems from the cultural pressure applied by the Japanese to their children from early infancy. These pressures, as will be seen later, do not occur during the first days of life, but are applied later.

In the development of *ko*, the father is proclaimed the titular and revered head of the family, while the mother, in comparison to the father and to the sons, especially the eldest son, is without status. Even the babe in arms cannot escape obeisance to the father. Filial respect and conformity are foisted upon him while he is still an infant: the mother pushes the head of the suckling into a bow as the father enters the room. Later, if he is not duly obsequious, the baby is chided for his infantilism and unfavorably compared with more dutiful children. If this fails, as a last resort the need for obedience is made clear to him by the burning of dried leaves on his skin. One subjection to this moxa cautery usually suffices, but if it does not, the second searing

17

or branding accomplishes the complete riddance of the child's self-assertiveness and full compliance to the institution of filial respect.

Over a hundred years ago Von Siebold observed that: "Children are trained in habits of implicit obedience, which, independently of any beneficial effects on the future character that may be expected, Japanese parents value as obviating the necessity of punishment."[35] Gorer[36] and Benedict[37] at first believed that this conformism was furthered by introducing the male child, at least, to early and rigid bowel training. Mildred Sikkema, writing in *Psychiatry*,[38] does not agree with Gorer and Benedict. (Neither of the latter, to the best of my knowledge, has been in the Orient.) Sikkema is half right and half wrong: bowel training is not as severe as described by Gorer, nor so late and lackadaisical as outlined by Sikkema.* On my recent trip to Japan, I investigated the subject and discovered, much to my astonishment, that Japanese men, even physicians and psychiatrists, knew little about bowel training practices, even as used by their own wives on their own children. By inquiring into sources that included Japanese mothers as well as physicians and psychiatrists, I learned that it is quite customary for the Japanese to start "holding the child out" when he is five or six months of age, at the time when he also begins to be exposed to the institution of *ko*. There is a network of small canals and ditches, and a child is held out over these waterways until his bowels move. However, contrary to Gorer's belief, the holding out is a benevolent gesture and is not ordinarily accompanied by physical violence. Sikkema may have been misled by the system used by the Japanese for establishing the chronological age of a child. When I asked at what age the Japanese introduced bowel training, the answer was invariably, "the first year or so." This puzzled me, until I learned that the infant, regardless of the month in which he is born, becomes one year of age on January 1. Thus, if a child is born on December 15, he is reckoned as one year old on the first of January.

In the course of the establishment of submissiveness to the father, the male child is permitted to vent his reactionary hostilities upon the female members of his family. He is even permitted to attack and beat his mother.

Submissiveness toward the father is transferred to the emperor through the institution of *chu*. In *chu*, self-effacing obedience is developed to such an extent that a Japanese, when inducted into imperial military service, becomes one already dead. He no longer has any right to his own life; it now belongs exclusively to the emperor. So far as individual strivings are concerned, the Japanese soldier or sailor must renounce them completely. The Meiji statesmen, with the development of mass compulsive obedience to authority, fashioned millions of males into tools for the furtherance of world domination, which finally eventuated in the Tanaka plan for world conquest. Through effective technical procedures, the Meiji statesmen intensified Japanese subservience; in this they were aided by the fact that, long since, a divinity had been ascribed to the person or figure of the emperor. Hirohito, grandson of the Great Meiji, is revered by the masses as a direct descendant of Amaterasu, the sun goddess, daughter of Isanagi.

Fascistic schemes of society and the controlling of the inter-relationships of people, as advocated by Plato, have actually been in active operation in Japan, gradually gaining momentum, since the commencement of the Yamato dynasty, several hundred years before Christ. The modern French writer Lecomte du Nouy advocates the complete suppression of individualism in children: "When we speak of beginning education in tender childhood, we mean in the cradle. We realize that this will shock the sentiments of many parents and especially of mothers, who will object that it is exaggerated or impossible. We do not think so; they do not realize the important part played by unconscious egoism in their love. The smile, the joy of their child, gives them so much pleasure that they do not have the courage to impose at the start the disciplines which will have to intervene one day, and will become more difficult and painful to apply as the child grows older. Even though they are ready for any sacrifice, they are often weak, and the moral formation of the child is thus rendered much more painful later on, both for themselves and for him. We will not speak of the laziness of parents which unfortunately often intervenes. It is much less tiring and nerve-racking to give a child its milk as soon as it cries, or take it up in one's arms, then to let it yell. If the mother weakens only once, the child does not forget and soon becomes intolerable."[39]

In fact, the *ko* to the father, the obsequiousness, is developed when the infant is in his precognitive era. The importance of this fact is becoming recognized by an increasing number of psychiatrists and anthropologists.

On his visit to Japan in the eighteenth century Thunberg made some observations regarding Japanese children which might still be remarked today: "I observed everywhere that the chastisement of children was very moderate. I very seldom heard them rebuked or scolded, and hardly ever saw them flogged or beaten, either in private families or on board of the vessels; while in more civilized and enlightened nations, these compliments abound. . . ."[40] "With respect to courtesy and submission to their superiors, few can be compared to the Japanese. Subordination to government and obedience to their parents, are inculcated into children in their early infancy, and in every situation of life they are in this respect instructed by the good example of their elders. . . ."[41]

Menpes observed the strict training of the Japanese children: "The science of deportment occupies quite half the time of the Japanese children's lives, and so early are they trained that even the baby of three, strapped to the back of its sister aged five, will in that awkward position bow to you and behave with perfect propriety and grace. This Japanese baby has already gone through a course of severe training in the science of deportment. It has been taught how to walk, how to kneel down, and how to get up again without disarranging a single fold of its *kimono*. After this it is necessary that it should learn the correct way to wait upon people—how to carry a tray, and how to present it gracefully; while the dainty handing of a cup to a guest is of the greatest importance imaginable. A gentleman can always tell the character of a girl and the class to which she belongs by the way she offers him a cup of Sake. And then the children are taught that they must always control their feelings—and if they are sad, never to cry; if they are happy, to laugh quietly, never in a boisterous manner, for that would be considered vulgar in the extreme.

"Modesty and reserve are insisted upon in the youth of Japan. A girl is taught that she must talk very little, but listen sympathetically to the conversation of her superiors. If she has a brother, she must look up to him as her master, even although he be younger than herself. She must give way to him in every detail. The baby boy places his tiny foot upon his sister's neck, and she is thenceforth his slave. If he is sad, her one care must be to make him happy. Her ambition is to imitate as nearly as possible the behavior of her mother towards her own lord and master."[42]

An Associated Press Newsfeature by Roy Essoyan appearing in the March 8, 1951 *Detroit Free Press* illustrates not only the excessive detail of training necessary to conduct the Japanese tea ritual, but also its lengthy existence in the culture: "(Quoting Masoki Sen, 15th generation descendant of Sen Rikyu, founder of the Japanese tea-drinking ceremonial 450 years ago) 'We teach the Japanese people how to develop character through tea-drinking. Many American officers and men have attended our school. It is even taught to policemen now, so that they, too, may acquire politeness and self-control. . . . The drinking of tea is only a background for discussion of the arts, flower arrangement, landscape architecture and aesthetics in general. It is the core of Japanese culture and art. The tea-drinking itself follows a rigid pattern.' " The AP writer proceeds: "There are usually five guests, one tea-master and one assistant tea-master present. The guests are seated in a line, according to their importance. Each utensil is brought in separately and commented on separately by each of the guests. Each cup of tea is brewed individually. Powdered green tea is always used. When receiving a cup the guest extends his right hand. The whole ritual . . . takes at least an hour. It was all decided that way, 450 years ago. Sen has written nine books about it."

(Observe that the ritual is unchanged either by the passage of time or by such minor upsets as the presence of the American Occupation forces. Moreover, Essoyan reports that Sen is "on the road," and will soon be teaching his ceremonial method in major cities in the United States.)

In 1949, when I lectured at the anthropological museum at the University of Pennsylvania, I saw an exhibit which Mrs. Masaru Harada had presented to the Museum of the University of Pennsylvania consisting of a collection of Japanese figurines of great warriors, their flags, and their insignia. The articles are emblematic of authoritarianism. Deliberately planned to inspire a fixed emotional attachment for the military, the collection is displayed in the best room of the house on May 5, Boys' Day. Girls' Day is celebrated by an exhibition of Japanese domestic gods.

There is a Japanese poem which sums up filial obligation:

> "Karasu!
> Karasu!
> Kanzaburo!
> Oya no on wo wasurena yo!"

"O crow! O crow! Kanzaburo!—never forget the goodness of your parents!"[43]

The Japanese child, more so the male child, is trained rather than educated to filial respect and to national duty. The concept of duty, and of following duty as the proper role of the Japanese, is constantly alluded to in literature on Japan and the Japanese people. The position of a leader, while on the surface anomalous, was actually clear-cut: it was he who voiced the principles and policies of some segment of leadership, military, national, or whatever. These leaders were relatively few, the bulk of the Japanese people being expected merely to follow this leadership blindly, without any expression of individual thought, and with action itself based upon the dictates of the leader. Moreover, as Sansom points out,[44] such loyalty as grew up around a leader transformed itself into a personal loyalty, not a loyalty toward the leader's beliefs. In fact, according to western concepts, the feeling of the Japanese follower for his leader was not loyalty as we know it, but blind identification (a psychological process which will be discussed at length in a later chapter).

Adams discusses the effects of the required and highly specialized training of *samurai* sons in special schools: "It made him loyal, rather than patriotic; his clan and lord were his idols, rather than his country and people."[45]

Longford quotes Article VII of The Laws of Shotoku Daishi, on the concept of duty, which is again an abnegation of the concept of self expression: "Let every man have his own charge, and let not the spheres of duty be confused. . . . In all things, whether great or small, find the right man, and they will surely be well managed: on all occasions, be they urgent or the reverse, meet but with a wise man, and they will of themselves be amenable. In this way will the State be lasting and the Temples of the Earth and of Grain will be free from danger. Therefore did the wise sovereigns of antiquity seek the man to fill the office and not the office for the sake of the man."[46]

3

CONFORMITY AND RAGE IN THE JAPANESE MALE

JAPANESE child training destroys the rights of the individual, as conceptualized by occidental psychoanalysts, and frustration of personal striving produces fear and rage. In the words of Dollard, ". . . the occurrence of aggressive behavior always presupposes the existence of frustration and, contrariwise, . . . the existence of frustration always leads to some form of aggression."[47] Rage can be equated with destructiveness or destructive intent. I know the controversy between those that believe that aggressiveness (used in the sense of destructiveness) is present in the child when he is born and those who believe that aggressiveness (destructiveness) is a reaction to frustration. Masserman puts it this way: "The dynamics of aggression have often been the subject of heated (and often aggressive) controversy between those who, like Nietzsche and Karl Menninger, believe that aggression is an inevitable manifestation of a universal 'instinct,' and those who, with Money-Kyrle, Dollard and others, conceive of aggression as one of many defense mechanisms against frustration and insecurity. Fortunately, appeals to purely aggressive motives are, at least in partly civilized cultures, ineffectual

25

or revolting unless by guarded invocation of tolerable degrees of fear as well as hatred. Our Army leaders quickly learned that the simple exhortation 'Kill!' was unacceptable to most recruits until it was expanded to 'Kill, or be killed by the (effectively described) "Krauts" or the—Japs!' "[48]

I am convinced that destructiveness is a reaction to frustration. The behavior of the Japanese supports this point of view. Not only is self-determinism repressed in Japan, but the rage consequent to the repression of self is not permitted spontaneous expression. The rage is only loosed on acceptable and specific targets. Hate supervised is not an idle speculation, and hate supervised can become hate internalized; internalized hate is demonstrable among the Japanese. In Tokyo-to (Greater Tokyo, population 5,500,000) in 1928 apoplexy accounted for 9.4 per cent of the deaths. Rempei Sassa says this is the highest figure of all the metropolises of the world.[49] Moreover, the figure is increasing. Sassa's studies are important because the constant polite repression of temper can cause high blood pressure. And the Japanese are the most polite nation in the world.

Indirectly, the somatization (or bodily changes due to repressed rage) known as allergy exposes another internal way in which the Japanese fixes hatred. Dr. Y. Kusama, Chairman of the Council on Medical Education, whom I met in Japan in 1949, informed me that the Tokyo Japanese are allergy-ridden. A study of hostility in allergic children made by Hyman Miller and Dorothy Baruch,[50] in Beverly Hills, California, disclosed that the allergic child is less likely than the non-allergic child to express spontaneous hostility, aggressiveness or hate. Their description of the allergic child fits the description of the average Japanese adult. The average

Japanese adult is incapable of a spontaneous retaliatory hostility; and the allergic child cannot express his hatred for his rejecting mother. The allergic child locks his hatred within his allergic symptoms, as the Japanese also fixes his hatred in an allergic matrix. In this way his allergy assists him in maintaining a non-spontaneous hostility. Anthony Yasutake told me that Japanese do not immediately revenge an affront, but smile politely. In the words of Edwin O. Reischauer: "The Japanese so successfully submerge their spontaneous emotional expressions or so warp them to fit their rigid rules of conduct that they have won for themselves the reputation of being a race of 'deadpan' robots, and many casual observers consider them as deficient in feeling as any people could be. The man . . . who submits to an unjustified berating without changing expression . . . seems to have no emotions at all."[51]

In the instance of the arterial hypertension and of allergic manifestation, the symptoms of each respective disease are barometers of internalized or repressed hostility. The high incidence of spontaneous Japanese suicides affords another glimpse into the operation of hate internalized; and at first glance it would seem strange that the non hara-kiri type of suicide often occurs when a Japanese feels the emotion of love for a member of the opposite sex. Of all the suicidal causes listed by Dr. Ryuji Nakamura, love complications were the most statistically significant.[52] These suicides are to be distinguished from the stylized hara-kiri, which connotes the ritualistic use of the self as a target for hate.

The blood-curdling hara-kiri of the pre-Meiji era is a seismographic indicator of subterranean pressures and hates in a nation that seems placid enough on the surface.

To understand more completely the stylized release of hostility in the sado-masochism of *hara-kiri*, consider Satow's description:

"Then the seven Japanese witnesses, Ito, Nakashima Sakutaro, two Satsuma captains of infantry, two Choshiu captains, and a Bizen ometsuke took their places. After we had sat quietly thus for about ten minutes footsteps were heard approaching along the verandah. The condemned man, a tall Japanese of gentleman-like bearing and aspect, entered on the left side, accompanied by his kai-shaku or best men, and followed by two others, apparently holding the same office. Taki was dressed in blue kami-shimo of hempen cloth; the kai-shaku wore war surcoats (jimbaori). Coming before the Japanese witnesses they prostrated themselves, the bow being returned, and then the same ceremony was exchanged with us. Then the condemned man was led to a red sheet of felt-cloth laid on the dais before the altar; on this he squatted, after performing two bows, one at a distance, the other close to the altar. With the calmest deliberation he took his seat on the red felt, choosing the position which would afford him the greatest convenience for falling forward. A man dressed in black with a light grey hempen mantle then brought in the dirk wrapped in paper on a small unpainted wooden stand, and with a bow placed it in front of him. He took it up in both hands, raised it to his forehead and laid it down again with a bow. This is the ordinary Japanese gesture of thankful reception of a gift. Then in a distinct voice, very much broken, not by fear or emotion, but as it seemed reluctance to acknowledge an act of which he was ashamed—declared that he alone was the person who on the fourth of February had outrageously at Kobe ordered fire to be opened on foreigners as they were trying to escape, that for having committed this offence he was going to rip up his bowels, and requested all present to be witnesses. He next divested himself of his upper garments by withdrawing his arms from the sleeves, the long ends of which he tucked under his legs to prevent his body from falling backward. The body was thus quite naked to below the navel. He then took the dirk in his right hand, grasping it just close to the point, and after stroking down the front of his chest and belly inserted the point as far down as possible and drew it across to the right side, the position of his clothes still fastened by the girth preventing our seeing the wound. Having done this he with great deliberation bent his body forward, throwing the head back so as to render the neck a fair object for the sword. The one kai-shaku who had accompanied him round the two rows of witnesses to make his bows to them, had been crouching on his left hand a little behind him with drawn sword poised in the air from the moment the operation commenced. He now sprang up suddenly and delivered a blow the sound of which was like thunder. The head dropped down on to the matted floor, and the body lurching forward fell prostrate over it, the blood from the arteries pouring out and forming a pool. When the blood vessels had spent themselves all was over. The little wooden stand and the dirk were removed. Ito came forward with a bow, asking had we been witnesses; we replied that we had."[53]

Parenthetically, however, it should be noted that under rare and significantly unusual circumstances, the hatred fulminates and escapes the rigid repression and usual patterns of discharge. In order to understand the nature of such an explosion, it is necessary to understand the biology of the male child in particular, and specifically that part of his early history having to do with the nature of the expression of anger toward his mother. If the boy becomes annoyed or angry, he is not permitted to discharge this rage in the direction of his father, the emperor, or *giri* bureaucracy; but he may, as an alternative, legitimately pound his mother's breasts.[54]

Dr. Koizumi tells me that there is a sort of once-a-year moratorium on decorum allowed the Japanese male. On New Year's, Japanese students may be invited to their professors' homes, where host and guests alike may proceed to get very drunk. But the resultant devastation—broken windows, furniture, etc.—is considered (once a year) to be forgivable. This is, analytically speaking, a reaction against the strict cultural restraints forced upon all Japanese men throughout the remainder of the year.

In Manila, after the return of the Americans and the establishment of their unprecedented dominance, the Americans became the power-figure which, in its abstract sense, precluded the possibility of the Japanese discharging the bulk of their rage. General Yamashita, a newcomer to the Philippines, had not yet consolidated the various Japanese military units spread out over the island of Luzon. There were a northern and a southern army under separate commands. The naval units were answerable to the admiralty. The Japanese were practically without leadership and direction from a consistent and single high authority. Thus rudderless, as it were, they reverted to the type of display of violence permitted them in their early boyhood: they corralled the Filipino women and ran bayonets sidewise through their breasts,* even as, in childhood, they had beaten the breasts of their own mothers. In both cases, their behavior, to any psychoanalyst, would be a comprehensible outlet for the discharge of hatred in a time of great confusion and frustration.

* * *

Wherever there is rigidity, there is always an underlying resentment, bitterness, or hatred; among the Japanese this may be seen in their more recent criminal codes and in their earlier attitudes toward criminal behavior. Capital punishment was common, even for relatively inconsequential crimes. It made little difference who committed the crime, as to rank; trial was speedy and retribution immediate. Such evidence of hostility represents one permissible outlet for hate: those who were on the side of justice could legitimately vent their hostility upon anyone who disobeyed the moral or legal codes or transgressed against the authoritarian. By remaining on the side of law and order, the individual not only proved that he was obedient, but was able to keep his own resentments and bitterness in check by using the "criminal" as a target. In the same manner, in time of war an enemy becomes a target for the accumulated hostilities of its foe; and often war drains off the accumulated tensions incidental to the development of hate following frustrations, or interference with the deterministic growth of individuals.

4

CONFORMITY AND RAGE IN THE JAPANESE FEMALE

I WONDERED about the women. They were docile enough and seemed to conform if considered from a statistical point of view. But they did not exhibit the same quantity of rigidity and conformity as did the male. Here and there a woman appeared among the inmates of the mental hospitals who raved with the spectacular and frantic abandon of a person in the manic stage of manic-depressive psychosis. The Japanese male even when insane was well behaved. This striking oddity of the pacific male insane will be discussed in the next chapter. I conjectured about these women and came to the conclusion that, being women, they were not, and never had been, considered important. Because they were unnecessary, they were not so assiduously repressed by their induction into *ko* to the father. An additional supporting item is expressed by the fact that Japanese women commit only a third as many suicides as the men.[55] This cultural finding should be of utmost significance to all.

Seemingly, it is a great catastrophe to be born a female in Japan, since even though women are not so regidly repressed by the institutions, they are nevertheless subjected to extreme degradation. Sidney Gulick observes: "The Japanese lady, at her marriage, lays aside her independent existence to become the subordinate and servant of her husband and parents-in-law, and her face, as the years go by, shows how much she has given up, how completely she has sacrificed herself to those about her."[56] A line from an old poem called "Dreary Things," written by a lady-in-waiting upon one of the early Japanese empresses, calls attention to one of the catastrophes that might befall the Japanese male:* "The birth of a succession of female children in the house of a learned scholar."[57] Von Siebold remarks that " . . . [women] are . . . held during their whole lives in a state of tutelage, of complete dependence upon their husbands, sons, or other relations. They are without legal rights, and their evidence is inadmissible in a court of justice."[58] Cornelia Spencer says: "Japanese wives . . . do not have the equivalent of the geisha houses. They stay at home and listen to the description of this girl or that, if anything is said about the matter at all, or else pretend no knowledge of it. Their marriage must completely absorb them and it is never thought that they, too, may have need of some of the kind of companionship which the entertainers afford their husbands."[59] Embree writes: "The selling of daughters as geisha and prostitutes is a prerogative of the father. A recent law says a girl's consent must be obtained, but in practice this is a mere formality. A girl is in no position to refuse her consent. Recent laws which have made it possible for women to own property have only resulted in aiding their husbands who are in debt. When the creditor comes, the man divorces his wife and puts his property in her name and is thus penniless himself. The creditor is balked.

Later the man may, and usually does, remarry his divorced wife."[60]

Adams, speaking from the Victorian period, expresses much the same ideas: "No one at least will deny that the Japanese women have been educated on a different principle from our own. They have been told to obey their parents implicitly in all respects; and as long as those parents kept them at home, and did not issue .heir commands to the contrary, they might be as pure in body as our own maidens. But each one knew that if to-morrow her parents directed that she should be sold to a stew. or should become the concubine of any given man, she had nothing to do but to resign herself, without a word or a murmur, to the fulfilment of their decree. And where the woman is looked upon as so inferior to the man, where she prostrates herself before him, serves him at his meals, and is little better than his slave —where, too, the vicious system of polygamy, or what is equivalent thereto, flourishes—can the same standard of chastity and virtue exist as with us? It seems to me that with the Japanese a woman is chaste, not from a religious point of view, not because it is right and natural to be so, but because she is ordered to be so by her parents. It is not with her a matter of principle, it is a matter of obedience. I should be glad if the contrary could be proved."[61]

It is evident that in a nation where the women cannot in normal society become overtly aggressive, violence on the part of a woman might be regarded by the Japanese as a manifestation of mental illness or antisocial behavior. The literature of the early Meiji period* gave much attention to murders committed by women. Yet in reality murder—by some such secret methods as poisoning—has long been almost the only outlet for the pent-up hostility of Japanese women. Dr. Koizumi informs me that many columns of newspaper space went into coverage of a famous sex murder by a Japanese prostitute within recent pre-war years (and was avidly read by most literate Japanese). One may safely assume that not a little of the attention given the case sprang from the fact that overt hostility in a woman, even on the part of a prostitute, was a curiosity in Japanese life.

However, despite the derogatory attitude universally expressed toward the Japanese woman,[62] there is still evidence that she is more spontaneous, flexible, and free-moving than the Japanese man. Not being considered important, she is not subjected to strenuous early infantile institutions. I have noticed that the laughter of Japanese women is more genuine, spontaneous, mirthful and less restrained than that of the men, and I am supported in this observation by Miss Roxane Lambie, who spent a year in Japan as a club worker with the American Red Cross from 1946 to 1947.

The men as children were subjected to severe self-discipline and disindividualization. Their indoctrination being more thorough was likewise more lasting in its effect than that of women.

5

JAPANESE CONFORMITY AND INSANITY

JAPANESE males, even when insane, conform to authority. In March, 1949, I had an opportunity to observe the effect of the early infantile discipline of the Japanese male. During my visits to Japanese insane asylums, one at Kyoto and the other about thirty miles from Tokyo, I observed a situation that was almost unbelievable: there were no special facilities for confining the insane; the most violent lived together in rooms that were separated by unsecured rice-paper partitions opening into long corridors. The windows were unscreened glass of ordinary thickness, waisthigh even for the Japanese. When I had first read reports[63] of the Japanese insane, I was skeptical, and at the Ko-no-dai National Hospital I kept insisting that the institution must house more violently disturbed males. The Japanese psychiatrist, trained at our own Boston Psychopathic Hospital, understood my disbelief, because he was familiar with American insane. Yet, in his willingness to help me, he practically gave me the keys to the hospital; and like a man from Missouri, I saw every room throughout the institution. What I saw confirmed the reports I had read: the male Japanese did not become rabidly disturbed. In this connection I must emphasize that it is not the practice of the Japanese to exterminate their insane, as is commonly believed by many Americans.

It is customary for occidental psychiatrists and psychoanalysts to expect unpredictable violent behavior from some categories of insane. It is likewise usual, for anyone cognizant of the psychology of insanity, to appreciate the wells of self-hate and anger that ferment in the heart of the insane person. Yet, with the culturally enforced degradation of the Japanese individual (a societal situation usually assumed to result in self-hate, rage, and insanity) it is astonishing that violent categories of insane are not encountered in the Japanese asylums. Further, insanity of any type in Japan is statistically insignificant. At the time I visited the hospitals mentioned, there were 2,700 Japanese hospitalized in all of the Greater Tokyo mental institutions—2,700 in a population of 5,500,000, or 49.1 per 100,000 (as compared with the United States figure of 400 per 100,000). Because the Japanese insane are so tractable and a high percentage of them managed at home, it is difficult to estimate the exact statistical importance of insanity for the Japanese archipelago; however, there is every reason to believe that psychoses are less frequently encountered there than in the United States.

In studying the problem, another surprising fact came to my attention: paranoid types of insanity are relatively infrequent in the total census of Japanese asylums. Dr. A. R. Manitoff, of the United States Military Government for the Tokyo area, supplied me with statistics demonstrating that the paranoid type of schizophrenia is encountered about one-sixth as frequently as other forms of schizophrenia. Berger made a similar observation of the Japanese army psychiatric casualties encountered in Korea after World War II.[64] He found that paranoid types of schizophrenia were numerically insignificant. When compared with figures from the United States, the statistical insignificance of Japanese paranoid schizophrenia is most astonishing.*

From information supplied me by Dr. Charles Barker, of Pontiac State Hospital (Michigan), it is immediately evident that in contrast with Japan, the United States reveals not only a statistically important number of paranoid schizophrenics, but—a source for socio-economic alarm—the number is rapidly increasing.

PATIENTS ADMITTED TO PONTIAC STATE HOSPITAL
AS OF OCT. 25, 1950

(Present Hospital Population, including Patients on Convalescent Parole Status)

Total Hospital Population		3722
Schizophrenia		
Simple Type	59	
Hebephrenic Type	360	
Catatonic Type	368	
Paranoid Type	832	
Unclassified	206	
Total		1825

Percentage of Schizophrenics in Total Hospital Population   49.0%
Percentage of Schizophrenics in Total Hospital Population who are Paranoid   22.3%

PATIENTS ADMITTED TO PONTIAC STATE HOSPITAL
JULY 1, 1949 TO JUNE 30, 1950

Total Admissions (including those previously admitted
    at Pontiac or elsewhere)   1139
    Schizophrenia

Simple Type	11	
Hebephrenic Type	86	
Catatonic Type	119	
Paranoid Type	348	
Unclassified	41	
Total		605

Percentage of Schizophrenics in Total Admis-
    sions 1949-1950   53.1%
Percentage of Schizophrenics Admitted 1949-
    1950 who are Paranoid   30.6%

Dr. Leopold Bellak, who is a leading authority on schizophrenia, says that "every fourth or fifth bed available in the nation (U.S.) is occupied by a patient diagnosed dementia praecox (as of 1948)."[65]

One would expect, in a patriarchy where love and emotions are suppressed and depreciated, where power and authoritarianism are exalted, that a high incidence of paranoid mental disorder would be encountered. Paranoid mental disease is usually spawned by a drive for power, when the individual believes that he is incapable of being loved. But if this is true, why did not the power-mad Japanese nation abound in paranoid schizophrenics?

My first-hand observations now reinforced the conclusions of other investigators whose findings I have previously remarked: "If one were to investigate other anthropological realms for confirmation of the fact that it is the pressure of the parent upon the child that fashions the child's character, one could point to the Japanese. Colonel Cotton and Colonel Ebaugh made a startling discovery in their survey of psychiatric hospitals in Japan. They discovered that the most psychotic of the institutional inmates often were separated from one another by a thin sheet of glass. Ebaugh and Cotton came to the conclusion that the Japanese had been indoctrinated in non-assertiveness so early in their lives that even when psychotic, they were incapable of individually sponsored, aggressive behavior.[66] In *The Cornelian Corner and Its Rationale* (1947), I ventured one answer to this question: "One might conclude that the projectional types of psychotic behavior would be relatively infrequent in an ethnic group which frowned upon personal aggressiveness. . . ."[67]

This attitude toward the question is further elaborated by Douglas Haring: "An underlying hypothesis of the recent anthropological-psychoanalytic studies, *sans* technical jargon, may be summarized briefly," he writes. "With due allowance for physical and regional limitations for cultural history, the unique aspects of any society are determined and maintained by emotional habits learned in infancy by a majority of the participating individuals. Much of this learning occurs before the infant learns to talk. Consequently, a variety of socially important emotional habits continues vague and indefinite, even unconscious, throughout every individual's lifetime. One knows only that certain types of social situations are congenial and he feels at home in them, while in other situations he is ill at ease, even violently disturbed. The experiences of early infancy, reinforced by subsequent events, have developed in him uncon-

scious criteria of social and cultural choice. Such pre-
ferences one takes for granted, despite fluent rationaliza-
tions, the ultimate criteria of his personal and social pre-
ferences lies beyond his ability to perceive objectively
and to describe verbally."[68]

In this frame of reference, one might say that the
Japanese emotional disease of neurotic conformism is
an almost universal character neurosis which protects
the Japanese from developing psychoses. So long as he
lives submissively in an authoritarian milieu, he operates
in a familiar setting such as Haring suggests, and his
ego integrations are adequate and characteristic for this
particular mode of life. At this time, although I am
in complete sympathy with Haring's point of view, I
believe that it leaves questions to be answered. Why does
the authoritarian milieu of the United States breed more
paranoid schizophrenics than does the even more authoritarian milieu of Japan?

To this question I think there is an answer: The
Japanese baby has an intimate relationship with his
mother from the time of birth. And despite the fact
that she later becomes rigid in her child training methods, her attitude is basically warmly maternal. The
warm motherly attitude of the Japanese woman is in
some way communicated to the infant. (See also "The
Primary Unit.")[69]

In the first five months of the Japanese child's life,
before the development of his conscious ego, he is per-
missively fed. Surprisingly enough, the Japanese have
long known, even if they did not realize it, how to treat
the Japanese mother to bring about a state of mind
which was most conducive to her becoming a motherly
person. Any woman must herself be mothered to become motherly toward her child; this fact is well known

41

to scientists today. Von Siebold shows us that the principle was followed by the Japanese as far back as 1841: "For one hundred days after her delivery, the recent mother is considered as an invalid, and nursed as such; at the end of that period only, she resumes her household duties, visits the temple frequented by her family, and performs her pilgrimage, or any other act of devotion that she may have vowed in her hour of peril."[70] Again, Von Siebold observed the early permissiveness of the Japanese: "The infant, immediately upon its birth, is bathed, and remains free from all swathing and clothing that could impede the growth and development of body or limb."[71]

It seems evident that there is no early mouth-conflict-with-the-mother memory patterns existent in the psyche of the Japanese that divides self-rights from mother-rights. Mouth-conflct-with-the-mother memory patterns are a necessary predecessor to schizophrenia. Mouth-conflict memory patterns are derivatives of an early lack of maternal supporting or maternal security-producing physical contact for the newborn. Such a lack tends to promote preconscious memorial oral displacements to the eye, which thus becomes the "mouth that sees" as well as the eye becoming the object that is eaten. Because the eye implies a physical detachment from the object seen, the latter becomes the target for projection—i.e., for ocular cannibalism. Since this process occurs beyond the pale of consciousness, paranoid foundations become implicit in this type of personality. Eventually, if the ego disintegrates or becomes distorted, the paranoid foundation may preempt and dominate the psychic operations of the individual. (This was further discussed in my article, "Some Simple Cultural Factors in the

Etiology of Schizophrenia," that was published in *Child Development,* September, 1951.) Because the ego of the Japanese is consistently, firmly and cohesively structured, the danger of splitting through regression to the oral dichotomy memory is minimal. René A. Spitz points out that "inconsistent, contradictory behavior of the mother makes the establishment of the adequate object relations impossible and arrests the child at the level of primary narcissistic discharge of its libidinal drive. . . ."[72]

In this regard it is important to describe another factor of Japanese child life that is not encountered in the United States. Even after the mother starts to institute *ko* (respect to the father), the baby is still in contact with the mother's body. The child rides in a sling on the mother's back, able to peer over her shoulder, and thus experiences a sense of security and physical satisfaction. I have described these advantages in "How to Cherish the Child and Free the Mother":

"When a baby is carried in a sling on the mother's back, facing forward, the child will see for himself and will experience for himself how grown-ups cooperate or get along with one another. . . . Through direct maternal inoculation the infant experiences the great human necessity of cooperation.

"If the child is carried on the mother's back, shoulder high, he is freed from the feeling of being a mite in a world of giants. Little children on the ground surrounded by grown-ups must fear being overshadowed by others.

"If the infant is able to look over the right shoulder from his position on the back of the mother, he is introduced to a flowing panoramic world that has significant spacial and time connections. In a crib, the world is introduced to him in piecemeal fashion. In his fixed crib position he does not gain the feeling that he too is a part of a moving world.

"In intimate contact with the sinuous rippling movements of the mother's warm back, the child is afforded a feeling of the flexibility and resiliency of the mother. This infant learns that the mother does not meet each outside situation with stiffness, the impression that would confront the child if tied to a cradle board.

"The child should face the mother's back, being made secure there by sashes or wrap-arounds which do not inhibit the mother's movements, or the child's arms or legs. In this position the infant is able to grasp the mother. The primate grasping reflex affords the infant the sense of security that he too is doing something active, that he holds his mother. He experiences a mutual relationship with his mother, his own activity contributing his share to the relationship.

"With the baby so intimately related to the mother, the mother too learns the ways and language of the baby. The baby is fed when he asks for food. A state of frustration does not persist. No need develops for the baby to turn to self for gratifications. The turning to the self for self pleasure leads to tight little circles . . . to thumb sucking, to masturbation, to tongue sucking, to devices that later on in life tie up quantities of important energy that, if freed, could be used for more appropriate and meaningful activities."[73]

In the American culture, there is a fractionation in early infantile experience. The baby can see, hear, and smell the mother. In each instance the mother is appreciated as a thing apart from the infant. The need for the baby's general body sensations to be exercised by actual contact with the mother's body (even tasting should be included) is given scant attention. Even when feeling-attention *is* given to the child, it is pin-pointed at various significant areas of the child's body. The ultimate in contact, skin-to-skin, is not customarily a continuous experience for the American baby; he is more likely to be related to the mother from afar. This state of affairs places a higher importance upon the eyes, ears, and nose as means of contact with the mother than upon the skin.*

I have given considerable attention to this matter in a previous publication** and since it is so basic to the understanding of character structure, I feel that it is important to restate my discussion here:

"Skin contact with the mother, particularly with a motherly mother, advances the development of the skin ego. An accurate and objectively correct memorable picture of the skin surfaces—in substance, an accurate and memorable picture of the body boundaries—promotes a sense of reality. The mother should stimulate all of the baby's skin, not merely those areas (such as mouth, anus, vagina, urethra) which, due to their physiological functions, call forth specific and exaggerated maternal attention. All of the surfaces of the baby's body should be stimulated, fondled, and caressed by a relaxed, motherly mother. The very young baby should be held against the mother's bare skin; for there is perhaps no other way in which the realness of the mother's body is so accurately and consistently registered upon the child. Consistent contact with the mother's body provides, through the sensory end-organs of the baby's skin, a valuable and unchanging picture of her actual texture. So important is the skin ego—the memorable skin schema—that everything possible should be done to develop it.

"Speaking still of our own culture, let us indicate what may occur in connection with the baby's other senses, in order to emphasize the importance of consistent skin contact between mother and infant. In the case of the ocular sense, the light rays striking the rods and cones of the child's retina are neither the mother herself, nor even a properly consistent fetishistic substitute for her. When the light rays are reflected upon the baby's retina, the child may be confronted with a confusing variety of mothers: bare-headed or hatted, rouged or unrouged, clothed or naked—some so extremely different from previous images that the baby may not even recognize her as the same person he has previously seen. Moreover, the source of light may alter the mother's appearance. She may be presented to the child's eye as an effulgent being one moment, and as a silhouette the next. Thus, through the ocular sense alone, the baby draws a constantly varying, potentially inconsistent, and hence incomplete fetishistic representation of his mother.

"The same situation exists in the case of the olfactory sense. The sensory end-organs in the mucous membrane of the infant's nose may again be presented, as in the case of the retina, with fragmentary and conflicting fetishes for the mother, since only the odors which emanate from her are actually present at the mucous membrane surface, not the mother herself. The baby may feel that he is surrounded by a swarm of mothers: the 'B.O. Mother,' the 'Ivory Soap Mother,' the 'Shalimar Mother,' the 'Mary Chess Mother,' confusing in the inconsistency of their various smells.

"Once again, through the auditory sense, according

to the changes wrought by the mother's varying emotions and even her clothing, the baby may draw from the sounds of her voice and garb another confusing series of impressions, other fetishistic representations of a variety of mothers: the angry-voiced, the contrite and dulcet-toned; the silent wool-clad, the rustling taffeta-clad, the crackling starched-cotton-clad. The sounds may be distant or near-at-hand—an angry outburst at fifty feet, followed by contrite murmurs in the baby's ear.

"If the mother is not a breast-feeder, even the taste of her, as conceptualized by the baby's formula, may change with every feeding.

"Whether the mother is represented to the baby through eye, ear, or nose, if he is not also in frequent contact with the mother's skin, he does not experience the real mother. However, when the skin of the infant is thoroughly stimulated by contact with the motherly mother's own body (and not merely by a ray of light, an odor, or a sound wave), there is a consistency and reality to the relationship which undoubtedly advances the adequate development of the child's body schema memory. The texture and temperature of the mother's skin varies little from one contact to another. Because a skin-to-skin relationship with the mother is consistent and real, rather than fetishistic and full of vagaries, the baby's sense of reality, his efficient skin ego, develops properly."

* * *

As a result of this separation of the child from the mother, I postulate that self-identity is blurred, because without excitation of the skin areas of the child, the sense of body boundary is not memorially recorded as being different from the memorial picture of the moth-

47

er's boundaries. This neglect of feeling influences or actually encourages the infant to set up part of his own body as a plastic representative of the absent mother. This in turn, as I have said, encourages narcissism, such as thumb-sucking, early infantile masturbation, hair-twiddling, tongue-sucking. By these devices the baby becomes the mother who gives love to the baby as well as the infant who is babied by the mother. The baby, by becoming the mother to himself, dominates all possibilities. He develops a domain of his own.

In the United States people do not tolerate intimate contact of skin or flesh or of the body, between two individuals over sustained periods of time. Everybody looks to the time that he can be by himself or get off by himself. In the development of the Japanese *ko,* the mother is physically related to the child, and this is preferable to having no physical contact with the child at all. To paraphrase what I have said in a paper published in *Child Development:*[74] ". . . it is fatal to neglect the child completely. To prevent the advent of psychosis, the mother should do something that touches the child with her presence even if touching the child means consistently rigid toilet training."

In brief, I theorize that the consistently good physical relationship between the Japanese baby and the Japanese mother reduces to a minimum the danger of the child ever developing a psychosis.

However, the fact that the Japanese type of child-raising forces the Japanese child to bind rage with allergic thongs or with other types of psychosomatic disease perhaps introduces a new approach to culture-personality studies. Observing the presence or absence of bound or free-floating fear-rage offers a short-cut to cross-cultural studies. In this connection, I would suggest comparing the capacities of the individual members of the ethnic group being studied for their expression of appropriate spontaneity in contrast with the demonstrable rigidities of criminalism and/or psychosomatic disease and/or insanity.

This cross sectional short cut has its advantages. A survey that compares the relationship between crime, psychosomatic diseases, and insanity in any given culture might indicate that this type of approach provides an efficient and relatively rapid method of evaluating the ethnos under study. The American scene can be assayed from the three angles. Without attempting anything other than to indicate a trend I might say that crime costs this country twenty-six billion dollars a year. Psychosomatically sick Americans occupy at least 80 per cent of our hospital beds. The American insane are numerous. Fifty per cent of all hospital beds are occupied by the insane; there are 400 per hundred thousand insane living, in the United States. The Okinawans present an entirely different statistical figure. Their crime figures prior to World War II were negligible. Psychosomatic diseases are rarely encountered among the Okinawans. And in Okinawa five years after the war there were about 9 insane per hundred thousand population. The Italians have about 200 per hundred thousand institutionalized insane. The Italian crime and psychosomatic statistics are not available at this time, but perhaps could be obtained, if a serious scientific study were undertaken. Eire provides an interesting situation for speculation. Juvenile delinquency is conspicuous, particularly in Dublin and the larger cities. However, adult criminals are not numerous; in fact they are perhaps fewer than in most cultures. But the insane rate is higher than any that I have ever statistically encountered (666.9 per hundred thousand). The frequency of psychosomatic diseases in the Irish culture is not known to me. Japan presents an interesting contrast. The frequency of crime is not spectacular. The insane number 49 per 100,000 for Tokyo-to. But the incidence of psychosomatic disease is exceedingly high.

Of course it is not the intent of this approach to do away with the very valuable behavioral and character structure studies.

6

PSYCHO-DYNAMICS OF JAPANESE HATE DISPERSAL

TO be sure, the maternal extermination of the baby's self-expression evokes its resentment toward the mother. The child takes out a token rage on the mother, but he dare not destroy her; she is too necessary to him. To preserve a giving mother-figure, the mother is divided in the child's psyche into two persons, the good and the bad mother. At first the bad mother *imago* or image is deflected to the father, who is the depriver. Levin describes the depriving father: "The killing of the father could be the result of his not being a good 'mother.' It would be generally agreed that the child does not recall the infantile period of frustration when he was deprived of his full measure of mother-love and oral gratifications. This loss of love is well locked in the unconscious and is forgotten. In fact, the mother, because of her domestic role, appears to be the one who gives the protection and care which is also the father's duty. But the dominant mental image of the father is that of authority and power; he is a prohibitor and denier—a depriver. As contrasted with mother-love his role symbolizes the authority which curtails the child's freedom. . . . These deprivations—

51

be they of the sexual freedom which could result in intercourse with the mother, or be they any other type of deprivation—are unconsciously equated by the mind of the child with the earlier deprivations by the mother. The algebra of the unconscious only knows simple equations. The mother is not killed because later—irrespective of how poorly she performs her domestic role—she comes to symbolize love and protection. That is, she is needed by the child. Her former acts of deprivation are now well forgotten and repressed. In our culture the father early becomes a competitor with his children, and, therefore, constantly reactivates the latent resentments against the mother. In accord with the psycho-dynamic facts, there should have been more mother-murder than father-murder had the unconscious been able to come out of its repressions."[75] But repressions exist, and Frederic Wertham writes: "I searched through crime bulletins and newspapers. Murder of a mother by her son is probably the least frequent of all kinds of homicide in the United States."[76]

Patricide is unthinkable in the culture of Japan; matricide, almost unheard of in the United States, is not readily condoned in Japan but is a great deal more tolerable there than the murder of a father. It is almost impossible to obtain statistics on the rate of matricides and patricides in Japan. However, in talking with Mr. Yasutake, who, in his journalistic work in Japan, read many court records involving criminal cases, I learned that his impression was that there are few murders of any sort, by American standards; and such as involve killings of members of the family are largely limited to the killing of sons for insurance, for the support of parents. Almost never is there a patricide, and when the almost equally rare matricide occurs, it is in Mr.

Yasutake's opinion, almost invariably because of the women's supposed interference in the marriage of one of her children, never for money. Dr. Robert Ward, Assistant Director of the Center for Japanese Study, University of Michigan, also talked with me regarding this matter. He not only confirms Yasutake's statements, but says further that the Japanese would be so ashamed of matricide or patricide (especially the latter) that the only statistics on the subject would be found in police records. From an article by psychoanalyst Heisaku Kosawa on "Two Types of Guilt Consciousness—Oedipus and Azase," we find a strong hint that there may be more matricide than patricide in Japan.[77] In his article, Kosawa includes the following bit of Japanese folklore demonstrating this point:

". . . the 'belief without foundation' of King Azase [began] in India at the time of Buddha. . . .

"A young prince gained victory after victory in his neighborhood. Upon the advice of Daiba, he incarcerated his father, since his longing for vengeance had become greater and greater. The prince went to the jail door and cagily asked the keeper, 'Is my father the king still alive?'

"The keeper told him everything [evidently that his mother had visited his father]. The prince flew into a rage. He swore at his mother and cried, 'My mother was a rebel, because she was the companion of my father, who was a rebel! The Buddhist priest was a devil, because he lengthened the life of the king by his devilish arts!'

"He reached out with his left hand and seized his mother's hair. Grasping his dagger in his right hand, he held it at his mother's breast. He would have stabbed her in no time at all. She was terrified, and folded her hands as if in prayer. She squirmed, bowed her head, and clutched her son's hand. Her whole body was bathed in sweat. Then she fainted.

"Suddenly [two] ministers of state . . . rushed into the room. They got between him and his mother and cried, 'O, Prince! We have often heard that in olden times there were many cruel kings. Many of them killed their fathers to get possession of the throne, but never have we heard of any ruler who was so cruel as to murder his own mother. If you, O Prince, should commit such a misdeed, it would bring dishonor and shame on our entire caste. It would be a deed worthy of the lowest caste, the fishermen. We would not be able to bear it if such a crime became known.' The ministers implored the prince to give up his intention.

"When he heard this counsel, the prince dropped the dagger and gave up the idea of killing his mother. However, he immediately gave orders to lock his mother up in the most remote corner of the castle.

"After Prince Azase had ascended the throne (after letting his father die miserably) he indulged his sensual pleasures. But after awhile his conscience began to bother him and he became mentally confused. Horrible ill-smelling sores developed all over his body. One could hardly go near him, and he kept saying to himself, 'In all of this the fruit of my deeds can clearly be seen, and it is certain that I am going to hell.'

"This was the climax of his dejection and sorrow. His body and soul were sick. Troubles and worries about the present and future weighed down his body and soul. . . ."

Kosawa ends his account of the story of Azase with the statement: "I would like to note that among neurotics and psychopaths, these psychic conditions [i.e.,

Oedipus (father-murder) and Azase (mother-murder)]
can also be terminated by religion [Buddhism]."[78]

In Japan the father does not long remain a target—
the "bad mother." By the mother's persistent development of and reverence to the father (*ko*), the father becomes tabu. The rage is then deflected to someone outside the family. To requote Muramatsu: "This intense
emphasis on in-group characteristics in feudal Japan
resulted in exclusiveness, cliquism, and hostility towards
outsiders. . . . Elaborate rules were set up to govern necessary out-group relations. From these developed those
elaborate patterns of etiquette which are often regarded
as characteristically Japanese."[79] Because of the uniformity of *ko, chu, giri, enryo, kodo,* and *bushido* training,
the Japanese have become most homogeneous. The performance of all Japanese people is virtually identical
with the performance of a single Japanese individual,
and what can be said of the psychology of the individual
can be said of the psychology of Japan. To quote
Kokutai No Hongi, "In our country, Sovereign and
subjects have from of old been spoken of as being one,
and the entire nation, united in mind and acting in full
cooperation, have shown forth the beauties of this oneness with the Emperor as their centre. The august virtues of the Emperor and the duties of the subjects con-
verge and unite into a beautiful harmony."[80]

This is important to know, because the psychic splitting of the mother into two persons—the good mother
and the bad mother—is a dichotomy long known to students of psychology, and without this knowledge it is
impossible to understand the workings of the Japanese
personality.

Hasegawa makes note of the Japanese provision in
their mythology for a good-bad dichotomy. He says:

"Another characteristic of the Japanese as reflected in their mythology is the cooperation of two opposing forces—the *ara-mitama* and the *nigi-mitama,* which mean 'a rough soul' and 'a gentle soul,' respectively. The *Nihon Syoki* contains, in an account of the Empress Zingu (170-269), a passage in which the Empress, when she was starting on an expedition against the three Korean states—Japan's first foreign war—is represented as having received an oracle promising her protection by these two divine souls. The *ara-mitama,* as the name shows, is the spirit of military force, and the *nigi-mitama* is its contrary—the soul of peace. This mythical interpretation of the cooperation of the soul of arms and the soul of peace promised on the eve of the expedition is certainly symbolic of the divine intelligence of deity and at the same time of the mentality of the Japanese. In Japanese mythology, strict injunction is given against any preponderance of either of the two souls. Susanoo-no-Mikoto [wicked brother of Amaterasu] was a god with a preponderance of the *ara-mitama.* He it was that worked injury to farming and textile industries. This guilty behavior, the first recorded offence in the history of Japanese criminology, was discussed before a conference of the gods, according to whose findings the offender was deported with confiscation of property."[81]

Rage, to be sure, exists in the Japanese individual. Collections of similar individuals constitute the Japanese nation. (A nation, according to one of Webster's definitions, is: "a people connected by supposed ties of blood generally manifested by community of language, religion, and customs." It is in this sense that I use the word.) Some significant objects, animate and inanimate, are inviolable, acting as stand-ins for the good mother. Others are violable (the bad mother) and can be and are

56

satisfactory and permissive targets for Japanese rage. These permissive targets are given more elaborate treatment in this chapter and in the following chapters.

Doing away with the Shogun in the Meiji Restoration did away with the cultural duality here outlined.* As a result, it became necessary for the Japanese to find outside targets for the expression of their hostilities in order to retain their duality system. Accordingly, they began to seek permissible outlets for these hostilities outside of Japan. To follow this process, it will be helpful to trace the whole question of hostility as it has affected the Japanese over the centuries.

* * *

Geza Roheim, writing on "The Psychology of Patriotism,"[82] quotes Petofi's "In My Country":

> "Thou plain ornate with sheaves of gold
>   And covered with sweet phantom bearing mirage
> Dost thou still recognize me
>   And really know thy son?

> "Where I once in my cradle's lap so soft
>   Tasted the sweetness of my mother's milk
> The day will shine again and make me thine
>   Thy child again, beloved country mine."[83]

Roheim comments on the meaning of Petofi's poem as follows: "In the quotation of the great Hungarian poet I gave as a motto, there are three striking trends: (1) the mother country is the mother; (2) it is a mother seen through the mirage of phantasy; (3) there is a desire to return, a nostalgia, a regressive trend."[84]

It should be noted that there are distinct feminine overtones to the Japanese patriarchy. The royal family are descendants of Amaterasu, a sun goddess. A detailed

57

description of this myth may be found in *Kojiki*,[85] or *Nipon O Dai Itsi Ran*.[86] Besides this significant connection with a female deity, there are other feminine characteristics which stem from the dynasty itself. The Fujiwara contribution of females to the royal line almost equals numerically the male contributions of the Yamoto family, and after the Fujiwara rule, Fujiwara males served as regents for the imperial line. In a number of instances in many generations, the old emperor abdicated in favor of his son, a minor. The maternal uncle, a Fujiwara, then ruled until the son reached majority.[87] The feminine overtones of the Emperor's relationship to the Japanese people are evidenced in *Kokutai No Hongi*: "Evidences of the Emperor's endless love and care for his subjects are constantly seen throughout history. The Emperor graciously treats his subjects as *ohmitakara* [a word meaning 'great treasures,' 'subjects' or 'people'], loves and protects them as one would sucklings. . . ."[88] While we are presented, externally, with an almost universal appearance of paternal dominance, the hierarchal power patterns being essentially patriarchal, we may presume the presence of significant maternal constituents in the picture of Japanese culture. The apparent over-exaggeration of masculine importance and the deliberate devaluation of the female position in the later Japanese patriarchal structures should direct anthropological attention to the powerful, if subtle, political influences exerted by Japanese women. Kenji Ohtski, a psychoanalyst writing for the *Tokyo Journal of Psychoanalysis* recognizes the feminine influence: "The racial characters of the Orientals are 'id-ic' and feminine as compared with those of the Occidentals, which are 'ego-ic' and masculine."[89]

The patriarchal pattern itself functions in a matriarchal setting. In fact, the training of the Japanese in adherence to the patriarchal institutions of *ko* (obligation to the father), *chu* (extreme obligation to the emperor), and *kanzan* (respect for authority), is a maternal responsibility. The rigid patriarchal structure is transmitted to the children through the interposition of an intermediary host, the mother; the tensions of the mother are transferable to the newborn infant.

Sibylle K. Escalona, of the Menninger Clinic, has remarked upon the disturbance of infants who have been managed by "tense, excitable, nervous, and insecure" mothers, where, as she says, the upset behavior of the child seems attributable directly to the emotional condition of the adult, rather than to faulty handling by her.[90] Ashley Montagu, Professor of Anthropology at Rutgers University, has expressed the same feeling in a personal letter to me. The mother's "frame of mind," he says, provides the child with the basis for its own orientation.

Later in the life of the Japanese child, maternal patterns and pressures are induced in the child because mother and child (and in particular the male child) are one and the same person. The proper reciprocal emancipatory process is cancelled by insistence upon the institutions of *ko, chu, kanzan, giri,* and *enryo.* In fact, these institutions are dramatized almost as post-hypnotic suggestions, induced by a maternal hypnotist; and later, triggered by the proper grouping of power estates previously rendered specially significant by the mother, the institutions fetishistically come to represent the mother herself. The Japanese patriarchy is, in its final analysis, a maternal accouterment or construct which mirrors with only slight distortion the mother's own reaction to her rigid environment. The pressures she exerts upon her offspring vary; she is most relentless and rigid in her attitude toward her oldest son, and in general more rigid toward sons than she is toward daughters. The mother manifests not only a selective inattention, but a selective attention, as well. In hypnosis, if a rigid bar is pressed against the flaccid arm of the subject, the arm will become rigid, like the bar, even if no word is spoken and no vocal suggestion made. The rigid Japanese patriarchy is like the rigid bar, but the bar is wielded by the phantom of the mother who originally indoctrinated the child with the patriarchal system.

A Viennese analyst noticed in the material of his Japanese patient a dominance of father material. This would not seem strange to anyone knowing the characteristics of Japanese culture.* However, this so-called father material actually represented mother material, the maternal attitude toward the analysand when he was an infant and child. The analytic aura of respect for the father expresses: "This is how my mother wants me to obligate myself to my father."

The dichotomous mother idea is quite well elucidated and dramatized by such characteristic combinations as: Emperor-Kwambaku;** Emperor-Shogun; Shogun-Shikken.*** Alcock has observed the detailed political or governmental duality when he wrote: "This double machinery of a titular Sovereign [Mikado] who only reigns, and a Lieutenant of the empire [Shogun] who only governs, and does *not* reign, from generation to generation, is certainly something very curious; and by long continuance it seems to have led to a duplicate system such as never existed in any other part of the world, carried out to almost every detail of existence. Every office is doubled; every man is alternately a watcher and watched. Not only the whole administrative machinery is in duplicate, but the most elaborate system of check and countercheck, on the most approved Machiavellian principle, is here developed with a minuteness and perfection as regards details, difficult at first to realise."[91]

Kokutai No Hongi further demonstrates the duality system: "Especially adaptable to the system of ultra-nationalism . . . have been those principles of loyalty and filial piety based on the five Confucian relationships of sovereign and subject; father and child; husband and wife; elder and younger brother (or sister) . . . ."[92]

* * *

The good and bad mother duality is particularly significant in the Japanese scheme. In this frame of reference the emperor plays a dual role which has contributed to the permanency of the Yamoto-Fujiwara combination. The emperor is a good mother symbol, a sanctified goddess mother (Amaterasu) and therefore inviolate. He is also the bad mother, now protected by the taboos and made unassailable by the growing power of the patriarchy, the father now existing as the protected bad mother. In "A New Interpretation of Hamlet," Laurence Rockelein and I pointed out: "Certain material which has recently come to the attention of the authors indicates the Oedipus complex may be a reaction to repressed matricide. Intensely repressed rage against the dominant, fearsome and unpredictable mother-figure in prehistoric matriarchal cultures may have been deflected through the millennia on to the weak and insignificant father-image. The father, reacting in self-defence, became strong, leading to the evolution of patriarchal systems. . . ."[93] It was Rockelein who called to my attention that in the Ona culture of South America, men arose in arms against the tyrannizing women, slew them, and allowed only the children, male and female, to live. The female children were then intimidated through the employment of ritual.[94] Before the Meiji Restoration, however, all functionaries had become a part of the Meiji unification and therefore protected by the ever-so-special Meiji or emperor tabu and by their identification with divinity. This splitting of the mother into two parts, the kind mother and the bad mother (father), in my mind is responsible not only for the rigidity, but also for the perpetuation, of Japanese institutions and the long life of the reigning dynasty, which is now in its one hundred twenty-seventh generation. Because of the sanctity afforded the emperor and the imperial institution, rage is not directed at him but is deflected to a target permissible under the Japanese system.

* * *

The regression of the leaderless Japanese in Manila to the level of attacking women brings up the whole matter of the urgent need for Japanese people to give vent to their repressed hatreds, and accordingly for the need for permissible targets for hatred within the patterns of their culture. While some of the targets for hatred might be considered "individual" ones in the sense that a single Japanese may permissibly vent his own internal hate against a particular target, in a broader sense a Japanese, being a disindividualized person, represents in his actions the hatred-venting required by the whole Japanese nation; and many instances of the use of permissive targets for this purpose involve mass attacks by groups —religious sects, dwellers of geographic areas, armies and the like.

In keeping with the rigid patterns observable at present in all departments of Japanese life, it is safe to say that under conditions prescribed by the authorities, avenues for limited discharge of hostilities, from a psychoanalytic point of view, are accorded the Japanese military men of today similar to those granted the old-time *samurai*. Alcock vividly describes the behavior permitted the *samurai*: "These are the classes which furnish suitable types of that extinct species of the race in Europe, still remembered as 'Swash-bucklers,'—swaggering, blustering bullies; many cowardly enough to strike an enemy in the back, or cut down an unarmed and inoffensive man;—but also supplying numbers ever ready to fling their own lives away in accomplishing a revenge, or carrying out the behests of their Chief. They are all entitled to the privilege of two swords, rank and file, and are saluted by the unprivileged (professional, mercantile, and agricultural) as *Sama,* or lord. With a rolling straddle in his gait, reminding one of Mr. Kinglake's graphic description of the Janissary, and due to the same cause,—the heavy projecting blades at his waist, and the swaddling-clothes around his body,—the Japanese *Samurai* or *Yaconin* moves on in a very ungainly fashion, the hilts of his two swords at least a foot in advance of his person, very handy, to all appearance, for an enemy's grasp. One is a heavy two-handed weapon, pointed and sharp as a razor; the other short, like a Roman sword, and religiously kept in the same serviceable state. In the use of these he is no mean adept. He seldom requires a second thrust with the shorter weapon, but strikes home at a single thrust, as was fatally proved at a later period; while with the longer weapon he severs a limb at a blow. Such a fellow is a man to whom all peace-loving subjects and prudent people habitually give as wide a berth as they can! Often drunk, and always insolent, he is to be met within the quarters of the town where the tea-houses most abound;

or returning about dusk, from his day's debauch, with a red and bloated face, and not over steady on his legs, the terror of all the unarmed population and street-dogs. Happy for the former, when he is content with trying the edge of a new sword on the quadrupeds; and many a poor crippled animal is to be seen limping about slashed over the back, or with more hideous evidences of brutality. But at other times it is some coolie or inoffensive shopkeeper, who, coming unadvisedly between 'the wind and his nobility,' is just as mercilessly cut down at a blow."[95]

There is evidence that in the early 1900's the abolition of the *samurai* was nominal, rather than actual. The *samurai* spirit persisted despite their legal dissolution. Augusta Campbell Davidson makes the following observation: "The samurai, moreover, are by no means things of the past; on the contrary, they, or some of them, are more to the front than ever. Under the old *regime*, indeed, they had in fact, if not in name, played the leading part in the affairs of the provinces of their several lords, who had, as a rule, become degenerate through the habits of luxury and effeminacy acquired in long centuries of peace. So in the commotions of 1868 the daimyos, as a class, weighed down by their own incapacity, sank to the bottom so far as participation in public affairs was concerned, and the most able of their samurai retainers, seizing on their opportunity, rose to the top, and have remained there ever since. Most of the prominent figures of modern Japan are men who began life as samurai not of the highest grade, though now they are noblemen like their former lords, the daimyos."[96]

This putative position is not supported alone by this knowledge of the Japanese's perennial addiction to sameness (despite the evidence of surface changes), but also by familiarity with the psychodynamics ubiquitously applicable to all human beings. A psychoanalysis of a festival event or ritual related to the discharge of the conscript from service provides material for the analytic deduction that the modern military man of Japan is accorded some of the privileges of the *samurai* of old. Again, we are indebted to Embree for an observation of the behavior of the Japanese woman who sets forth to greet the returning conscript: "The women of his *buraku* dress up in outlandish costumes, often as soldiers or tramps, and meet the returning procession by the bridge in the next *mura*. The women make obscene jokes as if they were men, try to rape the young school girls, and in general cause bursts of laughter and gaiety."[97]

Moreover, there is a variety of games which permit the discharge of pent-up hostility—*sumo* (Japanese wrestling), *kendo (gekken)*, fighting with bamboo staffs, mock-*samurai* sword duels and the like. And vicarious opportunities for the release of hatred are provided the Japanese masses today through the spectators identifying with the actors who portray *samurai* in certain stylized Japanese dramas. Among the most popular of such plays is the one which depicts the courage of the Forty-Seven Ronin. (A *ronin* is literally a "wave man," or one tossed upon the waves—actually a *samurai* who has become detached from his *daimyo* or lord.) The story, based on an actual event of the early eighteenth century, runs briefly as follows:

Asano Takumi no Kami, Lord of Ako in the province of Harima, along with another *daimyo*, was appointed to act as host at festivities feting an official of the emperor. Kira Kotsuke no Suke was appointed to instruct the two in the etiquette of such an affair. In the course of their lessons, Takumi no Kami was insulted by Kotsuke, and the former attempted to kill him. For this outrage, which was the more heinous for having taken place within the palace precincts, Takumi no Kami was forced to commit *hara-kiri*. For a year thereafter, Takumi no Kami's 47 *ronin* deviously maneuvered themselves until they were able to avenge their dead lord by killing Kotsuke no Suke and placing his severed head before Takumi no Kami's tomb. Thereafter, they all committed *hara-kiri* themselves, by order of the government, for their crime, having previously arranged with temple priests to be buried before their lord's tomb.

There is, however, a forty-eighth grave to be seen there—for in the course of the plot to lull Kotsuke no Suke into carelessness so that he could be killed, the leader of the *ronin* entered upon a life of apparent debauchery and forgetfulness of his dead master. A Satsuma man, seeing him drunk in a gutter, had stepped and spat upon him for his disloyalty. Now, after the *ronin's* accomplishment, he went before the grave of their leader and committed *hara-kiri* in apology for his insult to the man, and was himself duly buried with the *ronin* by a priest who had witnessed the act.

7

THE EXTRA-NATIONAL DISPERSAL OF
JAPANESE HATE

A BACKWARD look at a great historical upheaval in Japan, whereby the age-old feudal patterns seemed essentially torn out by the roots, will afford a picture of the effects of these changes upon the Japanese in their handling of their hatreds. Townsend Harris, the first American consul, concluded a treaty with the Japanese shogun in 1858. Not long thereafter, the Meiji emperor moved his capital to Yedo (now Tokyo). With the assistance of princes loyal to the old order, especially the prince of Mito, the emperor finally abolished the shogunate, which had been in the hands of the Tokugawa family, descendants of the Minamotos, for over 250 years. "The battlecry that ushered in the modern era in Japan was *sonno joi.* 'Restore the Emperor and expel the Barbarian.' [The 'Barbarian' originally meaning the Shogun, but later foreigners.]* It was a slogan that sought to keep Japan uncontaminated by the outside world and to restore a golden age of the tenth century before there had been a 'dual rule' of Emperor and Shogun. The Emperor's court at Kyoto [later moved to Yedo] was reactionary in the extreme. The victory of the Emperor's party meant to his supporters the humiliation and expulsion of foreigners. It meant reinstatement of traditional ways of life in Japan."[98] With the restoration of the Meiji to power, the so-called feudal epoch came to an end. Even though there seemed to be significant external changes, however, the internal architecture remained the same. Muramatsu notes that: "Many basic feudal conventions have continued relatively intact in family, school, and office, and especially in rural areas."[99]

The examples of continuing feudalistic behavior after the presumed end of the feudal period are numerous. Yanaga, for example, writes: ". . . Ito and other members of the Sat-Cho oligarchy rewarded themselves for their services to the clan-dominated government [by setting up a new peerage]. Plainly, it was a political maneuver to create a new privileged class whose support Ito needed, especially since the lesser *samurai* class had withdrawn support from the bureaucratic clan-government. At the same time, the new aristocracy was expected to furnish membership to the Upper House as a check on the power and actions of the Lower House. In a sense, the institution of the peerage was a contravention, if not a negation, of the principle of equality which was espoused by the government at the time when the feudal class system was abolished. It was a retrogressive step which set back the hand of time in the final achievement of true equality and popular rights."[100] Francis Adams writes that, after a massacre of French sailors (occurring after Perry's invasion) by a number of Tosa soldiers, a message from the ex-prince of Tosa to the French minister to Japan was dispatched: "It is an affair of which I certainly had not the slightest cognizance; my one wish has been to entertain friendly relations with foreigners. The act of violence which my retainers have committed has caused me to feel deeply ashamed. I am aware that foreign nations must feel grievously incensed. It hurts me to think that my people should have interfered with the Mikado in his projects for civilizing the country. I pray that Tosa alone, and not the whole country, may be rendered responsible for this act. . . . "[101] This is surely a document which smacks of continuing feudalistic relationships, yet it occurred in the spring of 1868.

With the beginning of the Meiji Restoration, Japan became unified and the feudal lords were replaced by the Kanbatso, who pledged absolute fealty to the emperor. Save for this absolutistic aspect, the new coterie of officials was quite similar to the old lords. The shogun was replaced by a premier. In 1884, 500 new peers were created to replace the *daimyos,* the lesser land-owners, and the two-sworded *samurai* of the feudal era. The *daimyos* became governors of the geographic sub-divisions of the country, accepting a marked reduction in revenue. There was, however, one significant, if obscure, difference in behavior between the old aggregate of feudal lords and the new bureaucrats and noble hierarchy: the Star (Army), Anchor (Navy), and Face (Very Important People), were enjoined against fighting among themselves. From 1874 to 1886 there were thirteen rebellions or disturbances in Japan, but after the unsuccessful Satsuma Rebellion in 1877, led by Saigo,* the imperial power was not again questioned. To be sure, a single premier was assassinated here and there, but there was no evidence of mass uprising. The Shogun-Harris debacle sensitized the emperor to the danger of almost any type of independent action which might originate among his officials. As before, Japan saved herself and maintained her sameness and her national safety through the process of disindividualization *(mimpi).*

All of this may have been fine for the emperor, but the Meiji Restoration and unification of authority unbalanced the internal situation in Japan. That the Japanese had feared such a sequence of events is pointed out by Captain Golownin, who wrote: "The inclination of the people to exchange ancient laws and manners for new ones, may, in the opinion of the Japanese government, prove ruinous to the empire, by causing revolutions in its political situation, the consequences of which might be civil war, and conquest by a foreign power."[102] Internal dissensions, instead of being permitted, were now repressed. There were no longer any intra-Japanese targets for the mobilization and expulsion of accumulated hostilities. Unfortunately, the removal of the targets did not remove the hostility.

Disindividualization frustrates the individual in his inclination toward maturation; frustration leads to fear; and thence to fear-rage. In order to deplete the fear-rage and the reservoirs of hostility, there must be a target for their externalization, and now in Japan there was no longer the Hogan War type of outlet; no longer the Peasant Revolution; no longer the internal Japanese targets employed by Akechi, Ashikaga, Ieyasu Tokugawa and Satsuma. Denied these internal targets, it became imperative that new ones be found, external to territorial Japan. On these must be vented the explosive bursts of accumulated, pent-up hatred. Seeking, therefore, for targets acceptable to the emperor, and supplied with the American blueprint for imperialism furnished them by the Perrys and the Harrises, the Japanese lost no time in entering upon imperialistic warfare. Their first target was their teacher, the United States.

Had we been alert, we might have learned from the

Russian, Golownin, what was inevitable; an astute and thoughtful observer of the Japanese, he wrote in the year 1824: "What must we expect if this numerous, ingenious, and industrious people, who are capable of everything, and much inclined to imitate all that is foreign, should ever have a sovereign like our Peter the Great; with the resources and treasures which Japan possesses, he would enable it to become in a few years the sovereign of the eastern ocean. What would then become of the maritime provinces of eastern Asia, and the settlements on the west coast of America, which are so remote from the countries by which they must be protected? If the Japanese should think fit to introduce the knowledge of Europe among them, and adopt our policy as a model, we should then see the Chinese obliged to do the same:* in this case these two powerful nations might soon give the situation of Europe another appearance. However deeply a horror of everything foreign may be impressed on the Japanese and Chinese governments; yet a change in their system is not inconceivable: necessity may compel them to do that, to which their own free will does not impel them! Attacks, for example, like that of Chwostoff, often repeated, would probably induce them to think of means to repel a handful of vagabonds who disturbed a nation. This might lead them to build ships of war on the model of those in Europe; these ships might increase to fleets, and then it is probable that the good success of this measure would lead them also to adopt the other scientific methods, which are so applicable to the destruction of the human race.

"In this manner all the inventions of Europe might gradually take root in Japan, even without the creative spirit of a Peter, merely by the power and concurrence of circumstances. The Japanese certainly would not be

71

in want of teachers if they would only invite them; I therefore believe that this just and upright people must, by no means, be provoked. But if, contrary to all expectation, urgent reasons should make it necessary to proceed otherwise, every exertion must be made to act decisively; I do not mean to affirm that the Japanese and Chinese might form themselves on an European model, and become dangerous to us now; but we must take care to avoid giving cause to our posterity to despise our memory."[103] Note the phrase—*"despise our memory."*

* * *

Religions have been officially recognized targets for Japanese extra-national hostility for generations. Buddhism has at least twice been singled out for mass hatred, first in about 552 A.D.[104] when the Japanese believed the Buddhist idol to be responsible for a pestilence; and again in 1571, when their great monastery on the shores of Lake Biwa was destroyed and the monks killed or banished. The former incident is recorded by Eliot as follows: (More as an indication of political mutuality of purpose than for any great urge to spread the Buddhist faith, the king of one of the three Korean groups presented to the Japanese emperor an image of Shaku Butsu, a Buddha, of gold and copper, along with a number of other gifts and a letter extolling the glories of the Buddhist faith.) "The presents and letters . . . engaged the serious attention of the Japanese Court. The Emperor, we are told, leaped for joy, but thought it prudent to consult his ministers. Opinion was divided. On the one hand it was argued that Japan ought to follow the example of other civilized countries, on the other that the native gods might be offended by the respect shown to a foreign deity. The cleavage of opinion was indicated at the first council held to discuss the

matter: the Soga family was for Buddhism, the Mononobe and Nakatomi were against it. They had old
grounds of difference with the Soga and held important
charges connected with Shintoism which seemed threatened by these religious innovations. It was finally decided that the Soga should take the image and worship it
as an experiment. But the experiment was not a success.
When Soga no Iname turned his house at Mukuhara into
a temple and installed the image there a pestilence
broke out. His rivals demonstrated that this was due to
the foreign cult and obtained imperial permission to
burn the temple and throw the image into the Naniwa
canal.

"But the gradual infiltration of Buddhism continued.
In 577 another mission arrived from Pekche with three
priests, a nun, a temple architect, and a maker of images.
Two years afterwards Silla sent . . . a Buddhist image."[105]
Subsequently a temple was built by Umako Soga, son of
Iname, an image installed, and three nuns maintained,
and then a second one, in 584; but "the next year (585)
Umako was taken ill and was told by a diviner that this
was a curse sent by the Buddha. . . ."[106] Now the rivals
of the Sogas got permission to have freedom to worship
Buddha revoked again due to a recurrence of the pestilence. "Mononobe went in person to the Soga's estate,
burnt the temple and the images, again threw the ashes
into the canal, and beat and imprisoned the unfortunate
nuns. But the anti-Buddhist arguments became less
convincing when, in spite of these summary measures,
the pestilence grew worse. . . . The Soga were then permitted to practice Buddhism as a family cult, but not
with too great publicity, and the three nuns were re-
leased."[107]

Early in the preparation of this manuscript, I was

disturbed by Robert King Hall's prefatory remarks in *Kokutai No Hongi*, which seemed to contradict the individualism-tenets of Zen Buddhism ("the nonexistence or nonreality of human ego").[108] But on rechecking the writings of the foremost Japanese Buddhist scholar, D. T. Suzuki (*Zen Buddhism and Its Influence on Japanese Culture*, Eastern Buddhist Society, Otani Buddhist College, Kyoto, 1938), I was convinced that individualism was indeed the keynote. Suzuki says:

". . . Zen is opposed to everything that goes by the name of science or scientific. Zen is personal while science is impersonal. What is impersonal is abstract and does not take notice of individual experiences. What is personal belongs altogether to the individual and has no signification without the backing of his own experience. Science means systematisation, and Zen is just its reverse."[109]

Several facets of Zen belief noted by Suzuki are especially important in consideration of Japanese culture, which is so obviously and highly stylized and where expression of individualism is in effect tabu:

"Deficiency or imperfection of form is held to be more expressive of the spirit, because perfection of form is likely to attract one's attention to form and not to the inner truth itself;

"The deprecation of formalism, conventionalism, or ritualism tends to make the spirit stand in all its nakedness or aloneness or solitariness;

"This transcendental aloofness or aloneness of the absolute is the spirit of asceticism, which means the doing-away with every possible trace of unessentials;

"Aloneness translated in terms of the worldly life is non-attachment. . . ."[110]

The foremost occidental authority on Japanese Buddhism, Sir Charles Eliot, in his writings on Zen Buddhism, supports the contention that this religion is of a basically individualistic nature. Eliot writes:

"It was not a suitable religion for Japan in the seventh or eighth centuries because what was needed then was a clear and decided creed which could school and civilize a people among whom the masses were in a rudimentary stage of culture."[111]

"The main idea is that the mind should be kept 'empty,' that is, clear, unprejudiced, and ready to follow any inspiration."[112]

" . . . Zen . . . laid . . . little stress upon scriptures and ceremonies and so much upon mental • discipline."[113] "It was . . . exceedingly pliant and appealed to classes who had little taste for dogma or ceremony."[114]

"[Zen] . . . became . . . the religion of the military class [in Japan]. In China, where soldiers are not much respected and often not distinguished accurately from brigands, such a transformation was unthinkable, but in Japan, though strange, it is explicable, for Zen as a system demands above all things individual discipline. It makes light of learning (in spite of having produced an enormous literature) and of all attempts to found a spiritual life on scriptural knowledge, and bids those who would become adepts cultivate such virtues as courage, perseverance, and clear insight, all of which are as useful to a soldier as to a priest."[115]

"[The object of Tinzai, a sect of Zen] . . . is apparently to insist that the mind of the seeker after truth must be absolutely free and untrammeled, and he expresses himself thus: 'If you meet the Buddha, slay him: if you meet the Patriarch, slay him . . . for this is the only way to deliverance. Do not get entangled with anything, but stand above, pass on and be free. . . .'"[116]

Even today there is room for intra-Japanese hostility in the area of Buddhist religion. "The belief of Jodo and Shinshu," says John Embree, "is called *tariki* or the reliance on a higher power as contrasted to *jiriki* or dependence on one's self (as in Zen) for salvation and enlightenment. . . . The Shinshu priest in Fukada maintains that, as Zen stresses the individual, it thus encourages self-centeredness and undermines the family system, a subtle bit of theological propaganda."[117]

There stood, in the middle 1500's, a tremendous Buddhist monastery, Enriaku-ji, on Mt. Hiei-zan, on the shores of Lake Biwa a few miles from Kyoto. There were said to have been 3,000 buildings in the institution, and the monks numbered many thousands. Their political power was tremendous, and they were able to obtain whatever concessions they desired from the government. They opposed the then-existing authority, coming to dislike and fear the vice-shogun, Nobunaga, who was appointed to serve under the Emperor Ogimachi in 1568; and when his enemies, Prince Asakura, of the Province of Echizen, and Governor Asai, of the castle of Itami, in the Province of Omi, led forces against the government at Kyoto, the Buddhists gave them shelter and supplies as they passed Lake Biwa. Nobunaga intercepted and defeated the forces of the prince and governor, but so great was his anger against the Buddhists that he turned on them in 1571, burning all of their buildings and killing almost all of the monks; the few who survived were banished. (Ieyasu partially restored the monastery later, but limited its size to 125 buildings, and never afterward was it a political force.)[118]

St. Francis Xavier established the first—and warmly received—mission in Japan, when he arrived at Kagoshima, Province of Satsuma, on August 15, 1549. The prince gave him permission to preach, and great interest in the new faith was evidenced, both by the commoners and royalty. He was aided in this mission by two Japanese who had been rescued from attackers by a Portuguese ship and had been turned over to Xavier's care and subsequent conversion; they returned with him to Japan after their conversion, and worked in the mission. Xavier remained in Japan for two years and three months,* where, for the most part, he met with success, except in Kyoto, where he abandoned his efforts at proselytization.[119]

In Nagasaki, in 1567, nearly all the citizens were Christians, as was their ruler, the prince of Omura. At the request of Portuguese traders and priests, the port city was ceded to Portugal in 1573 and placed under its jurisdiction. The Portuguese tore down Buddhist monasteries and temples in the city, and most of the sites were used to build Christian churches.[120]

Because the Buddhists had sided with his enemies, Nobunaga began to show favor to the Jesuits. The latter did not understand the political basis for this friendship, and remained puzzled that Nobunaga never embraced the Christian faith. Under his patronage, however, a church was built in Kyoto and one at Azachi on Lake Biwa, near where Nobunaga built his home. The church rose under his patronage to its greatest prosperity, numbering an estimated 600,000 communicants.** In 1582 a mission was sent to the Pope, including some Japanese Christian princes. After being feted en route in Spain and Portugal, they were enthusiastically received in 1585, first by Pope Gregory XII, who died suddenly during their stay, and by his successor, Sixtus V.[121]

There was an ominous significance (for the Japanese) to the pilgrimage to Rome. It proved beyond the shadow of a doubt that the Christian religion was not one which could be absorbed or taken over by the Japanese, but was rather the product and possession and under the absolute dictation of an outgroup. Its very deep well-spring was Rome, thousands of miles from Japan; and it was obvious that the Christians felt fealty toward, and in fact drew their direction from, foreigners in a foreign city, and not from any person or group or place in Japan.* Robert King Hall bears out this contention in his introduction to *Kokutai No Hongi*, where he states that "Christianity is often linked with Westernism and individualism in Japan, and accordingly is the antithesis of the belief in the divine origin of the Empire and infallibility of the Imperial Line. Hence, by implication, christianity is part of the ideological threat** to the ultranationalistic Japan. . . ."[122]

In 1585, Gregory XIII ordered that no religious teachers except Jesuits be allowed to enter Japan, because they were enjoying such success in their work that he did not want any competition to retard their progress. This brought about envy of the Portuguese Jesuits among the Spanish Franciscans. Accordingly, the Spanish governor of Manila wrote a letter to Hideyoshi, Nobunaga's successor, asking permission to trade with certain Japanese ports. Four Franciscans attached themselves to the party bearing the letter. Hideyoshi, pleased by the elaborate gifts of the Spaniards, allowed the Franciscans to establish themselves in Kyoto and Nagasaki. Now the Jesuits objected, on the grounds that the Franciscans were defying papal orders, but the Franciscans replied that they had come as ambassadors, not as religious teachers, and that, since they were already in Japan, the pope's ruling did not require them to leave.[123]

The Franciscans at this juncture claimed that the Jesuits were responsible for the opposition they encountered: ". . . they openly avowed that the Jesuit fathers through cowardice failed to exert themselves in the fulfillment of their religious duties, and in a craven spirit submitted to restrictions on their liberty to preach."[124] While this was going on, a Portuguese sea-captain told Hideyoshi that the King of Portugal would begin by sending priests, would wait until they had effected conversions, and then would send armies which, with the aid of the converts, would take over the country. Hideyoshi, recalling that similar events had taken place in China, India, and the East Indies, in 1587 issued an edict ". . . commanding all foreign religious teachers on pain of death to depart from Japan in twenty days."[125] Portuguese trade was still permitted, but ships and merchandise were to be confiscated if "any foreign religions" were brought to Japan by the traders.[126] "In consequence of this edict, in A.D. 1593 six Franciscans and three Jesuits were arrested in Osaka and Kyoto and taken to Nagasaki and there burnt."[127] (Sansom's account of the episode places the date at 1596, the manner of execution—crucifixion, the number killed at 26: six Franciscans and 20 Japanese catechists.)*

As in Europe under King Philip II of Spain and Portugal, the Japanese princes who had embraced Christianity took "the most forcible measures," prior to the 1587 edict, "to compel all their subjects to follow their own example and adopt the Christian faith."[128] Konishi enforced the acceptance of Christianity and robbed the Buddhists of their temples and lands; Omura and Arima, and to some extent the princes of Bungo, followed Jesuit advice* and used their political power to enforce Christianity.[129] Sansom writes: "The early missionaries in Asia, thinking only in terms of religion and not realizing that religion in most countries is an expression of national temperament, found themselves confronted in Japan, as well as in India and China, by the difficult problem of reconciling their own principles with other people's practices."[130]

"To . . . [Taiko-Sama] it [the edict] was purely a political question. He had no deep religious impressions which led him to prefer the precepts of the old Japanese faith to those of Christianity. These systems could not apparently live together, and it seemed to him the safest and most sensible way to extinguish the weaker and more dangerous before it became too strong. Hence he began that policy of repression and expulsion which his successor reluctantly took up."[131]

In 1606, Ieyasu issued a warning proclamation that ". . . it was for the good of the state** that none should embrace the new doctrine; and that such as had already done so must change immediately."[132] In contravention, large numbers of Christians proceeded to put on extravagant parades and celebrations*** to mark the beatification of Ignatius Loyola, in 1609, both in Nagasaki and in the Province of Arima. Ieyasu thereupon had a number arrested, banished, and their estates confiscated on grounds of ". . . bribery and intrigue on behalf of the Daimyos of Arima."[133]

In 1614, Ieyasu issued a still stronger edict, against the practice of Christianity by either foreigners or natives.[134] Offenders were ordered sent to Nagasaki, whence Japanese Christians were deported to the northern extremity of the mainland; and in the case of Takeyama, who had already been banished by Taiko-Sama, to Manila. ". . . ten thousand troops were sent to Kyushu, where the converts were much the most numerous and the daimyos in many cases either openly protected or indirectly favored the new faith."[135] "As many as three hundred persons are said to have been shipped from Japan October 25, 1614. All the resident Jesuits were included in this number, excepting eighteen fathers and nine brothers, who concealed themselves and thus escaped the search."[136] There followed a period of witch-hunting characterized by frightful tortures of all sorts, and the institution of a reward system for informers against Christians. "At what time this practice began it is difficult to say, but that rewards were used at an early period is evident from the re-issue of an edict in 1655, in which it is stated that formerly a reward of 200 pieces of silver was paid for denouncing a father (*bateren*) and 100 for denouncing a brother (*iruman*); but from this time the rewards should be: for denouncing a father, 300 pieces; a brother, 200 pieces; and a catechist, 50 pieces. In 1711 this tariff was raised, for denouncing a father to 500 pieces, a brother to 300 pieces, and a catechist to 100 pieces; also for denouncing a person who, having recanted, returned to the faith, 300 pieces. These edicts against Christianity were displayed on the edict-boards as late as the year 1868."[137]

It is interesting to note that Murray makes no mention of a period between 1598 and 1615, during which Ieyasu relaxed his persecution activities. Sansom writes: "He had more urgent matters to deal with and he was a cautious ruler who knew how to bide his time. He was much interested in foreign trade and therefore disposed to keep on good terms with both Spanish and Portuguese at least until he could develop his own merchant marine. He even approached the Spanish gov-

81

ernment of the Philippines, through a Franciscan intermediary, offering to open harbors in eastern Japan to
Spanish ships, proposing reciprocal freedom of commerce, and asking for naval architects. He also gave it
to be understood that he would not enforce the anti-
Christian edicts. The missionaries made good use of the
respite afforded to them. Valignano, writing in 1603,
said that by 1600 all the residences and most of the
churches had been rebuilt and great numbers of new converts had been made. He put the total number of Christians at 300,000, the population of all Japan being at that
time probably about 25,000,000."[138] Whether Murray
omitted this information through a lack of knowledge,
or whether he failed to see the larger implications of the
attitude of the Japanese officials toward Christianity is
not evident. However, it seems important for our present purposes to realize that persecutions were sometimes
of a more local character than Murray implies, and that
there were, as just indicated, long respites therefrom,
and politico-economic sidelights.

One of the most astonishing of all aspects of Christian persecution by the Japanese government was a practice current in and after 1616, which Sansom describes
as "so extreme as to be scarcely rational."[139] "The . . . formula [by which apostates gave up their Christianity in
order to return to the good graces of the Japanese gov-
ernment] is an involuntary tribute to the power of the
Christian faith, for the converts, having abjured their
religion (generally under duress),"* writes Sansom,
"were by a curious logic made to swear by the very powers that they had just denied: 'By the Father, the Son,
and the Holy Ghost, Santa Maria and all the angels. . .
if I break this oath may I lose the grace of God forever
and fall into the wretched state of Judas Iscariot.' By an

even further departure from logic all this was followed by an oath to Buddhist and Shinto deities."[140]

An interesting aspect of early Christianity in Japan was the masochistic nature of the Japanese which it displayed. Sansom writes, "All the Jesuit observers are agreed in describing the Japanese as a people whose traditional manners and customs so predisposed them to a disregard for life that it was necessary for the missionaries to preach to them vigorously against suicide. The Jesuit letters refer frequently to their devotion to the cross, their love of Christ crucified, and their cruel flagellations, which made the blood flow. 'It was difficult to moderate their spirit of love and penitence. . . .' To most people in . . . Eastern Asia . . . the doctrine of atonement was repugnant. They were shocked by the idea of a divine person undergoing torture and death and disliked a symbolism that had to do with blood. This was particularly true of Buddhist countries, and it is somewhat surprising to find a masochistic strain in Japan, where the religious ascetic usually mortified the flesh only by living frugally in a mountain hut or by practising such minor austerities as bathing in very cold water. But it is an undoubted fact that the Japanese people throughout their history have been remarkably ready in peace as in war to suffer as well as to inflict death; and this may account both for the ferocity with which the Japanese Christians were persecuted and for the fortitude with which they went to martyrdom."[141]

In 1626, Nagasaki had 40,000 Christians; by 1629 there were none who acknowledged Christian belief.[142]

Kaempfer wrote of the Imperial Proclamation of 1637 prohibiting the departure of Japanese from the country. This, he says, was "signed by the chief Counsellors of state, and was sent to the Governors of Nagasaki, with orders to see it put into execution. It was then the Empire of Japan was shut forever, both to foreigners and natives. Thenceforward no foreign nation should have leave to come into the country, and none of the Emperor's subjects to go abroad, as appears among others, by the following positive orders contained in the Proclamation aforesaid.

"To Sakaki Barra Findano Cami, and to Babu Sabray Sejimon.

"No Japanese ship, or boat whatever, nor any native of Japan, shall presume to go out of the country; who acts contrary to this, shall die and the ship, with the crew and goods aboard, shall be sequestered till further order.

"All Japanese, who return from abroad, shall be put to death. . . ."[143]

Also in 1637, Christians from scattered areas joined forces with oppressed *samurai* farmers and took over a castle, which they provisioned with rice seized from government stores. They held the castle against a siege by government forces for 102 days. (Prior to the siege, some of the insurgents had endeavored unsuccessfully to take the castle of Tomioka and suffered complete defeat; it was another band of them, under more skilled leadership, who took and held the castle of Shimabara.) The government forces were led by Itakura Naizen and reinforced upon order by troops of the *daimyos* of Kyushu—a total of 160,000 men. On April 12, 1638, the insurgents surrendered and were slaughtered. Japanese estimates place the number killed at about 40,000, but Murray feels this much too high. (Sansom speaks of 37,000 slaughtered.)[144] It is interesting to note that the Yedo also ordered that the daimyo of Amakusa, whose misrule immediately precipitated the rebellion, be stripped of most of his holdings, and he was still so hated in the areas he still controlled that he committed *hara-kiri*. Also, "The daimyo of Arima whose misconduct and neglect had driven the *samurai* farmers into their fatal rising, was also permitted to take his own life."[145]

The Dutch merchants in Japan, upon request by the Japanese government, supplied powder, cannon, and one ship which were used, to no great effect, in the siege.[146] This caused resentment among the Portuguese, who favored the Jesuit cause. Of this action, Dutch historian Geerts says that the Dutch did only what they had to, and did it to protect their interest in Japan. Aid was requested by the Japanese against rebellious subjects, not against Christians; and the Dutch did not participate in the final massacre.[147]

Following the Shimabara tragedy, Christianity went underground or existed in scattered remnants; yet, while there was a *kiri-shiten bugyo* (Christian inquisitor) with an active and numerous staff, with headquarters in a building which had once held Christian prisoners in Yedo, Christianity still survived. In 1865, in villages around Nagasaki, ". . . there were . . . not only [Christian] words and symbols which had been preserved in the language, but even communities where had been kept alive for more than two centuries the worship bequeathed to them by their ancestors."[148] Graves of martyred Christians were always decorated by flowers, although no one knew who put them there.

A truce to anti-Christian persecution was declared in Japan in 1873; in 1889, a law granting freedom to worship according to the Christian religion was enacted.

The Taoist philosophy, emphasizing freedom of the

individual, never succeeded, as did Christianity, in gaining a foothold in Japan. Incompatible with Japanese ideology were such beliefs of Taoism as ". . . the importance of keeping the original simplicity of human nature, the danger of over-government and interference with the simple life of the people, the doctrine of *wu-wei* or 'inaction,' which is better interpreted as 'non-interference' and is the exact equivalent of *laissez-faire,* the pervading influence of the spirit, the lessons of humility, quietude and calm, and the folly of force, of pride, and of self-assertion [as opposed to collectivism]. All these will be understood if one understands the rhythm of life. It is profound and clear, mystic and practical."[149]

* * *

As has been clearly indicated heretofore, hostility toward foreigners has affected an exceedingly lengthy history and affected all aspects of traffic with non-Japanese, religious, commercial, and political. Perhaps Golownin stated as precisely as anyone the reasons for this —or perhaps he over-simplified the matter—when he described a talk with some Japanese in which: "They explained to us the grounds on which their laws prohibit them from reposing any trust in Japanese subjects who have lived in foreign countries. The great mass of mankind, said they, resemble children: they soon become weary of what they possess; and willingly give up everything for the sake of novelty. When they hear of certain things being better in foreign countries than in their own, they immediately wish to possess them, without reflecting that they might perhaps prove useless, or even injurious to them."[150]

In 1862, there occurred an attack upon four foreigners, one of whom was injured and then brutally hacked to death, which indicates the reckless manner in which the Japanese made use of their hatred of foreigners as a target for their hostilities. The event is colorfully described by Alexander Michie:

"The victims were a party of three gentlemen and one lady from Yokohama. . . . The party proceeded from Kanagawa towards Yedo, not intending to go farther than Kawasaki, which was the limit of authorised excursions in that direction. On the way they met the *cortege* of a Daimio [Satsuma], the first indication of which was several *norimono* (the heavy palanquin in which the nobles of Japan travel) with armed attendants, forming an irregular train with considerable intervals between. When passing these *norimono* the foreigners walked their horses. . . . Then a regular procession was met, preceded by about a hundred men marching in single file on either side of the road. The foreign party thereupon proceeded at a foot's pace, keeping close to the left side, until they reached 'the main body, which was then occupying the whole breadth of the road.' The English party halted on approaching the main body, according to one of the survivors; but according to another, they were stopped 'when they had got about twelve men deep in the procession,' by 'a man of large stature issuing from the main body,' who, swinging his sword with both hands, cut at the two leading foreigners, Mr. Richardson and Mrs. Borrodaile, as their horses were being turned round, and then rushed on the other two. Whereupon the advance-guard, who had been described as marching in single file, closed in upon the retreating riders. They were all able by the speed of their horses to get clear of their assailants; but Mr. Richardson was so terribly hacked that after going some distance he fell from his horse, dying, or, as his companions thought, dead. He lived, however, until the Daimio's procession reached the spot, when several of his retainers proceeded to butcher and mutilate the dying man in the most shocking manner. . . . [The woman] escaped substantially unhurt, though a sword-stroke aimed at her head cut away her hat as she stooped to avoid the blow. She saw Mr. Richardson fall, and her two wounded companions, unable to render help, urged her to ride on. She miraculously arrived at Yokohama, bespattered with blood and in a state of very natural agitation. Mr. Clarke and Mr. Marshall, exhausted by their wounds, managed to reach Kanagawa, where they were properly cared for at the American consulate."[151]

There were, however, exceptions to the prevalence of antagonism toward anything foreign among the more astute. Not enough attention has been paid to the perspicacity of Lord Hotta who addressed the emperor's court on March 19, 1858, seeking permission to consummate trade and other diplomatic treaties with the United States. Payson Treat quotes from his speech as follows: "Either a war has to be fought, or amicable relations have to be established. . . . Among the rulers of the world at present there is none so noble and illustrious as to command universal vassalage, or who can make his virtuous influence felt throughout the length and breadth of the whole world. . . . To have such a ruler over the whole world is doubtless in conformity with the Will of Heaven. . . . In establishing relations with foreign countries, the object should always be kept in view of laying a foundation for securing a hegemony over all nations. . . .

"When our power and national standing have come to be recognized, we should take the lead in punishing the nations which may act contrary to the principle of international interests, and in so doing, we should join hands with the nations whose principles may be found identical with those of our country. An alliance thus formed should also be directed toward protecting harmless but powerless nations. Such a policy could be nothing else but the enforcement of the power and authority deputed (to us) by the Spirit of Heaven. Our national prestige and position thus ensured, the nations of the world will come to look up to our Emperor as the great ruler of all the nations, and they will come to follow our policy and submit themselves to our judgment."[152]

If Hotta were an American, he would have been revered for his wisdom and vision. We learn from John W. Foster that this astute statesman was aware of the dangers that threatened Japan from foreign sources. "It has been seen that the Japanese were as artless as children in the practice of diplomacy, and accepted submissively the treaties which Commodore Perry and Minister [formerly Consul] Harris prepared, as well as those of the other nations patterned after them. But the statesmen of Japan were sagacious and highly patriotic, and they early discovered that the nation had been led into a thralldom, a release from which would require the greatest wisdom, persistency, and forbearance."[153]

Yet in fact, Hotta's intent came to be included in the Japanese nationalist philosophy. Hall points out that: "These [ultranationalistic] interpretations [of the original intent of *Kokutai No Hongi*] were characterized by a doctrine of total subservience of the individual to the State, by a belief in the divine mission of Japan in East Asia and in the entire world, and by an admiration of and proficiency in the military arts."[154]

There were, to be sure, occasional Japanese thinkers who, like Ieyasu himself (who reversed his own position temporarily in easing his anti-Christian persecutions), departed from the main line of Japanese policy. Sansom cites an interesting example of a man who, about a half century before Hotta, and possibly for quite different reasons, took a stand much like his:

"Among the important and effective critics . . . were certain thinkers of a new sort, whose interests were scientific rather than literary. Perhaps the most influential and certainly one of the most interesting among them was Honda Toshiaki (1774-1821). He was an extremely gifted man, a samurai born in Kaga, on the west coast, in a Tozama fief remote from Yedo influences. There he developed an interest in sea voyages and learned about conditions in Yezo. He studied mathematics and astronomy and opened a school in 1797. He worked at the Dutch language and went to sea in command of a small coasting vessel on a voyage to the northern parts of Japan. He wrote a number of works on shipping, conditions in western countries, and the conservation of natural resources; and he addressed himself to matters of national policy in his *Keisi Hisaku (A Secret Plan of Government),* which proposed state control of industry, commerce, and shipping together with the expansion of national strength by means of colonization. He was much concerned by the difficulty of adjusting population and food supply and was perhaps the first Japanese thinker to see clearly that the closed economy of Japan, a country with only modest natural resources, was incapable of supporting the standard of living to which the people had become accustomed unless foreign trade was increased. He therefore did not hesitate to argue for a merchant marine capable of overseas traffic, and specifically proposed trade with Russia. . . .

"He, . . . like the National Scholars, was opposed to Confucianism. He was even inclined to think that Christianity might be useful. He said that the most important things needed by Japan were gun powder, metals, ships, and colonies. It will be seen that his views were such as would be abhorrent to the Bakufu, especially those which concerned Christianity, a hatred of which was a canon of Tokugawa doctrine on international affairs. His opinions were much in advance of the times and most of his books remained unpublished during his lifetime."[155]

There were later Japanese whose awareness of the menace of western powers likewise led them to endeavor to awaken the government to the exigencies of the moment. Such a man was Shuhan Takashima of Nagasaki, of whom Okuma writes: "In the forties . . . [prior to Perry's arrival], Shuhan Takashima . . . urged that (like her neighbor, China, which had been so utterly defeated by European forces through her defences being altogether out of date) Japan, if she did not reform her weapons and art of war, would fail to defend her own coasts from a foreign invasion, and that nothing was of greater importance to the empire than to make a radical change in its military system. He went so far as to obtain some guns from Holland, and with his followers, whom he had trained in their use, came to the Shogun's capital to show the new tactics and to urge upon the Government the necessity of adopting Western methods of organization. The authorities were too short-sighted to give full hearing to him, although his petition served to attract to a certain degree the attention of the Shogunate and of many far-sighted warriors who began to study under him, and in the end his petition actually proved to be the dawn of the reorganization of the military system of the empire. Takashima went so far, in cooperation with Egawa, one of his pupils, as to cast guns and elaborate measures for the national defence, but his only reward was that the conservative authorities arrested him in 1842 and put him in prison."[156]

There was also Fukuzawa Yukichi, who protected his own status as a liberal by consistently refusing to enter government service. He studied Dutch and English and went to the United States with the Embassy to exchange ratifications of the treaty of 1858, and in 1867 went to Europe and the United States. Two years later he published *Conditions in the West*, which sold in the thousands of copies. He advocated the natural rights of man and took a generally liberal attitude toward government. "Fukuzawa," writes Yanaga, "contributed immeasurably to the development of Meiji ideas and institutions in his multiple role of critic, publicist, journalist, educator, businessman, feminist and philosopher. In the intellectual life of the nation, no other person of his day contributed as much as the 'Sage of Mita' to the liquidation of the old and the building up of the new Japan in the early years of Meiji."[157]

Men of the rare flexibility and emotional maturity of Toshiaki, Takashima, Yukichi and a few others were rare. Most Japanese could not have been able to understand, let alone subscribe to, the celebrated musing of Freud: "It does not seem as if man could be brought by any sort of influence to change his nature into that of the ants; he will always, one imagines, defend his claim to individual freedom against the will of the multitude."

After Perry and Harris, a number of Japanese missions were sent to the occident to learn the "Western Way." Those Japanese who wound up in Bismarckian

Germany found themselves more comfortably ensconced than those Japanese who studied in other foreign countries. It is not surprising that the rigid teutonic German influence brought back to Japan by Ito dominated not only the Japanese political scene but Japanese medical institutions as well.

8

THE ACADEMIC AND LEGAL STATUS OF JAPANESE PSYCHOANALYSIS

THE Nipponese are thrown into a state of consternation when confronted by an innovation. The Nomonhan Incident,[158] a conflict on the Manchurian border in which Russians used flame-throwers against Japanese troops, perplexed the Japanese government. Their troops were seared by the flame-throwers, but previous to this harrowing experience they had not known that such weapons existed. There was a numerically important and powerful aggregate among the Japanese who wished to ignore the incident, contending that the durability of the Nipponese soldier was proof against such weapons. This group, imbued with the ideologies of *giri* bureaucracy and evidencing a belief in the immutability of Japanese disindividualization, provided a cultural block that was finally overcome by the more realistically-minded Japanese of influence. But the incident, now famous in the recent history of Japan, illustrates in a negative way their reluctance to take cognizance of a technological development that could suddenly disturb their way of life.

There was, therefore, a natural interest on my part in the reaction of the Japanese to a potentially disturb-

94

ing development such as psychoanalysis. I found, in pursuing this interest, that one question inevitably recurs: In the light of the foregoing observations on the psychology of the Japanese, what can be the therapeutic aims of the Japanese analysts? Having learned something about the possible conflict between Japanese psychoanalysis and the *giri* bureaucracy while on Okinawa in 1945, I determined to continue my investigation. One day in April, 1949, I addressed the Tokyo Psychiatric Society. Well fortified with two translators, Tsuneo Muramatsu and Heisaku Kosawa, I attempted to learn all I could about the Japanese psychoanalytic therapeutic objectives. Dr. Kosawa, a psychoanalyst, was the only physician-member of the Tokyo Psychoanalytical Society. Muramatsu spoke excellent English. He had studied psychiatry in this country, at the Boston Psychiatric Hospital, as well as in Germany.

In my interview with the Society, I outlined the difficulty: the contrast between the therapeutic aim of individualism and the therapeutic aim of a strict adherence to constituted cultural patterns. In America, interest is theoretically focused on the individual and psychoanalysis is directed toward making the person a better individual. Would psychoanalysis in Tokyo be directed toward making an individualized Japanese conform to the cultural pattern of Japan, or would individualism in a Japanese setting constitute an illness? Would the Japanese psychoanalyst require his patient to respect authority (*kanzan*) and to debase the individual (*mimpi*)?

Kosawa assured me that the Japanese therapeutic objectives are identical with American therapeutic objectives. The Japanese analyst strives to free his patient, strives to make him into an individual. But even as he assured me, he bowed, scraped, and sucked in air through his teeth. This bowing and scraping and sucking in air through the teeth communicated through a muscle or postural-language a message diametrically opposite to his verbal avowal of individualism. My caution was justified: I was a representative of the Surgeon General of the United States Army; Kosawa may have been doing a little *enryo*. Again, he may have been afraid to step on the shadow of his "superior." (After returning to the United States, I learned that Kosawa refrained from stepping on the shadow of his own analyst, even though that custom had been abandoned by the Meiji many years ago.)* Perhaps it was simpler than that; perhaps Kosawa had his tongue in his cheek when he dealt with psychoanalysts, especially American ones. At any rate, not entirely satisfied with his reply, I decided to establish, if I could, the attitude of the Diet toward the Japanese psychoanalytic societies, and also to seek out the answer to my major question about psychoanalytic aims, by reviewing actual case reports and articles written by Japanese psychoanalysts.

* * *

To investigate the Diet's attitude was justified for more reasons than one. As amply demonstrated above, for generations the Japanese had actively resented either internal or external interference and had resisted change. Truculently resurgent, they battled influences tending to disturb the Japanese way of life. Psychoanalysis, properly administered, can lead to cultural change. Pursuant to my realization of this fact, Shinji Arai (a Japanese lawyer, Director of Japan Foreign Trade Council, Inc.) was contacted at my request by Clark Gregory, of the Legal Section of the Far East Command. Shinji Arai, after an investigation, gave the following opinion: "As to the attitude of the Meiji government toward psychoanalysis, may I report that: (1) Psychoanalysis has never been very seriously studied in Japan, and there is no evidence, as far as I can ascertain, that any of the successive governments since the Meiji Restoration has shown any very keen interest in the relationship between the scientific conclusions of psychoanalysis and individual rights; (2) It appears that the establishment of a chair for psychoanalysis has never occurred in any university or college in Japan, psychoanalysis having been considered as one of the divisions of the science of psychology. It may be inferred that this field of study has not been considered of great importance to the government, and in fact that no Japanese government has concerned itself with the relationship of psychoanalysis to the core of human rights."

Dr. Muramatsu, a younger man than Kosawa, asked the latter whether he had had any difficulty or interference from the imperial government in his practice of psychoanalysis under the pre-war government, and was told that Kosawa had not. Muramatsu later stated, in a letter to me dated July 11, 1950 that "it seems to me that there has been no trouble from the government because there have been very few psychoanalysts [as opposed to psychiatrists] in Japan." In the same letter Muramatsu, himself a psychiatrist, goes on to say: "I myself usually help patients to readjust to their environmental conditions, and it depends upon their own, as well as their family's attitude or circumstances, how far to lead them 'gesellschaftlich' [or into an expression of individualism]."

Dr. Kiyomi Koizumi is at present at Wayne University College of Medicine, on a scholarship for graduate study in physiological chemistry awarded her by the

Medical Branch of the Presbyterian Board of Foreign Missions. She informs me that nothing was taught of psychoanalysis in the psychiatric course which she took in 1947 at Tokyo Women's Medical College. She says that the name of Sigmund Freud, while known to most students through their extra-curricular reading, was not included in the regular outline of the course, although on one or two occasions, departing from the outline, the professor mentioned Freud in class. Dr. Koizumi says, however, that Freud was discussed in her psychology classes in the Pre-Medical Division of the Tokyo Women's Medical College, where she had her pre-medical training. The assumption seems justified that psychoanalysis, even in modified form, was practically ignored by Japanese legal and academic circles. For the Japanese, so anxious to learn about the occidental way of life, to thus neglect Freudian psychoanalytic procedures poses a puzzling problem.

9

DO THE JAPANESE INTEGRATE, OR MERELY COPY WESTERN PSYCHOANALYSIS?

THERE was another possible factor in Kosawa's claim that analytic aims were the same in Japan as in the United States, and that was the well-known habit of copying.* My personal observations, as well as what I had read of the Japanese behavior throughout the ages, made me wonder whether perhaps Japanese analysts might be copying but not actually integrating, the *techniques* of analysts in other countries, even though their aims were different. To understand the psychological significance of the modern Japanese copying, it is important to know something of the history of this trait, insofar as it can be seen to have affected relations with other nations.

The experience of Fernam Mendez Pinto, a Portuguese traveler who visited Japan in 1542, illustrates the obstinate and ominous inflexibility of Japanese copying. The handwriting was plain upon the wall when the feudal Yamotos gained oligarchic ascendancy through the employment of better and more numerous iron weapons. Pinto made a present of a single harquebus, with the formula for making gunpowder, to the prince of Tane-Ga-Shima. "And a few years later he was assured that there were above thirty thousand in the city of Fucheo, the capital of Bungo, and above three hundred thousand in the whole province."[159] (William E. Griffis says that there were six hundred guns or pistols in use by the Japanese within six months of Pinto's present to the prince.)[160]

Dr. Thunberg, a Swede, writing on his Japanese travels in 1796, during the closed door era, noted a reaction against copying. It was as if, sensitized by their disastrous experiences with the Christians, the Japanese somehow knew that their culturally determined propensity for copying might eventually destroy their identity, and so they rebelled against it. Thunberg said of this epoch: "They have hitherto never suffered themselves to be corrupted by the Europeans that have visited them: rather than adopt any practice from others, which might be actually both useful and convenient, they have chosen to retain their ancient and primitive mode of life, in its original purity; into which they would not even insensibly introduce any usage or custom, that in the course of time might become useless to them, or detrimental."[161] However, forced to recognize their helplessness due to their intimidation by Perry, the Japanese turned again to copying in the astonishingly detailed form in which we generally think of it, indicating their psychological identification with the enemy.

Nitobe writes: "Immediately after Perry's squadron had left the Japanese waters, the rulers of the country, whether actuated by clear foresight and comprehension of the moment, or whether impelled by that mental confusion which attends sudden awakening from slumber and apprehension of the next moment, were aroused to immediate activity. Schools were opened for the study of foreign languages; academies shot up, where youths

100

could receive instruction in military and naval tactics; raw recruits were drilled; foundries and smithies sprang into existence, and belfries were molested to furnish metals for arsenal."[162]

Payson Treat records the keen observation and careful drawings by the Japanese of every detail of Perry's equipage and the behavior of his men: "The visitors to Perry's flag-ship studied with interest the weapons, from Colt revolvers to Paixhan cannon; they descended into the engine-room and watched the machinery in motion; and they observed the manoeuvers of the crew at general quarters. . . . [The drawings] were prepared for the use of the Yedo [Tokyo] officials and certain of the daimyos."[163]

Townsend Harris noted in his journal that in 1857 the Japanese ". . . sent over two handsome brass howitzers, exactly copied in every respect from one Commodore Perry gave them; every appointment about the gun, down to the smallest particular, was exactly copied: percussion locks, drag ropes, powder or cartridge holder and all. . . ."[164] "They added that Commodore Perry had made them a present of a brass howitzer gun; that they had made many after that model, and that the salute should be fired from their copies of the American gun."[164a] (When Perry returned to Japan a year after his first trip, in 1854, the Japanese had already made a number of copies of the original gun.)

L. Adam Beck is quoted by Harris as follows: " 'Here too (at Shimonoseki) was the destiny of Japan again decided when the allied fleet of the United States, England, France and Holland in 1864 thrust the civilization of the West in the face of her repulsion. A relative of my own, still living, was present. . . . I stood by the swirling, dangerous currents of Shimonoseki and mar-

101

velled, remembering that to the hand of this man who still lives was given the first breech-loading Winchester rifle turned out by Japanese workmen [the original of which had been given the Japanese by an English admiral] with the request, proudly made, that he would show it to the British Admiralty. He did this and adds: "But I do not recall that any interest was taken in the circumstance." Admiralties are not intuitive; one would think (that) that rifle might have interested them a little.' "[165]

Not only should, "that rifle have interested them a little," but also all foreigners should have been alerted by the precision techniques of the Japanese copying. Detail was religiously imitated. Yet one might suspect that much that they copied in guns, ships and cannon was inevitable, and of a decor that was meaningless to them. This loyalty to detail in their copying was a source of great satisfaction to the Japanese. They could proudly boast that they had been most faithful following extravagant detail. That they did not know the meaning of the detail did not always matter.

However, the facility for copying and their compulsive need to imitate exactly the products of the Western nations revealed an ominous element in their mechanical provess that should have sounded a tocsin not only to the occidental countries but to the Japanese nation as well. This "ominous" element is explicit of masochistic submissiveness, and demonstrates or at least indicates that Japanese copying was not integrated.

10

THE AMERICAN BLUEPRINT COPIED BY
JAPANESE IMPERIALISTS

STUDENTS of dynamic anthropology form their reconstruction of Japanese sociology from present
material and material collected in retrospect.* But
most fail to comprehend the prophetic import of the
feverish imitative activities of the Japanese. In fact,
there are very few people who realize that the United
States supplied the Japanese with the design for their
surprise attack on Pearl Harbor—even perhaps, to the
small detail of the date, December 7.

In 1853, Commodore Matthew Perry, younger brother of Oliver, of Lake Erie fame, made his "sneak attack"
upon Tokyo harbor, gun-ports bristling and ready for
anything, demanding that Japan open her ports to
United States trade. Millard Fillmore's message to Congress on December 6, 1852 spoke of ". . . great extension,
and in some respects a new direction, to our commerce
in the Pacific Ocean. A direct and rapidly increasing
intercourse has sprung up with eastern Asia. The waters
of the northern Pacific, even into the Arctic Sea, have of
late years been frequented by our whalemen. The application of steam to the general purposes of navigation
is becoming daily more and more common, and makes
it desirable to obtain fuel and other necessary supplies
at convenient points on the route between Asia and our

Pacific shores. Our unfortunate countrymen who from time to time suffer shipwreck on the coasts of the eastern seas are entitled to protection. Besides these specific objects, the general prosperity of our States on the Pacific requires that an attempt should be made to open the opposite regions of Asia to a mutually beneficial intercourse. It is obvious that this attempt could be made by no power to so great advantage as by the United States, whose constitutional system excludes every idea of distant colonial dependencies. I have accordingly been led to order an appropriate naval force to Japan under the command of a discreet and intelligent officer of the highest rank known to our services. He is instructed to endeavor to obtain from the Government of that country, some relaxation of the inhospitable and anti-social system which it has pursued for about two centuries. . . ."[166]

As David Murray puts it: "The question of landing by force was left to be decided by the development of succeeding events; it was of course the very last measure to be resorted to, and the last that was to be desired; but . . . the Commodore caused the ships constantly to be kept in perfect readiness, and the crews to be drilled as thoroughly as they are in the time of active war."[167]

Historian Herbert Gowen, convinced that Perry was expected to use force if the Japanese did not comply, notes that: ". . . this was the current impression among those Americans who did not either ignore or ridicule the expedition. . . ."[168] In support of his statement, he quotes from *The New York Herald*: " 'The Japanese expedition, according to a Washington correspondent, is to be merely a hydrographical survey of the Japanese coast. The 32-pounders are to be used merely as measuring instruments in the triangulations; the cannon-balls are for procuring the base lines. If any Japanese is

foolish enough to put his head in the way of these mete-
orological instruments, of course nobody will be to
blame but himself if he should get hurt.' "[169] ·

It is easy to understand what prompted our breaking
of Japan's private Monroe Doctrine. But, perhaps because our behavior was so reprehensible, or because, in
light of current developments in American history, the
mere extension of our mercantile interests pales by comparison, little or no attention is given to the Perry affair
in many of our high school history texts. One of the
most highly regarded books, a standard history in Detroit
and well-to-do suburban high schools, David S. Muzzey's
A History of Our Country, makes no mention of Matthew Perry in index or text. There is, in fact, but a
two-sentence allusion to the race with British shipping
for the tea and spice trades of the Far East, and of an
$858,000 subsidy given the Collins Line to compete
with the Cunard Line in this contest during the
1850's.[170] Perry and his cohorts receive no notice whatever—not even "credit" for opening the closed doors of
Japan. The *Encyclopedia Americana* (Edition 1922)
says of the Perry-Yedo Bay episode: "In 1852 he was
entrusted by President Fillmore with a letter to the
ruler of Japan for the purpose of establishing diplomatic
and trade relations, and was given command of a squadron which reached Japan in July, 1853. He delivered
President Fillmore's letter at Kurihama and returning
to Japan early in 1854 concluded, at Yokohama, the
treaty which inaugurated a new era in the history of
Japan." Charles and Mary Beard, in their American
history published in 1944, perhaps touch on the true
spirit of the Perry episode in their chapter "The Breach
with Historic Continentalism" when they say: "This
is not to say that no Americans—in thought, ambition,

and enterprise—had gone beyond the continental borders. Keels of American ships had plowed the waters of all seas bearing masters and merchants in search of foreign markets and opportunities to garner in large profits from foreign trade. American warships had bombarded many ports in distant foreign lands in retaliation for native interference with the operations of American traders. Ambitious naval officers, such as Commodore Matthew C. Perry, who opened to American commerce the barred gates of Japan, had dreamed of and proposed the seizure of islands and territories in far-off lands; and indeed a hold was established in the Samoan Islands by 1889."[171]

Interest in trade with Japan had begun as early as 1791, when American fur-traders unsuccessfully endeavored to sell otter pelts in Japan, and in 1812 Commodore David Porter tried to interest Secretary of State James Monroe in opening Japan; but not until the 1820's did whaling replace the fur trade and involve trade with Pacific islands and the Asiatic Coast.[172] A New York merchant, Asa Whitney, later asked Congress to act on the construction of a railroad from Chicago to the Pacific Coast, hoping such a road would draw the trade of the Far East.[173] And George Wilkes cast his longing eye upon the "opulent empire of Japan," trade with which nation would be of tremendous value to the United States, in his opinion.[174]

Subsequently, in addition to the hue and cry of the traders, the ship-wrecked sailor theme began to be heard. Chitoshi Yanaga writes: "On February 15, 1845, following the publication of the Cushing correspondence on the China treaty, Congressman Pratt of New York introduced a resolution in the House calling for immediate measures to effect commercial arrangements with Japan and Korea, but it passed unnoticed. The time was not yet ripe for such an undertaking. When the American whale ship *Manhattan* visited Edo [Yedo] Bay in April, 1845, to return shipwrecked sailors, it was accorded hospitable treament, although it was permitted to remain only a few days."[175]*

The director of the American and Foreign Agency in New York, Aaron H. Palmer, in January, 1851, urged Fillmore to send a special envoy to Japan along with a strong naval squadron. Daniel Webster discussed the matter with Palmer; and at the same time Commander Glynn had brought to New York reports of good harbors and supplies of high-grade coal in Japan. In June, Glynn pressed Fillmore to negotiate a trade treaty with Japan, using force if necessary. "He emphasized, however, that it should be made clear to the Japanese that the United States entertained no intention of interfering in their internal politics or religion and that she was interested only in freedom of trade."[176]

Yanaga tells the story of the first American plan to use shipwrecked sailors to gain the good will of the Japanese: "On February 21, 1851, the American bark *Aukland* put into San Francisco with seventeen Japanese sailors who had been rescued at sea. Commodore John H. Aulick, who had also seen the need of opening Japan, suggested to the State Department that the repatriation of these sailors would provide an excellent opportunity for the opening of relations with Japan."[177]** Aulick was duly given special-envoy rating and assigned to the job of returning the Japanese sailors, although, because of a diplomatic tangle he had precipitated in South America, he was relieved of his assignment, unbeknownst to himself, while en route to Japan. It fell to Perry to take over Aulick's command, though his mission was not to be carried out for another two years. Daniel Webster, as Secretary of State, received historical credit for implementing the Perry achievement.[178]

To put it bluntly, our need for coaling stations, with the increasing use of steam vessels, gave rise to the Perry sneak-attack on Yedo Bay. To cover for our imperialistic move, Japan was scathingly denounced as a cruel nation which tortured shipwrecked American sailors. President Fillmore's First Annual Message, on December 2, 1850, said: "Among the acknowledged rights of nations is that which each possesses of establishing that form of government which it may deem most conducive to the happiness and prosperity of its own citizens, of changing that form as circumstances may require, and of managing its internal affairs according to its own will. The people of the United States claim this right for themselves, and they readily concede it to others. Hence it becomes an imperative duty not to interfere in the government or internal policy of other nations."[179] But of Perry's assignment, Fillmore said: "A discreet and intelligent officer of the highest rank has been directed particularly to remonstrate in the strongest language against the cruel treatment to which our shipwrecked mariners have been subjected and to insist that they shall be treated with humanity. He is instructed, however, at the same time to give that Government [Japan] the amplest assurances that the objects of the United States are such, and such only, as I have indicated and that the expedition is friendly and peaceful. Notwithstanding the jealousy with which the Governments of eastern Asia regard all overtures from foreigners, I am not without hopes of a beneficial result of the expedition."[180]

That the charges of torture were trumped up as a "smoke screen" for our true interests is quite evident from two events which had occurred prior to the Perry incident. Commodore James Biddle, arriving at Uraga in the summer of 1846 with two ships, ignored the Japanese demand that he dismantle his weapons and proceeded to attempt to interest them in translations of treaties concluded with China, England, France, and the United States. The Japanese claimed Biddle had no authority to discuss treaties, but while they refused to negotiate, they did supply Biddle's ships with necessary supplies.[181] And two years later, Commodore Glynn was sent to "rescue" fourteen imprisoned shipwrecked American sailors, of whom word had been received by the Dutch at Nagasaki. He found that in fact they were deserters from the whaler *Lagoda,* and nine of them were not Americans, but Kanakas; one was a half-breed Indian adventurer who had landed from another whaler (and had obtained a house at Nagasaki, taught English to the natives, and attracted much interest by his use of candles to illuminate his home). All were turned over to Glynn who, having "adopted an assured and severe manner," demanded their release.[182]

The futility of American attempts to return shipwrecked sailors to Japan can easily be seen in light of the Japanese law forbidding emigration from the Japanese archipelago. Indeed, the Japanese even have a phrase indicating the unimportance of the individual human being, (*mimpi*), which is part and parcel of their attitude toward their shipwrecked sailors: *Miwa Ichi dai. Nawa matsu dai.* ("Life is only once. But name is forever.") Murray has already been quoted on the law against emigration; Thunberg, too, wrote that: "No Japanese is allowed to leave his native land and visit foreign countries; this being prohibited, under penalty of death,"[183] and pointed out that therefore the art of navigation had declined among the Japanese. (It is known that subsequently their ships were constructed in such a way that in severe storms their fan-tails would be ripped out, so that the craft could not be blown out to sea and the sailors would find refuge within the archipelago.) Thunberg recounts the return by two Chinese junks of several Japanese blown ashore on the China coast during his visit to Japan, and remarks that they were immediately confined to their "native places."[184] (Apparently they escaped the death penalty, perhaps because they had not been influenced by contact with Christians.) Wassily Golownin tells of the Japanese thanking the Russians for returning a group of Japanese sailors, but informing them (the Russians) that: "They may either leave them or take them back again, as they shall think fit; for, according to the Japanese laws, such persons cannot be forcibly detained, since those laws declare that men belong to that country on which their destiny may cast them, and in which their lives have been protected."[185] The Japanese believed that a rescued man owed *on,* or obligation, to the people who had saved him.

The Japanese feared that these "humanitarian exploits" concealed plots to violate Japan's desire for isolation.* There is, for example, the case of the *Morrison,* a ship owned by Olyphant & Co., of Canton. In 1837, the *Morrison* undertook to open negotiations and missionary opportunities in Japan, using as an entree the repatriation of seven Japanese sailors she had picked up at Macao. The Shogunate, learning her multiple purpose, ordered the Morrison away and opened fire on her.[186]

The Japanese altered their policy somewhat in 1843, permitting shipwrecked Japanese to be returned, but only in Dutch or Chinese ships.[187]

Once Perry effectively opened the doors of Japan, Townsend Harris was appointed consul and commenced negotiations for a trade treaty. (The history of his nefarious activities as recorded in his own journal and by Payson Treat, et al, is in part a commentary on United States policy, but also upon the warped personality of the man. In any case, the facts in regard to what he did had profound effect upon the Japanese, who were taking lessons—i.e., copying—from him in how to deal with other nations.)

Harris, like Perry himself, insisted on transacting business with the emperor, the *Ichi-Bun*.[188] His confusion as to who was, in point of fact, the actual ruler of Japan, and his own stubbornness on the whole matter, helped to delay approval of the trade treaty.* He inflated his own ego by representing to the Japanese that the message he bore was directly from the President of the United States to the emperor. (Actually it read: "To All to Whom These Presents Shall Come, Greetings.") Harris' official authorization to act as United States consul stated that he had ". . . full . . . power . . . to meet and confer with any person or persons duly authorized by His Majesty the Emperor of Japan, being invested with like [i.e., equal to Harris'] power and authority, and with him or them to agree, treat, consult and negotiate. . . ."[189]

Harris told the prince of Shinano that the United States asked no favors, merely demanding its "rights," that his mission was for the good of Japan, which should regard the sending of Harris as a favor conferred on them by the United States President.[190] He said the United States made no threats, but rather warned of the dangers to Japan, and pointed out a way not only to avert danger but to enhance Japan's prosperity.[191] At the same time he recorded in his journal the wish for warships to reinforce his demands,[192] and later threatened the Japanese with the might of the British fleet, through a skillful reading-out-of-context from a letter to himself from Sir John Bowring, Governor of Hong Kong. Sir John expressed himself as deeply concerned about Japan, and stated that if he felt sure of a friendly reception and of obtaining desired trade-treaties, he would not feel it necessary to bring a large fleet, as would be necessary if he anticipated stubbornness on the part of the Japanese. As Harris says, "reading [this extract] produced a marked sensation [upon the Japanese]. . . ."[193]

The consul demanded that American citizens committing crimes in Japan be tried by the American consul and punished according to American law.[194] He refused to accept the Japanese rate of exchange on gold, insisting that, while the Japanese had the right to set their own standard for their own people, they had no right over a foreigner, and ". . . to attempt to exercise such a right over him would in effect be a confiscation of his property."[195] (After the treaty was signed, the exchange was so rigged against Japan that she was nearly stripped of all her gold. It became common practice for foreigners, under protection of the treaty, to trade in gold, making certain profits of 200 per cent. Ultimately the Japanese government managed to intervene, stopping gold export and readjusting the domestic ratio of gold and silver. The *jo-i* barbarian-expelling party began to be felt as a force in Japan, backed this time by an increasingly aroused and incensed Japanese public.)[196]

Typical of the misunderstandings and confusions in the whole process of negotiation was the Japanese misunderstanding of the wording of the proposed treaty. The following explanation of what occurred in this situation was supplied me by Drs. Locher and Hall, of the History Department, University of Michigan: "It would appear that Article II of the Kanagawa Treaty which concerned the American appointment of consuls and agents at Shimoda, and in particular the phrase 'provided that either of the governments,' was incorrectly understood by the Japanese. This is shown by documents included in the Japanese Documentary Collection, *Documents Relating to Foreign Affairs at the End of the Shogunate,* Vol. V, Tokyo, 1914, p. 454. [This volume] gives the official translation of the English [rendered] into Japanese, prepared by the Dutch translator, Commodore Klerk. This translation is correct and specifically uses the phrase, 'provided that either one of the governments.' In Vol. V, p. 468, in a reply to the English from the Shogun's councillors, Kayashi Daigalm-no-Kami, the Japanese negotiator of the treaty, expressed the opinion that the American appointment of a consul or agent was a matter to be decided by further discussion. The implication was that the Japanese could refuse to permit such a move."*

Harris stood firm on his demands to conclude treaty arrangements in a meeting with the "head man," who by now was represented to him by the exalted position of the Shogun, and 18 months after his arrival in Japan, on December 7, 1857, "After a week of hospitality and exchange of courtesies, in which Harris was in charge of eight noblemen appointed as 'Commissioners of the

Voyage of the American Ambassador to Yedo,' he was received . . . in a most dignified manner by the Shogun."[197]

William E. Griffis, author of *The Mikado's Empire* and other books, and a pioneer educator in Japan in the 1870's, sums up their period of Japan's unwilling entry into the life of the outside world. In his life of Millard Fillmore, he writes: "In a word, the Japanese did not seek us. We sought them, and, almost by main force, dragged them out of their seclusion, in order to win their trade and enrich California and the United States. After we had taken their gold out of the country, and as soon as we gained their secrets, of tea, silk, ceramics, and what not, we built up tariffs against them."[198]

It is interesting to note, parenthetically, that the pattern for the Japanese exclusion acts did not originate with the Japanese, but with China, whose early influence upon Japan is well known. After the last of the great Ming sea voyages conducted by prominent Chinese eunuchs in 1405-1433, ". . . China withdrew once more into seclusion. Her people were forbidden to leave the country or to communicate with foreigners, and Chinese ships could no longer make ocean voyages. This attitude towards the outside world was maintained for more than three hundred years and influenced the course of Far Eastern history in important ways."[199] But even this ban had been preceded by an earlier one. The first Ming Emperor ruled (1404): ". . . that the 'people should not go down to the sea in ships'; and although these strict rules were from time to time modified or disregarded, for a long period it remained the official view that foreign trade and foreign relations in general were unnecessary and dangerous."[200] On the other hand, ". . . once the Tokugawa family had established a central government,

114

they carried out their exclusion policy with ruthless thoroughness. No Japanese official would dare to tolerate infractions of the law."[201] Thus we see that the Japanese "closed-door" pattern was a copy of the exclusion policies laid down by China almost 200 years prior to the Japanese edict of 1639. However, the fact that the Chinese act had never been withdrawn, though Chinese trade with Nagasaki was active prior to the Japanese edict, is an indication of the flexible and even *laissez-faire* attitude of the Chinese as contrasted with the compulsive authoritarianism with which laws were applied by the Japanese.

11

JAPANESE IDENTIFICATION WITH THE ENEMY

IN instances where individual strivings are, from earliest infancy, consistently suppressed, there results, as a natural consequence, an exaggeration or over-emphasis of mimetic responsiveness in the suppressed person. Mimicry supplants appropriate spontaneity.

Identification* is a psychological mechanism that develops out of a need to escape the anxiety stemming from the presence of a threatening authority. Well known to all psychologists and psychiatrists, it is recognized as a device which springs from a sense of weakness. The need for strength results in identification with the authoritarian for the purpose of neutralizing the threatening presence.** Identification is fraught with danger to the individual or group which employs it. This psychological mechanism involves the psychological process of indiscriminate copying.

There is much to be learned about the Japanese character structure from our first war with Japan, and much to be learned about mother-occasioned character rigidities and cultural inertia. The *daimyo* of Choshiu in 1863, loyal to the emperor at Kyoto, followed orders and fired on American and other foreign ships as they passed through the narrow straits of Shimonoseki. (The prince of Choshiu, who had obeyed the emperor and ordered the firing upon foreign ships at Shimonoseki, was later repudiated by the shogunate, and an actual state of war was declared by the Tokugawa government against him.)[202] The American ship *Pembroke's* commander averred that she had sustained $11,200 worth of damages (for "loss of time"), and the American minister forced payment of this sum by Japan.

Even so, indignant at this attempt upon the part of Japan to defend herself against invading foreigners, the combined fleets of France, Holland, England, and the United States joined against Shimonoseki. The straits city was blasted to bits. The *daimyo* of Choshiu capitulated, and Japan paid an indemnity of $3,000,000 to the nations participating in the bombardment. To do justice to our common people, it should be recorded that the citizens of the United States forced this government to return to Japan our share of the loot ($785,000), though we officially avowed that the money was returned because the handful of sailors in the one chartered vessel employed by the United States Navy in the joint attack occasioned the American people no appreciable expense.

We continued to "needle" and intimidate Japan. In 1865, the Englishman Parkes, known as an exponent of the "gun-boat policy," persuaded a number of foreign powers, including the United States, to conduct naval demonstrations off Hyogo as a means of inducing the emperor to ratify certain treaties and also to secure regulation of tariffs and the opening of Hyogo and Osaka to trade. Tyler Bennett terms the treaty one of the most un-American ever ratified by our government.[203]

When forced to capitulate, the Japanese identified

with the enemy. Still copying Perry's, not to say Parkes', style, Japan secured Korean treaties eleven years later by a display of naval power. In this connection it is to be noted that American Marines had previously invaded Korea, thereby establishing an important precedent that was followed or copied by the Japanese. And in 1874, using our "shipwrecked sailor" technique for masking imperial ambitions, Japan sent an expedition via Amoy to seek redress for the murder of Ryukyu sailors. The "culpable" Chinese were forced to pay an indemnity. Schwartz makes note of an odd political twist in the affair: though the Ryukyus were ostensibly Chinese-owned, the closer practical ties (commerce, for example) were with Japan. Schwartz puts it thus: "In December, 1871, a Loo Chooan junk was stranded on the southern coast of Formosa, and fifty-four of its crew were murdered by the head-hunting savages of that island. The Loo Chooans, in their hour of need, appealed not to father China, but to mother Japan. . . . The expedition against Formosa sailed in 1874. China protested against it, and for a time war between China and Japan over the incident seemed inevitable. Diplomacy, however, prevailed, and the two governments entered into an agreement at Tientsin in October, 1874. In this brief document the justice of Japan's proceedings is acknowledged, and China agrees to pay 'an indemnity of one hundred thousand taels for the relief of the families of the *subjects of Japan* who were murdered.' "[204] This demanding indemnity or money for relief of the families of the "subjects of Japan" who were murdered was a practice copied originally from the English. It was customary for the English to exact indemnity from the Japanese for any Englishman murdered in Japan. (The Ryukyuans, of course, were not actually

Japanese; they never did, and do not to this day, consider themselves such. In fact, the Japanese looked down on the Ryukyuans, regarding them, in the words of Newman and Eng, as "uncouth rustics. . . . The epithet 'Pork-Eater' is applied to Ryukyu people by the Japanese, and may involve another criterion of their racial prejudice—'the unpleasant body odor attributed by most Japanese to a diet including considerable amounts of meat.' "[205] The Japanese spheres of influence became more evident after the restoration of the Meiji, at which time the last king of the Shoyan Dynasty was removed to Japan.)

* * *

In a later conquest of China, Japan engaged in expansion activities, again in accordance with the American blueprint for imperialistic endeavor. On April 14, 1895, she extracted from China official signatures to the Treaty of Shimonoseki, in which China granted Korea full independence, ceded Pescadores, Formosa and the Liao-tung Peninsula to Japan. China also paid an indemnity of 200,000,000 taels to Japan, opened four treaty ports and the Yangtse-kiang to navigation, and negotiated a new commercial treaty.[206] Gaining momentum, Japan continued her imperialistic efforts, conquering Russia in 1904, participating in the defeat of Germany in 1918, and swallowing Manchuria in 1931.

The Japanese pre-World War II trickery was designed by the United States. Matthew Perry kept his guns trained on the Japanese reviewing stand, and when the Japanese moved it to a safer spot, Perry moved his ship so that his guns again pointed at the stand. Perhaps he was merely being cautious; but what about the diplomatic caprices of Consul Townsend Harris? Harris actually coerced the Shogun by recounting the predatory effectiveness of the English fleet upon China. At any rate, he implied that, as a civil functionary, he was in a position to effect a more lenient agreement with the Japanese than if the treaties were concluded under military pressure and with military personnel. Harris pointed out that, since the opening up of Japan was inevitable, the Shogun might as well conclude the first treaty with the United States, a great power with which he was already familiar. This was done, and similar treaties were soon effected with Russia and England.

* * *

The history of the United States and Japan in Hawaii further demonstrates the Japanese imitation of American methods. After the reign of Queen Liliuokalani, the Hawaiians for a time attempted a non-monarchic government. This government became an unintentional necessity, for President Cleveland refused to accept the islands as a territorial possession of the United States on the grounds that the revolt had been improperly assisted by diplomatic representatives of the United States, backed by the U. S. Marines. Foster describes Cleveland's stand as follows: "One of the first acts of Mr. Cleveland after his inauguration for a second term was to withdraw the treaty of annexation from the Senate. He was impressed by the declaration of the queen that she had been dethroned through the presence of the United States troops and against the will of a large majority of her subjects, and he sent a commissioner, Hon. J. H. Blount, to Hawaii to investigate and report upon the causes of the revolution and the sentiments of the people towards the provisional government. After a lengthy investigation Mr. Blount reported that the party which supported the new government constituted the intelligence and owned most of the property on the islands, that the greater part of the natives were in favor of the ex-queen, and that the revolution succeeded through the support of the United States minister and troops."[207] Meantime, the Japanese, having been urged by King Kalakaua of Hawaii, in 1881, to permit Japanese to emigrate to the islands, finally agreed to do this four years later after first dispatching a Japanese emissary to the Hawaiian government. By 1890 there were 12,360 Japanese in Hawaii, by 1900 there were more than 61,000.[208] (Foster notes that this was 39.7 per cent of the total population of Hawaii,[209] which we know may have included Okinawans.) Obviously Japan now had a justifiable interest in the Hawaiian Islands.

The manner in which the emissary was dispatched to the islands was patterned after Perry's "visit" to Japan: the dignitaries approached Oahu in a ship of war, and made their demands in the same fashion as Perry and Harris had made theirs upon Japan. The Japanese wanted to see the head man, the *ichi bun*.

During the period of heavy Japanese migration into the Hawaiian Islands, the United States was stealthily negotiating (in 1898) with the Hawaiians for a transfer of the islands to the United States—at the same time reassuring the Japanese officials that no such plan was under consideration. Deceived, the Japanese made note to remember; and years later, on December 7, 1941, as their aircraft carriers raced towards Hawaii, their emissaries in Washington, Nomura and Kurusu, ridiculed the idea of war and blandly talked of peace.

* * *

That was the beginning of what might seem to the Japanese a back-firing of their copying, the point at which they were no longer served by their teacher, the unadvertised (in the United States) American Way.

Imitators are blind, their actions reflex, total and non-discriminatory. As has been observed, there was no humanitarian basis for the Japanese concern for ship-wrecked sailors. Not only were the Ryukyuan sailors not even of their own racial stock, but, in fact, the Japanese despised them. So well aware were they of the death penalty for leaving the archipelago, that Japanese who were wrecked were exceedingly loath to be returned to their fatherland. Payson Treat cites the example of Dentichi, a shipwrecked Japanese sailor who joined an American expedition to Japan in the 1850's as a translator and took the name of "Dan Ketch." Treat says: "He was afraid to land in Japan lest he be beheaded under the law forbidding Japanese to leave the country."[210] Later Dentichi did land in Japan and was short-ly killed by one of the *ronin*. He may have been killed for any of three reasons: either he was too arrogant, or he now represented a foreign nation, or he had not paid the penalty for leaving the shores of Japan.

The catastrophe that befell Japan is tantamount to the devastating self destructive process that sooner or later occurs in every instance of immaturity. If one does not grow up, he grows in.

Japan, as we have said, *identified* herself with her enemies. This mechanism, known to all psychoanalysts, became her means of self-preservation. She accumulated available information about the methods used by the Western powers. By using these methods she hoped to perpetuate her identity. The French were employed to teach military tactics; the English taught naval strategy; the United States provided demonstrations of imperial-ist methods* and also supplied ships, arms, military specialists, artisans, and technicians.[211]

It might be said that there was a "last gasp" from

the westernizers in Japan in the last decade or so of the nineteenth century. Yanaga describes the battle of the Japan nationalists vs. the proponents of westernization as follows: "The movement for the preservation of 'national virtues' developed into an advocacy of strong nationalism after Mori succeeded in making it the basic concept in education. This reactionary trend was aided by the promulgation of the Constitution in 1889 and the Rescript on Education the following year. Thus, Japanism became the battle cry of those opposed to Westernism. In this period of reaction, Professor Kume Kunitake was forced out of the Tokyo Imperial University for a statement that Shinto was an ancient ritual of the worship of heaven. However, the prophets of chauvinistic nationalism, like Takayama Chogyu and Nishimura Shigeki, were opposed by Tokutomi and others who denounced superficial Westernism and advocated democracy. Saijoni, on assuming the post of Education Minister in January, 1898, expressed his view to an editor of the *Kokumin Shimbun* that the regulation and control of national morality on the basis of narrow, intolerant, and reactionary ideas would bring ruin to the country and that the State alone as an ethical basis was too narrow a concept. He stressed that if Japan were to take her place among the powers of the world, she would have to keep in step with world trends and not to go against them."[212]

To note again the Fillmore message previously remarked, and whose significance as a pattern for the Japanese became evident just a bit over a century later: "Among the acknowledged rights of nations is that which each possesses of establishing that form of government which it may deem most conducive to the happiness and prosperity of its own citizens, of changing that form as circumstances may require, and of managing its internal affairs according to its own will. The people of the United States claim this right for themselves, and they readily concede it to others. Hence it becomes an imperative duty not to interfere in the government or internal policy of other nations."[213]

On December 7, 1941, Kurusu and Nomura handed to Secretary of State Cordell Hull in Washington the following message: "It is the immutable policy of the Japanese Government . . . to enable each nation to find its proper place in the world*. . . . The Japanese Government cannot tolerate the perpetuation of the present situation since it runs directly counter to Japan's fundamental policy to enable each nation to enjoy its proper station in the world."[214]

The spirit of the message delivered simultaneous to the attack on Pearl Harbor was the same as that of Fillmore's message; the deception similar to that of the United States in the matter of Hawaii in 1898; as has been remarked, even the date, December 7, perhaps had conceivably been borrowed by the Japanese out of history, since it was on December 7, 1857, that Harris forced the initial conference of the Shogun.

From the Official Ministry of Education Policy on Instruction, under "History,"[215] it can be clearly seen that the Japanese still chafed, less than a decade ago, under the memory of such historical events as the Perry attack. It seems far from impossible that, in the light of such memories, and the total nationalist philosophy, the Pearl Harbor attack was outlined in the governmental mind much earlier than 1943, when the document was published:

[Item 4] "By presenting a comprehensive view of the rise and fall and prosperity and decline of the nations and races of East Asia and the world up to the present time and by delving especially into the activities of and historical facts about the peoples of East Asia and the truths about European and American invasion of East Asia, the historical significance of the establishment of Greater East Asia shall be elucidated and the mission of our Empire taught."[216]

Again for emphasis it might be added here that the psychologic procedure called "identification with the enemy" is a process that carries its own straight jacket. The rigidity of this special type of behavior is always accompanied by a look of appropriate spontaneity that characterizes emotional maturity.

12

THE PSYCHOANALYTIC MOVEMENT
IN JAPAN

FOR the past six years I have endeavored to find out as much as possible about the history and practice of psychoanalysis in Japan, because understanding Japanese psychoanalytic aims would, to my mind, throw more light on what makes the Japanese "tick" than any other approach to the problem. That I have encountered some difficulty in achieving this end is not surprising. According to Robert Textor: "Huge obstacles to finding and appraising the facts are to be found in the Japanese culture itself. The Japanese have been 'standing inspections' for a thousand years longer than we. They have had centuries of experience in pleasing their 'superiors.' Their deep sense of hierarchy, their frequent preference for propriety over 'rectitude' and sometimes over logic lead them to give answers to the casual American visitor which are not always in line with objective fact. There are vast areas of behavior about which the ordinary Japanese may be unwilling to talk freely. Some types of questions in the realm of government or sociology that a Westerner in official capacity would gladly answer in detail, his Japanese opposite number will tackle reluctantly or not at all. The Japanese official's main motivation may spring from a desire to prevent shame or loss of 'face' for his organization or for himself (and his family). As I have learned from many unsatisfactory interviews, 'rapport' is often achievable only after prolonged contact with a Japanese."[217] From the confusing and sometimes incomplete replies I obtained to questions put to various seemingly logical sources of information in Japan, it is indeed apparent to me that it is difficult to obtain direct answers, and even, in some cases, to get any answer at all.

An article, "History of Psychoanalysis in Japan," in English in the March-April, 1941, issue of *Seishin Bunseki* (prepared by Kenji Ohtski for newspaper publication and reprinted in the journal) supplies skeleton information on the origins of the psychoanalytic movement in Japan:

"Psychoanalysis was first imported into Japan in 1912 in the form of introductory treatises by Kaison Ohtski and Kyuiti Kimura which appeared in the psychological journal, *Sinri-Kenkyu* (*The Study of Psychology*), edited by Yoiti Uyeno. The first book published in Japan on psychoanalysis was Dr. Yasuasaburo Sakaki's *Study of Sexuality and Psychoanalysis,* printed in 1919. *The Study of Psychology* lasted for thirteen years, during which time ten articles on psychoanalysis appeared in its pages. From 1925 to 1929, however, general interest in psychoanalysis was suspended [for reasons not stated].

"Toward 1929, popular curiosity about the field was again aroused, and two separate publishers brought out Japanese versions of the collected works of Sigmund Freud, but their publication represented a transitory vogue rather than a serious scientific interest. However, Dr. Kiyoyasu Marui, professor of medicine at Tohoku

University, in Sendai, started a periodical called the *Psychoanalytical Bulletin,* which contained reports from his classes and is still being issued twice a year [1941].* Dr. Marui is hailed as one of the authorities on psychoanalysis in Japan.

"The first issue of *Seishin Bunseki* (*Tokyo Journal of Psychoanalysis*), edited by Seiya Hasegawa, Kenji Ohtski, et al, came out in 1933 and is still being published. It boasts a regular exchange with the journals of other countries.

"The Freud Prize is awarded annually to the contributor of the year's outstanding article in the Tokyo Journal of Psychoanalysis. The Prize was the suggestion of Prince Iwakura, a principal member of the Tokyo Institute for Psychoanalysis, of which Kenji Ohtski is president, and a founder, with Yaekichi Yabe, Hasegawa, and Kenji Tusima.

"Publication of the Shunyodo version of Freud's works was the first effort of the Tokyo Institute for Psychoanalysis. Translation was handled by the four founders of the Institute, under the general direction of Ohtski, who assisted in translation, editing and publishing, and also produced over ten volumes of original work on sexual psychology, characterology, economics, politics and literature, from the scientific point of view.

"There are three [psychoanalytically oriented] clinics in Japan for the treatment of neurotics: Tohoku Imperial University, Psychiatric Department, under Dr. Marui; the Psychoanalytic Society [now inactive, 1951], under Yabe [deceased, 1945] and the Tokyo Institute for Psychoanalysis, under Ohtski." (All of these men were psychoanalysts.)

Having been under the impression that only a very few Japanese psychoanalysts had themselves been analyzed outside of Japan, I have made an effort to discover whether my impression was correct. Dr. Florence Powdermaker informs me that she was told by Dr. Kosawa that he had himself spent only three months in Vienna, during which time he was an analysand of Dr. Richard Sterba. This would have been of course too brief a period to be considered a complete analysis by present occidental standards. Kosawa himself wrote me in 1952 that he had been in Vienna a full year however. In correspondence with Kenji Ohtski, I asked what information he had on the matter, and received the following reply: "So far as I know, only one analyst (Mr. Yaekichi Yabe) was analyzed, in England, by Dr. Edward Glover."* Yet a letter from Dr. Ernest Jones says that he himself analyzed Yabe! In reply to my query as to whether the first analysts in Japan were not analyzed,** Ohtski wrote: "Mr. Yabe, now dead, was the first analyst in this country and he was analyzed as mentioned above, though the analysis was not, it seems, so effective, on account of differences in language, life, feelings and customs."***

It is interesting to note here, in light of Ohtski's criticism of Yabe's analysis, what was said of Yabe in a caption under his picture in *Seishin Bunseki,* No. 32, 1950: "Received A.B. in America [college and year not mentioned], in experimental psychology. Returned to Japan and worked as labor psychologist for the National Railroad Bureau. Resigned and became psychoanalyst. In 1930 went to Vienna, studied under Freud. Went to England and had training analysis under Dr. Glover.**** Returned to Japan and became head of Japanese branch of International Psychoanalytic Association and began many new works. However, he could not accomplish what was expected of him because of the weakness of his character.* His principal book is *Theory and Practice of Psychoanalysis.* His principal translations are *The Theory of Libido* and *The Ego and the Id,* both by Freud. He died on August 4, 1945, of pneumonia, at the age of 70."

Although not mentioned in the above quotation, Yabe was a heavy contributor to *Seishin Bunseki.* Among his articles were "Crime and Guilt-Feelings," "Psychic Mechanisms of Hysteria and their Sublimation," "Wish Fulfillment by Means of the Dream and Nightmare," "The Characteristic Dream Symbolism of the Japanese," and "Psychoanalytic Therapy." Three others by Yabe which I have had translated (portions of which will appear in the following pages) are "Super-ego, Criminality and Religiosity," and "The Psychoanalysis of a Sleep Phobia," and "Personal Impressions of Dr. Edward Glover."

After receiving Ohtski's communication, I sent an inquiry to Dr. Ernest Jones in England, who is a past president of the International Psycho-Analytic Association. Having visited, in the summer of 1951, with Dr. Marui in Amsterdam and in Sussex, Dr. Jones wrote to me: "Dr. Marui . . . studied at the Phipps Clinic, Baltimore, for two and a half years from 1917 to 1919, was Professor of Psychiatry at the University of Tohoku in the Province of Sendai for thirty years, and for the past four years has been President of the University of Hirosaki as well as Professor of Psychiatry there. . . . He was analyzed in 1933 for a month by Paul Federn in Vienna, to whom Freud had sent him, [probably for analysis by Eitingen] then visited Berlin for two weeks, and then visited me in London at the end. He is without doubt the most reliable and serious analyst in Japan. His Society has 25 members, all of them medical except for four psychologists. Ten of them have been analyzed by Dr. Kosawa, who has been analyzed by Marui, and who now practices in Tokyo with a small group of four or five doctors around him. Ohtski, the leader of the other group in Tokyo, is a journalist and all of his members are lay. . . . The only one of that group who has been abroad was Dr. Yabe, who died in 1945. You have it down that Glover analyzed him and that he did controls with me. This is a reversal of the actual facts.

"I have no doubt myself that the Hirosaki Society, which for years has been a constituent Society of the International Association, will at our next Congress be recognized as the Official *Japanese* Society."

Dr. Marui was described by Dr. Yashiyuki Koga in a letter to me as "the most prominent Freudian in Japan." Dr. Muramatsu wrote to me about Marui as follows, the information confirming what Jones had said: "Dr. Marui is the leader of the orthodox Freudian group in Japan. There are only about five orthodox analysts in Japan, and they seem to be very loyal to Freud, and not to be willing to modify any idea or technique originated by him. 'Dr. Marui, who studied psychiatry in the U.S., organized the Sendai Branch of the International Psycho-Analytical Association of Tohoku University School of Medicine in 1934. It numbered only about 12 members." Dr. Marui is currently one of the editors of the International Journal of Psycho-Analysis, and is president of both Hirosaki University and of the Sendai Psychoanalytical Association. The branch of the International Association, which Marui founded, now meets at Hirosaki, rather than Sendai, and is called the "Japan Branch of the International Psycho-Analytical Association," according to Muramatsu. Dr. Marui himself informed me that there are 23 members in the

Sendai Psychoanalytical Association. He added that there are many analysts outside the Association, how many he did not know.

Ohtski wrote, in the summer of 1951, that the "Japanese Psychoanalytic Association is not yet established" —which curiously conflicted with a later letter from Dr. Kosawa, who is Director of the Kosawa Psychoanalytical Hospital. Dr. Kosawa wrote that there was a "Nippon Psychoanalytical Association," (which would be the same as the "Japanese Psychoanalytical Association") and that he was himself a member of the Tokyo branch of this organization. A letter from Kosawa dated January 11, 1952, supplies the clue to this series of statements and counter-statements. It appears that a Japanese Psychoanalytic Society was in the process of formation, perhaps without Ohtski's knowledge, and that, in July, 1951, the Society sent its Prospectus to *Imago,* evidently with the intention of notifying analysts in other countries of the Japanese Society's existence, and seeking their interest, support, and criticism. It is of interest that the Society includes "psychiatrists, sociologists, educators and religionists" among its members.

The "Prospectus for the Establishment of the Japanese Psychoanalytic Society," which Kosawa enclosed with his letter to me, is of sufficient interest to be quoted here *in toto:*

"In 1947 [*sic*] the 80th birthday of Dr. Sigmund Freud on the 6th of May was celebrated by the whole world, and his home, Vienna, became the Holy land of psychoanalysis. But alas! Suddenly a political storm occurred in the following year. German-Austrian union destroyed all this. Such was the destiny of the great Dr. Freud's enterprises.

"As a result of the World War II, Germany and

Japan surrendered, and from among the weeds and ruins there arose a new Japanese psychoanalytic society, born in the interest of the reconstruction of peace.

"The great efforts of the Occidentals have made the human being emerge from scientific dualism and given him back the opportunity of seeking a single god. Mephistopheles, the atomic bomb, has appeared before us announcing the coming of a new god.

"What could the new god be but the ideal of the United Nations? Japan's present relations with the other nations of the world indicate her faithful fulfillment of the Potsdam Declaration, her renunciation of war and intent to contribute to human democracy.

"To establish democracy it is necessary to make the individual ego, as well as the social ego, secure; and for the establishment of the social ego, the existence of the individual ego is absolutely essential.

"The Japanese people have variously expressed their individual egos through the teachings of Chinese Confucianism, Indian Buddhism and Western civilization, but our natural environment is too serious to establish it satisfactorily. We failed both in individual and social accomplishment.

"However, the opportunity has been given us, through our surrender to America, to receive her leadership represented by her sublimated Puritan idealism and her pioneer spirit.

"It is time to begin the salvation of our souls through the building up of our inner egos, enlarging them to become a part of a world-wide social ego and hence to contribute to human good fortune. It is for this reason that we think it imperative that we set up the Japanese Psychoanalytic Society and its laboratories.

"Our activities will consist of meetings of members

interested in research, publication, translation and general seminars."

Muramatsu says that a member of "so-called 'eclectic' groups" are being formed at present among young psychiatrists and psychologists, since the younger men are less prone to accept the orthodox Freudian concepts. He does not state, however, whether there are similar analytic groups forming.

In perusing a collection of issues of *Seishin Bunseki* from the beginning of publication to 1941,* one finds a vast number of references to Sigmund Freud, who carried on an active correspondence with Ohtski (some of his letters being reproduced in the *Journal*), and who also contributed many articles to the publication. Freud's theories were extensively discussed by various writers in *Seishin Bunseki,* his picture appeared frequently, and, as mentioned above, a prize bearing his name was established. The latter constituted an annual money-award, accompanied by a medal, statue, or similar work of art done by a different Japanese artist each year. A Freud Institute, evidently for psychoanalytic study, was also established, some of whose graduation exercises are pictured in the magazine. An "In Memoriam" at the time of Freud's death was printed in English.

Other Occidental psychoanalytic figures whose pictures were published or whose works received attention in the Journals include Ferenczi, Jekels, Jung, Glover, Wittels, Brill, Anna Freud, Reik, Hitschmann, Bergler, Rivers, Stekel, Flugel, Eissler, Piaget, Abraham, Rank, Alexander, Adler, Klein, Eitingen, Bose, Coriat, and Kris.

Throughout the magazines are a number of pictures of gatherings of the Tokyo Institute for Psychoanalysis.

the Tokyo Psychoanalytic Society, and miscellaneous meetings of analysts for specific purposes. Most of the groups include a number of women and an occasional Occidental. Dress of the members pictured, no matter what the occasion, includes a generous sprinkling of kimonos; and some of the banquets are conducted in Western-style, with tables and chairs, while others are in the Japanese manner (low tables, with the guests kneeling around them). Some of the people shown with the analytic societies (whether members or not was not clear from the captions) are in military dress, and one member we know from the above history to be a prince.*

From all of this it is apparent that there is a notable admixture of Western with Oriental culture in the Japanese psychoanalytic movement, an influence which, as I shall try to make clear in the following pages, has nevertheless left quite untouched certain basic Japanese ideologies, even among the more scientifically trained nationals of that country.

Before moving to other matters, it should be observed that there is this justification for the seeming superficiality of analyses such as the ones mentioned which were less than a year in length: All analyses of Freud's early associates were a good deal shorter, and considerably less intensive, than occidental analyses today. However, the more important point is that as a group Japanese analysts have not been sufficiently analyzed or sufficiently trained to practice effective psychoanalysis themselves.

An even more serious defect, which can best be illustrated by the final paragraphs of Kenji Ohtski's latest (January, 1952) summation of postwar psychoanalysis in Japan, is the amazing capacity of Japanese analysts to syncretize religion, the life and death instincts, Freudian-ism,—in short, most new thinking that comes their way. Says Ohtski:

"Therefore psychoanalysis in Japan may be expected to develop differently from psycho-somatic medicine [which is apparently accepted as synonymous with psychoanalysis] in America. The Orientals are fundamentally different from the Occidentals, as Dr. J. C. Moloney wisely suggests, since the former stand generally on an unconsciously synthetic [I had used the word "syncretic"] principle, while the Occidentals as a rule adhere to the consciously antithetic point of view." (I had not used the word "antithetic.")

He also reiterated his earlier statement (see his "History of the Psychoanalytic Movement in Japan," quoted in the first pages of this chapter) that "Psychoanalysis is . . . somewhat akin to Buddhism." This statement bears comparison with the "Prospectus for the Establishment of the Japanese Psychoanalytic Society" quoted above.

* * *

In recent correspondence with Japanese analysts, I have learned something of their present methodology. There is no indication that it has changed since before the war, and it seems to be, by and large, a fair imitation of the methods laid down by Freud, most of which are in rather general use throughout the Western world today—with a few notable Japanese innovations which will be remarked.

I questioned my correspondents as follows:

1. *Does the Japanese analyst have the patient lie on a couch?* Lay analyst Ohtski replied: "I do not let the patient lie on the couch, but both analyst and patient sit on chairs, though not face-to-face." Dr. Kosawa said:

"I do, but I do not know whether all Japanese psycho-analysts do so." Dr. Marui wrote: "We let the patient lie on a couch." Psychiatrist Muramatsu said: "As far as I understand, the Japanese analysts who belong to the orthodox Freudian school usually have the patient lie on a couch. I myself do, sometimes."

2. *Is the free-association technique used in Japanese analysis?* Both Mr. Ohtski and Dr. Kosawa answered in the affirmative. Dr. Marui wrote that "in analysis we lay heaviest weight on the free-association technique." Dr. Muramatsu concurred that this technique is in general use among Japanese analysts.

3. *Do Japanese analysts use dream-interpretation?* Ohtski replied: "Dream analysis is very much availed of." Kosawa said: "Yes, I use dream interpretation." Dr. Marui said: "I use dream-interpretation only as a sub-sidiary method." (This was interesting, from a renowned leader of Japanese Freudians.) Dr. Muramatsu said that Japanese analysts made no great use of the technique.

4. *How many times a week does a patient come for analysis?* Ohtski did not reply to this query, but Kosawa answered in some detail: "The number differs according to the kind of mental illness. For example: obsessional neurosis is 3 times a week; depression is 6 times a week; schizophrenia is once a week; etc." Dr. Marui said: "According to the circumstances of the patient and the analyst, three times a week, or every day except Sunday." Muramatsu said that patients might come once, twice, or three times a week.

5. *Is the patient seen for a fifty-minute period each time?* All replied that the period was usually fifty minutes to an hour.

6. *How many months or years does a person remain*

under analysis? Kosawa replied: "The term of analysis differs according to the kind of illness. For example: symptom neurosis is three or four months; character neurosis is eight or nine months; light depressive psychosis is seven and a half months; etc." Muramatsu placed the time at about six months, in most cases. (This is astonishing, since Western analyses often run for three, four, or five years.)

To recapitulate: As complete as possible an understanding of the Japanese psychoanalytic movement is a vital adjunct to the comprehension of the goals of Japanese psychoanalysis; and as I have already said, such knowledge should make more apparent what makes the Japanese "tick" than any other single body of information.

We have seen here something of the origins of the movement—something of the training and general focus of Japanese analysts. Let us now consider the cultural matrix in which Japanese psychoanalysis has had to function.

13

THE KEY TO THE UNDERSTANDING OF
JAPANESE PSYCHOANALYSIS

IT would be well at this point to recapitulate some of the basic concepts of Japanese culture, before launching into a final analysis of the goals of Japanese psychoanalysis. It will be remembered that Tsuneo Muramatsu has pointed out the *bun* (prescribed status in society to which every Japanese is born); the *ie* (family or house), which Muramatsu calls "the most important symbol in life"; the *oya bun* (parent-role) and *ko bun* (child-role), which connotes the relationship of employer to employee; *giri* (obligation toward family, society, and/or individuals); and *sekentei* (face).[218] Also to be borne in mind are such symbols as *mimpi* (signifying the nothingness of each individual Japanese); *ninjo* (warmth of human feeling); *kanzan* (respect for authority); *ko* (obsequiousness toward father or parent substitute, as in *kobun*); *chu* (obsequiousness toward emperor or ruler); *kodo* (obsequiousness to the emperor's way); *enryo* (be reserved, hesitant, modest, forced shyness); and *jicho* (doing what is expected of one); *musubi* (harmony).[219] These are probably for present purposes the most significant concepts of prescribed Japanese behavior or culture.

For a discussion of *minken* (popular rights) versus *kokken* (national rights), I refer you to an article in *The Far Eastern Quarterly*—"An Historical Study of Japanese Society."[220] "In 1881 Okuma was driven from the government and the *minken** ideals were repudiated by the remaining leaders. The government, while giving public expression to liberalism, began the authoritarian structure which revealed itself in the Constitution of 1889 and the Imperial Rescript on Education. A second turning point came in 1895 with the conclusion of the war with China. Victory over China was disastrous to the popular rights movement. During the war the opposition parties had sold out to the government, while after victory many liberal leaders saw nothing further to strive for. The *minken* movement was thus nearly extinguished, leaving only the socialists to continue the fight. On the other hand the war brought a surge of nationalistic fervor which transformed the *kokken* forces into virulent imperialists. It is from this point that Murayama dates Japan's modern tragedy; flushed with victory, Japan began to play the part of a world power before her time. The discrepancy between internal reform and military expansion spelled defeat in 1945."

In addition to an understanding of these terms, it is also imperative that we have some comprehension of the policies which have governed Japan in recent years. For example, what Ike says of political associations applies largely throughout Japanese life: "The cement binding together in [a political] association was not common interests or common principles. Rather the ties between leaders and followers were such external factors as love of wine, the ability to play chess, or the fact of having been born in the same village, town, or prefecture.

The behavior of an individual was not governed by his analysis of the choices open to him and his conviction that a particular course of action was morally right. Instead, it was blind obedience to the persons in positions of authority, and hence there could be no sense of individual responsibility."[221] In light of what has been said in preceding chapters, it is clear that there has been no great shift in Japanese national thinking; but it is for that very reason that it is significant here to discuss in greater detail than previously the content of *Kokutai No Hongi—the Cardinal Principles of the National Entity of Japan.*

A word should perhaps be said about the book, *Kokutai No Hongi,* itself: Unadulterated propaganda of the most extremely nationalistic sort, it was published in 1937 by the Japanese Ministry of Education, and only found its way into the English language a short time after World War II, although it was known and suppressed by American Intelligence during the war. Combining a glorification of Japanese national history with politico-philosophic dogma and even with predictions of imperialistic activity, it was significant not only as an obvious propaganda medium, but as a device for the intelligent consumption of things foreign—since intelligent Japanese foresaw that the copying of manners and methods of foreigners, and identification with their enemies, might well lead to the eventual dissolution of the Japanese empire.

From *Kokutai No Hongi* we learn, for example, the Japanese concept of "coevality." By the expression "coeval with heaven and earth," the Japanese level individuality and equate the Japanese person with heaven, emperor and earth: "Ordinarily, words such as 'eternity' or 'endlessness' convey simply the ideas of perpetuity in secession of time; but the so-called expression 'coeval with heaven and earth' has a far deeper significance. That is to say, it expresses eternity and at the same time signifies the present. In the great august Will and great august undertakings of the Emperor, who is deity incarnate, is seen the great august Will of the Imperial Ancestors, and in this Will lives the endless future of our nation. That our Imperial Throne is coeval with heaven and earth means indeed that the past and the future are united in one in the 'now,' that our nation possesses everlasting life, and that it flourishes endlessly. Our history is an evolution of the eternal 'now,' and at the root of our history there always runs a stream of eternal 'now.' "222 Coevality also implies a unity between emperor and people in every aspect of Japanese life which is clearly expressed throughout the book. For example: "The manifestation of our national entity . . . [applies] in the case of our military affairs. Since ancient times the spirits of the deities in our country have fallen into two groups: the spirits of peace [*nigi-mitama*] and the spirits of warriors [*ara-mitama*]. Where there is a harmonious working of the two, all things under the sun rest in peace, grow, and develop. Hence, the warrior spirits work inseparably and as one with the spirits of peace. It is in the subduing of those who refuse to conform to the august influence of the Emperor's virtues that the mission of our Imperial Military Forces lies; and thus we see the Way of the warriors that may be called Jimmu [Divine Warrior].* In an Imperial Rescript issued by the Emperor Meiji there is a passage which reads: 'Our national entity which has paid tribute to chivalry since the days of Our Imperial Ancestors.' "223

Kokutai No Hongi goes into further detail in explaining its ideology of the relationship between individual and state in developing the theme of national entity: "Human beings are real existences as well as historical existences linked with eternity. There are, furthermore, egos, as well as correlated existences. That is to say, their existences are ordained by a national spirit based on history. This is the basic character of human existence. Its real worth is found where this concrete existence as a people is kept in view and people exist as individuals in that very state. However, the individualistic explanation of human beings abstracts only one aspect of an individuality and overlooks the national and historical qualities. Hence, it loses sight of the totality and concreteness of human beings and deviates from the reality of human existence, the theories departing from actualities and running off into many mistaken channels. Herein lie the basic errors underlying the various concepts of individualism, liberalism, and their developments. The nations of the West have now awakened to these errors, and various ideologies and movements have sprung up in order to overcome them. Nevertheless, these ideologies and movements will eventually end in regarding collections of people as bodies or classes, or at the most in conceiving a conceptual State; so that such things will do no more than provide erroneous ideas to take the place of existing erroneous ideas, and will furnish no true way out or solution."[224]

Related to the idea of national entity is the process of syncretization. According to Webster (ed. 1948), to syncretize means "to become fused or united." In Japan, syncretization has become the process by which foreign manners, ideas, doctrines, etc., have been assimilated, so that they have been rendered compatible, rather than being in conflict with Japanese ways. This syncretization is consciously done; the process is exemplified in the formation of the Ryobu Shinto sect of Buddhism[225] by the monk Kukai in the seventh century, through the amalgamation of Buddhism and Shintoism.[226]

An example of the purposeful, premeditated use of the syncretization process, we read in *Kokutai No Hongi*: "Every type of foreign ideology that has been imported into our country may have been quite natural in China, India, Europe, or America, in that it has sprung from their racial or historical characteristics; but in our country, which has a unique national entity, it is necessary as a preliminary step to put these types to rigid judgment and scrutiny so as to see if they are suitable to our national traits. That is to say, the creation of a new culture which has characteristics peculiar to our nation can be looked forward to only through this consciousness and the sublimation and assimilation of foreign cultures that accompanies it."[227]

Returning to the concept of identification, whose psychological mechanisms have already been discussed in an earlier chapter, it should be remarked that perhaps Lord Hotta first (see page 88), and then the Compilation Committee of *Kokutai No Hongi*[228] and Ito Enkichi[229] were aware of the Japanese' unconscious capacity for identifying with the enemy. At least the great Meiji was aware of the dangers of foreign influence on the Japanese: "... if ... foreign ways are copied without due thought ... the great principle binding the Sovereign and his subject ... will in course of time be forgotten."[230]

Kokutai No Hongi says: "Following the Meiji Restoration Occidental cultures poured in with a rush, and contributed immensely toward our national prosperity;

but their individualistic qualities brought about various difficulties in all the phases of the lives of our people, causing their thoughts to fluctuate. However, now is the time for us to sublimate and assimilate these Occidental ideologies in keeping with our national entity, to set up a vast new Japanese culture, and, by taking advantage of these things, to bring about a great national development."[231] Further, it is stated that ". . . in the fields of *mental sciences,** too, there is the same precision and logical systematization and the shaping of unique cultures. Our nation must increasingly adopt these various sciences, and look forward to the advancement of our culture and national development. However, these scholastic systems, methods, and techniques are substantiated by views of life and of the world peculiar to the West, which views are due to the racial, historical, and typographical characteristics of the Occident. Hence, in introducing these things into our country, we must pay thorough attention to these points, scrutinize their essential qualities, and with the clearest insight adapt their merits and cast aside their demerits."[232] Foreign knowledge of all kinds was, according to the national entity program, to be incorporated, processed, and assimilated—as food is assimilated by the body after it has been eaten. "Our present mission as a people," states *Kokutai No Hongi,* "is to build up a new Japanese culture by adopting and sublimating Western cultures with our national entity as the basis, and to contribute spontaneously to the advancement of world culture."[233]

The Emperor Meiji's attitude toward individualism is clearly delineated: " 'It is the teaching of Our Ancestors, the spirit of our national laws, and what is looked upon by the entire nation as a model of teaching, to

count as most vital in education and studies the following
of the Way of mankind by clarifying the Way of humanity and justice and of loyalty and filial piety, by exhaust-
ing the resources of knowledge and of talent, and accom-
plishments.

" 'Howbeit, there have of late been not a few who
have given weight solely to knowledge, talent, and ac-
complishments, not fathoming the real purport of civilization and enlightenment, breaking the laws of ethics
and corrupting public morals. This is to be accounted
for by the fact that toward the early part of the Meiji
Restoration the good points of Western countries were
at one time assimilated and daily progress made with the
excellent idea of breaking away in the main from old
abuses and of adopting knowledge from all over the
world. Nevertheless, it is feared that if, as an unfortunate result, foreign ways are copied without due thought
—with ideas of humanity, righteousness, loyalty, and
filial piety set aside—the great principle binding the
Sovereign and his subjects, and the fathers and their
children, will in course of time be forgotten. This would
not be in keeping with the primary purpose of our
education and studies.'

"This behooves us," adds *Kokutai No Hongi*. "indeed to reflect on matters deeply, with the present times
viewed in the light of these factors."[234]

Speaking of the effect of western educational ideas
upon the Japanese, *Kokutai No Hongi* says: "Since the
Meiji Restoration our nation has adapted the good elements of the advanced education seen among European
and American nations, and has exerted efforts to set
up an educational system and materials for teaching.
The nation has also assimilated on a wide scale the

scholarship of the West, not only in the fields of natural science, but of the *mental sciences,** and has thus striven to see progress made in our scholastic pursuits and to make education more popular. The progressive spirit that sought knowledge all over the world, in obedience to the Charter Oath in Five Articles, and by breaking away from old abuses, brought about rapid progress in this sphere, too, thus reaping tremendous results. However, at the same time, through the infiltration of *individualistic** concepts, both scholastic pursuits and education became liable to be taken up with a world in which the intellect alone mattered, and which was isolated from historical and actual life; so that both intellectual and moral culture drifted into tendencies in which the goal was the freedom of man who was to become an abstract being and the perfecting of the individual man. At the same time, these scholastic pursuits and education fell into separate parts, so that they gradually lost their synthetic coherence and concreteness. In order to correct these tendencies, the only course open to us is to clarify the true nature of our national entity, which is at the very source of our education, and to strive to clear up individualistic and abstract ideas."[235]

Kokutai No Hongi lays the responsibility for the beginning of the concepts of individualism current in the west at the doorstep of the ancient Greeks, and implies that it was this concept which brought about the downfall of Greece: ". . . Occidental ideologies spring from Greek ideologies. Greek concepts, whose keynote is the intellectual spirit, are characterized by being rational, objective, and idealistic. Culture was shaped centering around cities, leaving to posterity philosophies and works of art rarely to be seen in human history; but toward the end of their days, individualistic tendencies gradually appeared in their ideologies and modes of life."[236]

Undoubtedly the collection of Japanese scholars who prepared *Kokutai No Hongi* were also aware of the practical significance of basing their operational program upon the Amaterasu-Ohmekami myth. The practical application of myths has been elucidated by Malinowski, to whom my attention was drawn by A. J. Levin. Levin writes as follows, quoting Malinowski (whose work is known and alluded to in various articles by Japanese analysts, according to Mayer-Oakes): "The myth is a 'statement of primeval reality which still lives in present-day life and as a justification by precedent, supplies a retrospective pattern of moral values, sociological order and magic belief.' The 'ideas, emotions, and desires associated with a given story are experienced not only when the story is told, but also when in certain customs, moral rules, or ritual proceedings, the counterpart of the story is enacted.' Here the practical purpose served by the hero myths was to make life more tolerable in an atmosphere of rejectors and rejected."[237]

Reed and Murdoch add to the substance of Malinowski's statements and clarify the conflicts of some of the philosophers with what were plainly the principles not alone of the recent pre-war Japanese government but of the rulers of hundreds of years ago as well: "The *Nihonki* [one of the most sacred books of Japan, completed in 720 A.D.] philosophizes, Chinese fashion, about the Producer Gods, as we call them, representing respectively the positive or negative principles. But Motoori repudiates these ideas, and says that they would lead one to look upon Izanagi and Izanami as mere abstract principles, whereas they are really 'living powers.' "[238]

Motoori (1730-1801) was a physician and philosopher at Ise, ". . . the great body of whose work was instinct with latent political tendency highly menacing to the domination of Yedo [i.e., the Shogun]."[239] Murdoch points out that Motoori used the interpretations of Confucianism worked out by Sorai as "weapons of attack" in his own writings.[240] Sorai (1666-1723), a follower of Shushi who went to the original Confucian writings for his inspiration, had regarded Confucianism as essentially political, writing: " *'Morality is nothing but the necessary means for controlling the subjects of the empire . . . [and] may be regarded as a device for governing the people . . .* [lacking the quality of true greatness when] men, . . . like our Ito Jinsai and others aspire to figure as sages [i.e., as individuals] how vain is the attempt. . . To try and adopt the ideas of the great teacher and carry them out in daily life, this, one can do, but this is very different from setting oneself up as an authority.' "[241]

Authority, or perhaps better authoritarianism, is the theme heard over and over again emanating from the cultural record of Japan. Reischauer in discussing Genro, the Elder Statesman created in 1892, said: ". . . the young founders of the new government, now grown to solid middle age, still controlled Japan. They had become 'elder statesmen,' the surviving leaders of early Meiji days, who added the prestige of long years of rule to their native political talents. They controlled the Privy Council and thus spoke for the emperor. Parties were formed, but they were dominated by the personalities and views of the old oligarchs."[242] Reischauer also indicated one way in which the Japanese oligarchy was perpetuated when he listed the Premiers who came from among the founders of the Meiji government: Ito, Kuroda, Yamagata, Matsukata, Okuma—a *samurai* from northern Kyushu—Katsura, Saionji, Yamamoto, and Terauchi.[243] Said Reischauer: "Although the oligarchy had moved from the closed committee room to the open floor of the Diet, it still held the reins of government. Japanese administration had been westernized, but in spirit the government had hardly departed from the traditions of a paternalistic, authoritarian state."[244]

* * *

It is instructive to find that the more perceptive writers of commentaries upon post-World War II Japan give conclusive evidence of the syncretization process, the identification with the enemy, which is in practice today under the American Occupation. Robert B. Textor, in an ominous little volume called *Failure in Japan,* writes of the "Old Guard,"* as he terms the pre-war, nationalistically-oriented, un-reconstructed residue of Japanese leadership: "It is interested in maintaining its power position despite the Occupation's reforms in the legal power structure. Often the best technique for securing its end is to go through the motions of complying with G.H.Q.-sponsored changes in the legal structure, then capture the altered edifice, and proceed leisurely to sabotage the purpose for which G.H.Q. had demanded a restructuring. Sometimes other techniques are indicated. Whatever may be the best technique, the Old Guard has usually found it. Its success . . . has been impressive."[245]

Textor also suggests another aspect to the problem —a possible way in which an "Old Guard" might function, when he quotes John M. Maki: "Much of the real government of Japan is invisible. In 1868, out of a decaying feudal situation, a new government was created by 'a group of men who designed it so that they could dominate it with a minimum of interference from the people. The creators of the modern state in Japan were reactionary in their philosophy of power, for they were as reluctant to widen the base of government as their (feudal) predecessors had been.' This philosophy of power still prevails in its essential respects today."[246]

It is quite evident that the Japanese policy is for the most part a policy that dissolves ego boundaries of the Japanese person, or in less technical jargon, the Japanese policy disindividualizes the Japanese. Their policy encourages a confluence of disindividualized persons into a homogeneity having no beginning nor end and is coeval with heaven, earth, and the person of the emperor.

At first sight one would be inclined to believe that the aim of occidental psychoanalysis and the aim of the cardinal principles of the national entity of Japan are so incompatible, so inharmonious, so far removed from one another that the two disciplines could never be reconciled. However, intelligent and adroit Japanese skillfully using the alchemy of symbols, abstract concepts and of words, conjured up on paper a Japanese version of Freudian psychoanalysis. In this version the emperor becomes inseparable from the superego. By exploiting coevality they explain the timelessness of the unconscious, and account for the existence of the id. To the Japanese, each individual "ego" becomes a part of a whole, each individual "ego" is a mosaic that fills into the general scheme established for the Japanese way of nationalistic life (*kokken*).

How adequately the Japanese have accomplished

this task will be discussed in more detail in the concluding chapters. At any rate, the study of psychoanalysis as it has been modified by the Japanese culture provides perhaps the best method of gaining accurate insight into the dynamics of the Japanese social system.

14

EXAMPLES AND INTERPRETATIONS OF
JAPANESE PSYCHOANALYTIC WRITINGS

W ITH the foregoing information in regard to the
influences at work upon all thought and action
in Japan under the highly nationalistic pre-war
regime (much of this actually originating centuries ago),
we are now equipped to consider the output of the
Japanese analytic writers without being superficial and
qualitative in our judgments. As a matter of fact, to the
casual western reader, much of the Japanese psychoanalytic literature appears itself to be superficial, naive,
imitative. He may be tempted, at first, to think of the
Japanese analytic organizations as little more than "hob-
by groups," with their membership heavily salted with
lay enthusiasts whose training ill equips them for scientific thinking. But it must be remembered that even
the best thinkers in Japan have been handicapped by
such governmental pressure-agencies as the Bureau of
Thought Control, and, even before the Bureau's existence, by the entire nationalistic concept which prevented
a true cross-fertilization of ideas, let alone an unfettered
application of true western methodology.

As I shall endeavor to show, much analytic literature
in Japan demonstrates a syncretic *adaptation* of termi-

nology and methodology, rather than outright *adoption* thereof. Much of it follows the line of the national entity program; much shows an acceptance of the concept of coevality; and the bulk of it is at least somewhat nationalistic in tone, or even in some cases extremely so.

Since this chapter will draw heavily upon materials I have had translated from *Seishin Bunseki*, I feel that a word should be said of my two principal Japanese translators. Dr. Kiyomi Koizumi, a native Japanese physician, has an unusual comprehension of, and vocabulary in, the scientific fields, especially medicine, in both Japanese and English. Mr. Anthony Yasutake, a Nisei, spent seven years in Japan before World War II as a journalist, and is familiar with the social structure of that country. Both are regularly employed as translators by Wayne University in Detroit, and are considered to be able and well-equipped. This being the case, I feel confident that their rendition of these articles into English is accurate enough to provide a fair basis for my interpretations. With minor idiomatic changes, the materials here used are as translated by them. (The articles printed in *Seishin Bunseki* in German were translated for me by Mr. John Winzen, naturalized American of German birth. Dr. Fritz Redl, a lay analyst and educator, translated the paper which appeared in Esperanto. Some of the articles were printed in English in the journals.)

A few of the articles or excerpts quoted here have been used merely to give an idea of the type and variety of contribution to *Seishin Bunseki* and call for little comment. It should be remembered, however, that those which were printed from 1937 through 1941 fell under at least indirect surveillance of the Bureau of Thought Control,* and that all pre-war articles were written under the influence of the growing nationalistic feeling which produced *Kokutai No Hongi* and finally culminated in the attack on Pearl Harbor.

Here is an article which appeared in Esperanto:

"The Psychological Point of View of Illness by Sigeaki Tukazaki

"It is difficult to define illness, because the concept of health itself is built only on a guess. What we call health is only that which finds itself without a symptom which would disturb daily life or give one a sense of suffering, and one cannot easily say that this is absolute health in a pathological analysis.

"Behavior does not open its surface like a quiescent volcano, nor does it remain only the sign of an old illness, like an extinct volcano. Such a state one ordinarily calls health-like, though in any case this may be an illness with severe significance. In other words, it is like being in a state of health.

"Chronic illness may go unrecognized, or in acute illness one has an incubation period, and to define convalescence depends upon the subjective [state] of the ill person. For illness, remarkably, has psychological significance; since the sick person's problem is his self-awareness of his state of illness, and only if the state of illness becomes conscious will the recovery of the disease itself be the latter. This is where the psychological value of allergy lies. Only if one forgets the principle of healing, then even our allergy cannot be reproached.

"Man is the carrier of illness, and independent of man there would be no illness. If one removes typhus from a person suffering from it, it is a bacterium, and the illness, typhus, recovers.

"A sick person is a man, and he must break the relationship with the outside world in order to attach his libido to illness. This is the conditon. Thus the sick person regresses to his infancy and is reigned by animism. At the same time, fetishism also raises its head and drugs assume a significance like witchcraft. One must not forget, in healing, the unconscious value of the drug, as well as its conscious value in reestablishing health.

"Would the Japanese proverb, 'Corporeal ill-health derives from spiritual ill-health,' also change, like the previously mentioned psychoanalytic thought?"[247]

A paper by Kenji Ohtski not only furnishes some interesting comments on Japanese cultural patterns, but, in the concluding paragraph, unwittingly supplies some insights into conflicts between western and oriental concepts:

"Character Defects of the Japanese and Their Cause
"Part I
"Racial Character and Its Analysis

"I firmly believe that there are differences in racial character of each race as well as in individuals. The difficult task is how to solve them in order to arrive at a fair conclusion. Even when scientifically analyzed, character studies are still far from conclusive, and if we seek proper solution through a study of philosophy, that, too, lacks reality; for we do not know just what is meant by individual character:

"According to a textbook in Philosophy written by Professor English of Ohio State University:

"1. *Character* is known as the *mark* of difference in individuals as well as in groups, and when *mark* is discriminated, it is not character but

156

characteristic—a just and proper term, but the two are confusingly handled.

"2. *Traits* represent the philosophy and specific motion of an individual.

"3. Many deeds are accomplished through one's tendencies toward motions and traits, regardless of obstructions according to one's standards of morality.

"Now Professor English has specifically divided into three phases his study of the word, 'character': (1) 'mark,' (2) a combination of 'mark' and 'trait' and (3) the will to do or accomplish. This analysis does not give us a clear picture. Although not in a practical manner, 'mark' may actually represent color of skin, height, and many other features visible to the eye; but it also seems to cover the philosophical character of a person. Hence it would be much simpler to divide it into (1) physical traits, (2) philosophic traits, and (3) moral traits. One may then ask how we can determine the difference between philosophic and moral traits, and the question whether morality is not philosophy—a very good question! We might say that philosophic traits have to do with the character of one's self, while moral traits have to do with the character beyond one's self. Therefore, I prefer to divide character into two parts: Physical Traits and Philosophic Motion, basing my theory on the standards of two specific motions.

"Hence, character study requires the noting of physical traits and, for other considerations, a discovery of its standard of philosophical motions. Of course, we do not believe that Mind and Body have two separate origins, and therefore Physical Traits and standards of Philosophy shall ultimately become a single factor. Some modern character studies are based on physical traits, but some go directly and deeply into Philosophy. I believe these two existing methods of character study are far from accidental.

"Part II
"Character Traits of the Japanese People

"In the past chapter we concerned ourselves with the broad study of character and its analysis of individuals, but not with that of Race or Group. The two sorts of study of course differ greatly. Physical Traits can be easily enough determined, but standards of Philosophy are much more complicated to determine, compared to the individual case. Various methods of study may be used.

"One method is to study History and Geographic Colors, and at the same time to include studies of Geographic actual daily living, and spiritual life as well. I shall use the simplest and most sufficient method, drawing my material from the simple daily life of the Japanese people. In this way, my method will be scientifically conclusive. All of the materials I have specified are more or less significant in the daily life of Japan; they are characteristic, original, and indigenous to the Japanese. Nevertheless, lest this method fail to convince, we shall re-analyze our conclusions in comparison to reality in a scientific manner.

"1. The Rising Sun is the national flag of Japan. I do not know the origin of this symbol, but there is a verse from a poem reading, 'Sun painted in bright red on a white sail.' It is an extremely simple and beautiful verse and the words

'Land of the Rising Sun' are definitely inspiring. Praise or criticism of these words is entirely beside the point when you find every person of Japanese race placing his sacred trust in the symbol of the Land of the Rising Sun.

"2. *Furoshiki* is a yard-square piece of material used in Japan by all classes of people in place of a suitcase. With it you can wrap an article large or small, square or round. When not in use, it can be folded and put into a pocket; or women may use it as a head scarf or muffler, since it comes in bright colors. It is, of course, simple, convenient and light-weight. Suitcases are bulky and hard to handle, although they protect their contents and are far better for storing-purposes than is the *furoshiki.* Books can be carried in the *furoshiki,* but they may be wrecked; while if they are carried in a suitcase they are protected, eliminating damage and worry.

"3. *Tenogui* is a one-by-three foot piece of light cotton material used to wipe wet hands, as a kerchief if need be, and also for a *furoshiki;* but it cannot be compared with towels, being less absorbent, nor with a kerchief, being rather embarrassing, and is small for a *furoshiki.* So by comparison its defects are about the same as the comparison of a suitcase and a *furoshiki.*

"4. The kimono's effect and defects compare to western dress identically with items 2 and 3 above. Tall, short, thin, or stout, the kimono is made so that it does not reveal the wearer's build, but western clothes look and feel fine. Kimonos are frail and soil easily, but are soft and graceful; they are not as practical as western clothing.

"5. *Geta* are Japanese wooden shoes. Their sound seems to impress western people as a sort of welcome. Perhaps it is approval, perhaps disapproval; it is difficult to say which. It is true that the noise is quite distressing, in a way, when walking on a stone or asphalt street, especially at a pier or train depot, but when you see well-dressed ladies or geisha girls walking on a dirt street which is typical of Japan, you are impressed with their truly romantic beauty and daintiness. It is believed that the idea of these shoes was inspired by horses' hoofs, and while wooden shoes are worn by some occidental peoples, their style and the manner in which they are worn is altogether different from *geta*.

"6. *Fundoshi* means loin cloth or jockey strap in western countries. Its significance in connection with the Japanese male character is great; for instance, the word *fundoshi* is spelled [Japanese ideograph]. This character is not Japanese at all in origin, but rather Chinese. Innocent as it may seem, it is divided into two parts and is sometimes used in two parts properly. The right half of the word *fundoshi* [Japanese ideograph] means 'army.' In other words, the army of any nation serves as a protective organization against outside harm to the nation, is its solid backbone; and so *fundoshi* serves in its function as a protector of the delicate male sexual organ, since it is located on the surface of the body, speaking in material terms. Spiritually speaking, the proper interpretation would be 'prepared' which is the right word at such a time as in a battle-front situation, in a political address, sports, poor business situation, or any situation which may require courage. If one asks another, 'Are you ready?' the answer is, 'I shall face it as soon as I tighten up my *fundoshi.*'

"Enthusiasm for wearing the *fundoshi* was highest in the Tokugawa era. The loin cloth was six feet long and became the symbol of Japanese character and courage, I gather from the history I studied; and there were specifications for other articles such as swords, cake, *shoyu,* fans, and rice cakes. Specific customs and habits included family, *sumo, hara-kiri,* tea etiquette, poetry, *kana* letters, the building of shrines of white wood, and the design of *torii.* Of course many specified items were imported, but completely Japanese and there is no conflict in saying that they [sumo, hari-kiri, tea etiquette, etc.] are of Japanese origin. As influential items, Mount Fuji, cherry trees and earthquakes were specified. To anyone familiar with the earthquake, the effect of its violence on Japanese character can easily be seen.

"Conclusions as to the character analysis from past articles on the Japanese race would be that they are: (1) simple, (2) pleasant, (3) honest, (4) progressive, (5) reserved. If we consider these as the good side of character, the defects would be that they are (1) childish, (2) not neat, (3) fickle, (4) shallow minded, and (5) not emotionally stable."[248]

To anyone familiar with the principles of the national entity program of Japan, there are several inferences to be drawn from Ohtski's conclusions. Let us consider what the author calls "weaknesses" of Japanese character in light of *Kokutai No Hongi,* bearing in mind that the article was written at a time when the pressures of the Bureau of Thought Control and of the national entity ideology would have been felt.

To be *childish* can be interpreted as meaning that Ohtski, as a Japanese, thought of his people as being children of the emperor, which was indeed a part of the governmental plan; yet, as an analyst, he knew that to be childish is incompatible with sound mental health, which instead calls for maturity.

Not to be *neat* is to express individualism. A great body of psychoanalytic information gleaned from innumerable sources has proved over and over again that untidiness and uncleanliness are often expressive of self-strivings. Here again we see that not to be neat is not to abide by the authoritarian dictates of Japanese culture; yet it is to express oneself, which is an end of western psychoanalysis.

A *fickle* person can be influenced by outside stimuli to act in accordance with occidental or foreign ideas, as opposed to those prescribed under the Japanese national entity program.

* * *

A basically Freudian article by Yabe, overlaid with Japanese ideology, shows something of the Japanese attitude toward super-ego, Buddhism, and family-worship:

"Super-ego, Criminality and Religiosity by Yaekichi Yabe

". . . the reaction of infants toward their parents is not one of gratitude; this feeling will be formed later on. The feeling of the infant toward his parents is at first that of response to superior power. Compared to the infant, the mother seems to have unlimited power, and this impresses him strongly. He senses that the father is helping the mother physically and mentally, and it seems to the baby that the mother obeys the father. Thus the infant develops his belief in the authority of the parents. Later, the infant has more experience and sees a wider world. He sees people other than his parents and finds some to whose power even his parents bow. As a result he begins to lose his belief in the power of the parents, which leads to a repressed stage at the age of two or three [western reckoning]. During this repressed period the child does not completely lose the feeling of the superior power of his parents, but it is relegated to the subconscious.

"The memory, in the pre-repressed stage, turns into fantasy or imaginings, with no time or space limitations; therefore, this memory can be transferred to any time or place and can easily be projected outside reality. The belief in the authority of the parents in the pre-repressed stage is transferred to a belief in something— a misbelief in something absolute. The faith in God or Buddha is based on this belief.

". . . the faith in God or Buddha is only internal. In order to find out the basis of a moral character we have to search this inner part. A moral character is formed from a core of belief in the power of the parents and all other memories added to it.

". . . ego is the ability to adjust to the environment, and the belief in the power of the parents is formed after the ego has developed to some extent. Ego grows as it absorbs things from the environment, and this action is called identification. The infant has a tendency to identify with the parents, to follow them, to imitate them, to become as powerful as they are. This brings about the development of the super-ego.

"When a child is two or three years old [western

reckoning], a part of the super-ego becomes repressed in the subconscious. We assume that the super-ego becomes repressed because it cannot exist with the ego. Infants believe in the power of the parents, but as they grow up they can find weaknesses in their parents, and the fantasy of parental power is repressed in the subconscious. When these repressed fantasies become conscious, they become the conscience. . . .

"Character based on memory of the pre-repressed stage is fixed by the stimulus of environment, so that a child who has a bad character becomes worse through each stimulus. Therefore punishment doesn't help the child. The main reason for this is that the punishment is external. Effective punishment must be based on internal reaction. The object of punishment should be that it effects the super-ego. Super-ego is conscience; therefore the guilty feeling of the conscience and regret should be the only punishment."[249]

In light of the Yabe article just quoted, it seems more appropriate here to mention the declared relationship between Japanese psychoanalysis and established religious principles. To the history of Japanese psychoanalysis given in Chapter 12 was appended the following paragraph: "Psychoanalysis corresponds on certain points to Buddhism, especially in the Nirvana Principle, and shares also some of the world viewpoints of Taoism—especially the high esteem for a deep, unconscious psychological life. It is therefore expected to have a very promising future in Japan and in the Orient at large. Moreover, it is believed and hoped that the cosmopolitan spirit of the science will contribute much toward the promotion of international friendship even during the present war."[250] (This, of course, refers to World

War II, in which the Japanese were not to become participants for another 18 months.)

To grasp the full meaning of the above statements, it will be well to pause at this point to indicate something of the philosophy of Taoism. Some aspects of the Taoist philosophy stress individualism and so, obviously, cannot be syncretized; but other aspects fit neatly into the national entity program and can be assimilated; "adapt their merits and cast aside their demerits," as *Kokutai No Hongi* puts it.[251] For example, to quote Lao-tse:

" 'Therefore the wise man in governing empties their minds [i.e., the minds of the governed] but fills their stomachs, weakens their wills but strengthens their bones.

" 'His endeavor is to keep them unsophisticated and without desire, and where there are those who have knowledge to keep them from presuming to act upon it. Where there is this abstinence from action good order is universal. . . .

" 'Heaven is long enduring and earth continues*. . . . He who is wise puts his own person last, yet is found in the foremost place; he treats his person as if it were foreign to him and yet that person is preserved.' "[252]

It is evident that the Japanese equate psychoanalysis with the Nirvana principle, which Potter explains as the "extinction of individualism";[253] this, of course, would be completely opposite to the goals of occidental Freudian psychoanalysis. This is their method of syncretizing psychoanalysis so that it is adaptable and assimilable in accordance with the national entity program. Since Nirvana means the "extinction of individualism," Japanese psychoanalysis must come to mean the same thing.

It is also of interest that a number of issues of *Seishin Bunseki* carry an advertisement picturing the four Shinto shrines with their *torii,* calling attention to the 2,600 years of continuous existence of the Japanese nation—an indication of the belief of the journal's presumably scientific-minded readers in the "coevality of heaven and earth," as well as further implying their interest in, if not identification with, yet another of the religions of Japan.

"The National Character of the Japanese People," by Kenji Ohtski, sheds further light on this concept: "The national family-system of the Japanese can be analyzed, biologically speaking, as the 'immortal bioplasma' [cf. the concept of *ie*] protected and surrounded by a constant supply of 'mortal soma.' [This is the Nirvana principle.] Because the soma is mortal, it lacks its own *raison d'être,* so it cannot be fortified in terms of each independent individual. This, I daresay, is a strong, as well as a weak point in the Japanese people. One of the characteristic marks of the Japanese is said to be their simplicity and naiveté. This may have originated from many causes, but as long as the existing family-system continues, this national characteristic [national entity] will perforce be retained—to the happiness or unhappiness of the Japanese and of the world, no one knows which! [Which is to say, the happiness or unhappiness of the Japanese, because of the Japanese intent to dominate the world.]"[254]

There are many examples of the coevality principle to be found in articles which have appeared in *Seishin Bunseki.* Kenji Ohtski presents us with an example of the syncretization of coevality of "God's Way" in an article in English, "On the Therapeutics of Insomnia"; "All Creatures of the earth, we dare say, only make use of [hibernation or sleep] for the purpose of fulfilling their sleep (death) instinct. This is a teleological assumption, but the assumption of instinctive desire is not purely teleological . . . as the instinct is nothing but a detachment of the blind (non-teleological) forces of the whole universe, which ever sleeps and wakes periodically for a purpose *God** only knows."[255]

Again, in an unsigned paper (printed in English), "Totalitarianistic Control in the Blocs and the Expected Peace of the World," we read: "Totalitarianistic control is not an easy task, nor is that of psychic control of the individual. Individual control can be had by securing harmony [masubi] among one's ego, super-ego, and id [by which the writer means that super-ego is the emperor, and harmony the adjustment of the individual to giri]; and so Ohtski says in 'The National Character of the Japanese People'[256] When harmony does not exist, the individual becomes neurotic. The situation is the same with the state. . . . Yet we cannot or need not decide whether the current control is morbid or sound, good or bad. It is rather a natural world-current [and the Japanese mean by this a *Japanese* world current, coeval with heaven and earth] which no one can defend or force back. We can only hope that the current will cause no more serious calamities among the human race. When the four great blocs of the world have finally established their respective controls so well that they do not conflict with one another [by which the writer means when Japan shall have devoured and assimilated the conflicting external national entities], then there should be world peace, a day we hope will come soon."[257]

Heisaku Kosawa, discussing guilt and the Oedipus and Azase Complexes, in another issue of the journal, (see also pp. 53-55, Chapter 6) unwittingly illustrates coevality and the syncretization process employed by Japanese analysts. He says that Freud attributes the origin of religious strivings to the guilt consciousness of the child who has killed or wishes to kill his father [which would be unthinkable in the Japanese ideology, because it is antithetic to *ko*]. Kosawa, however, feels that there are other causes than this guilt consciousness: "That which springs from the guilt consciousness of the child [in contra-distinction to that of the adult] is only the longing for religion [the child has not yet mastered *ko, chu, giri,* etc.] and not the already-reached religious psychic state."[258] (The child strives to become coeval with heaven and earth.) We have seen that Kosawa departed from the classical Oedipus complex of Freud because it implies father-murder, which is untenable in Japanese culture. He substitutes the Azase or mother-murder complex, because, though rare, it would be more comprehensible to a Japanese.

In describing what occurred in the life of Azase after he became king, Kosawa relates that Azase heard "a voice from heaven and no one knew whence it came." (Like St. Paul.) The voice, which proved to be that of his dead father, urged the king to hasten to Buddha to seek help before the latter went to Nirvana. Now, King Azase had feared he must go to hell for his misdeeds, but he finally sought Buddha, who received him compassionately and promised to keep him from going to hell although he had sinned. Kosawa says: "The explanations of Buddha cannot be interpreted in any other manner than that they took away the king's false belief and let him recognize the right one . . . [for at first] he believed that Buddha was very powerful, but he did not believe him powerful enough to help him."[259]

Azase, upon hearing Buddha's words, became contrite. He likened himself to an evil-smelling tree (Iran) from whose seed had sprung another, aromatic species (Sendom)—i.e., his new-found faith in Buddha. Because it sprang from so surprising a parent stock, Azase named his faith the "belief without foundation"—i.e., belief without cause, origin, or reason for its existence, coeval with heaven and earth, which, of course, embraces the cardinal principles of the national entity of Japan.

Observe that Sigeaki Tukazaki, in "The Psychological Point of View of Illness," already quoted, wrote: "A sick person . . . must break the relationship with the outside world in order to attach his libido to illness. . . . Thus the sick person regresses to his infancy and is reigned by animism."[260] This is an indication of syncretization, because breaking with the world means breaking with the Japanese way. Ohtski carries the Japanese psychoanalytic concept of health a step further: "Psychoanalysis makes one aware of the sense of illness [i.e., a sense of conflict with *giri*, a feeling of self-striving (*ninjo*)] at the very moment, and helps one to overcome it [to do *giri* or come into harmony (*musubi*) with the national entity] to reach the goal of further soundness of health."[261]

In an article "Hitler's Super-Ego," by Furosenin Shu,[262] we find the statement: "I say that Hitler's super-ego is minimal. . . . I firmly believe that the good [*nigi-mitama*] and evil [*ari-mitama*] personalities of Hitler derive from that sort of philosophy. Then let us question why Hitler's super-ego is minimal. First, there is his atheism." We may interpret Shu as meaning here that, having no super-ego to speak of, Hitler also displayed no *chu*, no reverence toward his emperor, which is to say that he had no belief in God. He goes on to speak of the lies and broken promises in Hitler's imperialistic endeavors and comments, "This sort of deceitful behavior will destroy the standard of human decency and will injure the respect and integrity of international morality, as well as bringing our civilization back to a primitive era. . . . But actually and seriously, the powerless middle class all over Japan have such an ideology. That is one reason why these people are treated so disrespectfully. It is easy to suspect the shallowness of their education and background, as well as their ideals. It is high time in this troubled world that we should learn to respect civilization [in Japanese parlance, the national entity] and also to speak up and declare our viewpoint." Here we see the implication that the Japanese middle class does not subscribe to the teachings of the national entity program, and that they are lacking also in devotion to morality. The author is undoubtedly trying to whip the middle class into greater submission to the emperor's "way"—which is to say, coevality, the Japanese "normal" state.

In Prince Tomohide Iwakura's article, "Self-Love and Super-Ego," we find a sentence which suggests the essence of the national entity program: "The mental attitude of both sexes becomes closely associated and through that association we are gradually engineered into complicated progression which is more supreme than is narcissism."[263] Here, in a line, we see the crushing of individualism and the supremacy of the "Way." Iwakura also writes, in the same article: "There is, of course, an early stage of narcissism, but in plain language self-love is basic and natural, as narcissism in children. A certain amount of libido will remain throughout life; however, in accordance with later progression a certain amount of the libido itself will be dissolved into narcissism and will prevail, but it seems to break down into characteristic forms: transformation of self-love to love of others, and transformation of self-love into (1) ego-ideal [*giri*]; (2) own ideal [*ninjo*]; and (3) super-ego [emperor]. Through these transformations of original narcissism comes the basic factor of contributing moralities [again, super-ego equals emperor]. In other tragically complicated cases, circumstantial morality established in early childhood due to the teachings of parents, relatives, neighbors, and other causes, becomes the common sense of the individual and will shortly become his moral standard [the development of *ie*—the loyalty to family or house]. Actually it began as a superficial rule, but eventually became the inner rule. According to a report from *Child Psychology*, super-ego and its foundations are already entrenched in a child's mind before he reaches five years of age. It can be seen from this report that it is an ancient and delicate problem to approach, and it is quite obvious that it is very difficult to impress an adult in these delicate matters."[264] Iwakura means that super-ego is established through intensive training in childhood—such training as has been noted previously: *ko, chu, giri,* repression of *ninjo,* etc.

Kenji Ohtski carries Iwakura's thinking a step farther in his article, "Psychoanalytic Observations on Morals."[265] Having given recognition to Iwakura's basic idea, that children's super-ego is largely developed by their parents during infancy, he goes on: "The love for others is another form of self-love. Love for others requires identifying oneself with others. . . . From the sociological standpoint, the conscience can develop more easily in a society where the relationship between individuals is complicated and close, because in such a society people can more easily identify themselves with others." Here we see a syncretization of the identification process as it is practiced within Japan—an identification with those who prescribe the moral code. It is interesting that Ohtski also says, in the same article, "as long as human beings live, morals will exist, though they may change in form"—connoting a coevality aspect to morality as it occurs in Japanese thinking. He even pleads the case for feudalism: "A society where life, production, and the soil are inevitably combined, i.e., a feudalistic, agricultural society, [a society in which the identification of peoples with each other mentioned above can most easily take place]. In capitalistic society, contact between individuals tends to be incidental in character. . . . Culture and customs are formed by people who have something in common. There must be similarity in emotional reactions, taste, education and interests among the people." Here are seen the concept of *mimpi,* the antithesis of individualism; a little of coevality; and a syncretization of that which exists with that which is desirable. Ohtski continues: "The individual person is closely related to society, and its morality [super-ego—emperor] is social morality in most cases. Particularly, individual morality is the morality of the home. . . . [Note that even in the home (*ie*), real individuality is denied.] Sometimes individual morality is contradictory to social morality. The morality of the nation contradicts that of the individuals in some cases. Everybody has suffered from the discrepancy between love for his country and international or class love." Thus Ohtski implies the conflict of individual with society, whose logical extension is the conflict of nationalism with internationalism. "Since the super-ego develops," he says, "out of narcissism, the demands of the super-ego are related to the love of self. In conclusion:

the moral man is the man who is obedient to the super-ego [emperor], and thereby also obedient to the demands of a true love of self. [A Japanese who does not perform *chu* and *giri* cannot love himself.] On the other hand, man also respects law because it brings some utility [utility in terms of national entity]. The old customs will fade away if no benefits can be obtained by following them. Therefore respect for moral law is another form of respect for utility. Utility is a characteristic of healthy morality." Ohtski thus makes clear the belief that coevality is threatened ("old custom will fade away") if obedience to the national entity ideology is allowed to diminish or disappear. Concluding his article on morals, Ohtski says: "The effort should be made to lessen the differences between classes in order to maintain a homogeneous social and moralistic order, because morality can develop only where people have similar emotions, interests, and values, and it will decline where homogeneity does not exist. From the psychoanalytic point of view, it can be concluded that in order to develop the moral sense in the individual, it is necessary to provide him with security in infancy so that the ego can develop in strength and in the capacity to respond to the demands of the super-ego." Like Shu, quoted above, Ohtski is disturbed by the tendency of middle-class Japanese to depart from the emperor's "Way." Quite obviously, in advocating homogeneity, he expresses the point of view not of western, but of Japanese psychoanalysis—a moral sense, a super-ego, a devotion to emperor and national entity which have nothing in common with the occidental psychoanalytic ideal of freeing the individual.

The prolific Ohtski has also provided us with a paper "On the Psychology of Jealousy and Revenge,"[266] wherein he produces further examples of the syncretic processes employed by Japanese analysts. Arguing the verity of Freud's claim that jealousy springs from the Oedipus, Ohtski suggests that it develops, rather, from narcissism. He then states: "A person in love transfers his love for his parents to his new love-object. Since it is thought that a child loves or should love his parents absolutely, it follows that the individual will have the same absolute love for his love-object."* This is pure syncretization: the adapting of the requirement of devotion to parents (*ko*) in Japanese culture insinuated into psychoanalytic thinking. In the same paper, he writes: "The person who is suffering from jealousy and longs for revenge should learn to balance his libido economy . . . [another object which is worthwhile to make up the loss of a love-object] can be found not only in the love of a person, but also in love of position, honor, money, etc." Note that "position" and "honor" are concepts incorporated in the basic idea behind national entity. Ohtski is recommending a form of sublimation which is in full accord with *Kokutai No Hongi.*

Yabe's article, "Analysis of a Sleep Phobia,"[267] makes very plain the importance of *giri* in the Japanese analytic procedure. A patient of Yabe's was torn between going to see a former doctor, with whom he had an appointment, and Yabe, whom he could not see if he kept the doctor's appointment. Yabe asked the patient how he had resolved the conflict, and was told he saw neither. Yabe discusses this behavior: "This is a symptom of compulsion. Here we can see an ordinary dilemma concerning the problem of *giri.* The patient discarded both *giris* to save himself. However, it led him to a second dilemma. By saving himself, he had a guilty feeling because he didn't follow the doctor's orders. . . ."

It is evident that Yabe saw nothing unusual in the idea that a patient should perform *giri* toward his analyst. It would appear that indecisiveness in the patient was of primary importance because it led the patient to "save himself"—i.e., to express his individualism—instead of *giri*, which connotes an attitude of respect toward his *superior*. (Evidently Yabe accepted the idea that both doctor and analyst were indeed the patient's "superiors.") Any expression of individualism, it will be recalled from the previous chapter's discussion of *Kokutai No Hongi*, constituted a "sin" against the national entity precepts, and the analyst thus viewed it as an illness.

One cannot overlook an item in Yaekichi Yabe's "Personal Impressions of Dr. Edward Glover."[268] In reference to his first appointment for didactic training with Dr. Ernest Jones, Yabe wrote: "English people are very punctual, especially Dr. Jones. (This seems to be very characteristic of anal characters.) [This seeming naiveté may not be far from the truth, when we analyze people to fit culture rather than their own expectations of maturity.] I worried so about the time because I could leave at 4:35 from Jones' office, but I had only ten minutes to go to Dr. Glover's."

In addition to many discussions which purport to be the original thinking of their authors, the Japanese analytic literature is full of articles which are apparently free translations of Freud or other western analysts. They are not necessarily translations of published papers. They seem often merely to reflect the exposure of the "trained" Japanese analysts to lectures and informal discussions experienced in travels abroad, or sometimes in the visits of occidental psychoanalysts to Japan. One such is "Psychoanalysis and Character Analysis," by

Rikitaro Takamizu,[269] a discussion of the oral, anal, and genital stages in infant development. The article is purely Freudian in concept, and is presented without argumentation or added comment by Takamizu.

Another article which in no wise conflicts with western thinking, and is entirely sensible by any standards, is a lengthy commentary on "Problems of Sexual Self-Indulgence," by Kenji Ohtski.[270] The author quotes a number of reputable occidental analysts on the subject and adds certain ideas and recommendations of his own. He is chiefly concerned with the neuroses caused or exaggerated by misinformation about the supposedly harmful effects of masturbation. When the Japanese became aware that social diseases might be contracted through the employment of prostitutes, at the same time that sociological developments in Japan made it impossible for mature men to find adequate sexual outlets, large numbers of Japanese turned to onanism. But this practice produced devastating emotional upsets, because onanism was in social disrepute. As Ohtski points out, physical education directors, physicians, and others preached against the practice, and a vast literature sprang up portraying the evils of masturbation. Ohtski very sensibly advocates the employment of onanism to reduce tension, but points out that men should be able to use this method without incurring social disapproval.

* * *

The advertisements in the journals are of interest to the western observer. A large share of them are devoted to books of various sorts, many of them having no direct relationship to the field of psychoanalysis. One which does relate to psychoanalysis recurs in several issues. It describes a book on a notorious sex-murder committed by one Sade Abe, a licensed prostitute who came from a high-class Japanese family. The murder is well known in Japan, even among laymen. The advertisement includes a photographic portrait of the murderess.

Another which occurs in many copies of the journal cannot but astonish an occidental. Side-by-side with serious articles by some of Japan's most authoritative psychoanalysts appears the following advertisement:

"Fuji's Therapeutic Instrument for Nervous Disorder
Invented by Dr. Momotaro Fuji

Patented in Japan, England, Germany and France
Good for any kind of illness
Simple and easy to manipulate
Giving no pain, leaving no scar
Health or illness solely depends on one's nervous
condition!
The perpetual use of the instrument will make one's nervous state normal, and gradually strengthen the natural power to recover, hence the happiness and rejoicing of millions of people since the advent of the instrument, though it it is not very long ego.
Price for one set: Yen 38.00
Parcel fee for Japan Proper: Sen 45
. . . . Japanese Territories: Sen 75
Notice: A Booklet of directions for, and explanation of the effect of, use will be sent gratis, when applied with postage (Sen 4) to —
Jitsugio-no-Nihon-Sha, Sales Dept.,
Nishiginza 1 chrome Kiobashi-ku, Tokyo, Japan."

Sometimes the quality of the editorial content seems little more appropriate: in the May, 1934 issue, there is an article on the psychology of the dog (which I did not have translated).

The illustrative material is sometimes startling: on the first page of No. 33 (March, 1950), *Seishin Bunseki* are two cuts labeled "Karl Menninger," and "his brother William." Both are pictures of Karl Menninger, taken from two different angles.

* * *

Dr. Koizumi informs me that the post-war issues of *Seishin Bunseki,* of which I have a special volume of reprints of representative articles, seem to be chiefly directed toward a sort of orientation of lay readers to psychoanalytic thinking. Thus it is not surprising to find, in the June and July, 1950, issues respectively, summaries of popular lectures such as "On Economic Psychology," by Kikuya Kimura, and "Main Currents in Modern Psychiatry," by Sichikuro Uyematsu. And in November of the same year, there is a review of *Educational Psychology: The Growth and Development of Human Beings,* published by the (presumably Japanese) Department of Education. The author of this review, Shigeru Kurabayashi, expends more space on a sort of didactic preface than on comment upon the book under review: "The field of educational psychology is as follows: (1) investigation of psychological characteristics and their development in infants and children; (2) psychological investigation of educational materials; (3) the relationship of educator and students, and all other relationships in the educational field; (4) studies of culture; (5) study of individuality and characteristics; and (6) study of the problems of education."

In the same journal, Kohsho Fukuda, in "The Psychology of Religion," suggests an instructional function; but at the same time it supplies a post-war example

178

of the syncretization of Buddhism and psychoanalysis which has previously been discussed in connection with pre-war writings: "The basis of religion is the life of emotion and will. Freud pointed out that religion has a compulsive neurotic phase and an erotic phase. But he did not study Buddhism. If he had lived longer and had become familiar with Buddhism, his opinion on religion would have changed. The relationship between the unconscious theory in Buddhism and psychoanalysis is a very interesting problem, and should occupy a more important place in the psychology of religion." Here, again, is the suggestion of the Nirvana principle applied in psychoanalysis.

Occasionally, throughout Japanese history, there have been "free thinkers" in politics, philosophy, science, religion, or art—thinkers who seem to have been born out of their time. Liberal, individualistic, international-istic, these hybrids or sports from the Japanese chrysan-themum frequently defied the government and indulged in thinking which was highly upsetting to the status quo, and often extremely dangerous to their own phys-ical well-being. Notable examples of these departures from the Japanese norm were Shiba, at the turn of the nineteenth century; Honda, in the early 1800's; Wata-nabe ("Kwanzan") and Takano in the mid 1800's; Prince Ito and Okuma, in the 1830's and after.[271]

This being so, it is not too surprising that *Seishin Bunseki* occasionally presents an example of similar de-fiance of the established Japanese patterns. Nevertheless, one is impressed—after reading paper after paper which is, if not analytically worthless because of the degree of syncretization, at least unsophisticated and lacking in depth and originality—very occasionally to find some-thing like "Unconscious Logic of the East and West," by Siujitu Tutiya, which is essentially intelligent, original, even quite compatible with traditional occidental analytic thinking:

"1. *Material and Mental Culture.*

"It has been thought that East and West are opposites. However, is there any basic difference between them? It is very important to find out about this problem from the standpoint of unconscious psychology.

"In our country, it is commonly considered that the Orient is mental [i.e., spiritual] and the West is material in culture. Maybe this conclusion has some truth, but it is based on some unconscious desire. When we try to discover some reality-concepts, our investigation itself is twisted by the unconscious wish to satisfy that desire. Material and mental culture are so closely related that it is more correct to consider that the Orient has its own mental and material culture, while the West also has its own. If we consider that the West is rich in material culture and the Orient in mental culture, it means that the Orientals despise Western culture, because in metaphysical philosophy the spirit is higher than the physical. I agree with the following sentence in *Chinese Thought and Japan*, by Sokichi Tsuda: 'It is meaningless to consider that culture can be divided into spiritual and material. Culture means the elevation and enrichment of human life by mental activity, but it is based on the life of human beings. Culture is neither merely spiritual or physical.' The reason why this mistaken idea has been accepted is that our present scientific culture is called material, and all other cultures are called spiritual. Also it is thought that Buddhism and Taoism are spiritual, and that morals and religions have been developed only in China and India. It is not understood that science is one of the best mental activities of human beings. The fact that science has developed in Japan does not mean that mental activity has developed. Rather the opposite is true.

"2. *The Revolution in the Methods of Production and the Resulting Mental Reaction.*

"In the Meiji Period, Western culture was introduced into our country and there was enthusiastic worship all over the country of all Western things. Later, when that Western culture was being absorbed and digested [Tutiya understands the Japanese habit of syncretizing!], we met with the world-wide panic of the capitalistic system. To escape from this danger some people went back to the old feudalistic age, and came to believe that the Orient is a mental culture and that the material culture was despicable. The tendency to curse capitalistic civilization even while living in it came about. And thus the idea of despising Western culture has both a historical and a social background. It also contained a concept repellent to Western civilization, based on the Oedipus complex and narcissistic feeling as devices for overcoming an inferiority complex. We cannot agree with the pathological attitude which blames or praises the capitalistic system too extremely, because capitalism is merely one period in social history, as youth is one period in individual history.

"Thus we reach the conclusion that East and West have followed the same process of social development; but the difference between these two is based on the social and psychological residue of the past, besides geographical and constitutional differences. The traditional spirit of the Orient catches the true image of life as a primitive form. Because of this, the techniques and theories of production in the Orient are archaic. On the other hand, the West has been driven by the power of life, and has progressed in theory and technical production. However, they lack the peace of mind which motivates the power of life, yet are committed to it. In this sense, we can say that the Orient has a mental culture and the West a material culture, and instead of making them opposites it actually unites them. [This is possibly an unconscious syncretization, but is clearly in line with the world-domination idea expressed by *Kokutai No Hongi,* whose concept of "one world" was a world absorbed by Japan.] The spiritual culture of the Orient cannot recognize its living spirit and complete itself without awakening from its peaceful sleep through the influence of Western culture. If Western culture does not accept Oriental culture, it cannot realize its insecurity, and cannot complete itself. Both cultures can be compared with the male and female, the Orient being the female and the West the male. This comparison is less thought than felt. But from an intellectual standpoint, both East and West have followed matriarchal patterns and then changed to patriarchal, feudalistic and capitalistic societies. In this process, we can recognize some differences based on emotional temperament.

"In sociology, the unique characteristic of the Orient is considered to be the so-called Asian production pattern. I believe this is the pattern of patriarchal society altered by a residue of matriarchal society. Some people believe that in the ancient Oriental countries there was no system of slavery such as existed in Greece and Rome. But it is thought that slave-labor appeared as a service to society in the Orient, because of the strong racial unity among Orientals. In fact, there actually were aristocrats, middle-class, and slaves in the ancient Orient. Such a system of society influenced the mental activity and ideology of the people. It can be seen in Shintoism,

Buddhism, and Taoism. The idea of basic Oriental thought is maternal [thus the relationship of the emperor to Amaterasu]. It is the psychology of a matriarchal society, where there is no external authority unconsciously, but where everything maternal is Alpha and Omega [the concept of coevality—no beginning and no ending]. On the other hand, in the West, the residue of patriotism is more distinctive. It can be seen most clearly in Christianity. That is, the most basic idea of the West is the patriotic one [the author's definition of patriotism is not clear; for by western standards the patriotism associated with nationalistic Japan would appear to have been greater than any we know]. Anything maternal or Madonna-like is repressed as original sin. God and Mary in Christianity are the projections of ideal parents, and Christ is the symbol of ourselves. In the social super-ego the Orient is feminine and the West is masculine; therefore Oriental women are maternal, while Western women are not. The super-ego of the man in the West has a realistic power, but the super-ego of the Oriental man is merely supported by superior feeling based on narcissism, which overcomes his inferiority complex; and he has less realistic power [here again the Amaterasu-emperor relationship]. The so-called repulsion of the Western female toward the male, described by Adler, is a jealousy of the male sex-organ, as well as a reaction against the desire to be mothered. Therefore chivalry in the West is the concession of the male to such a feeling of repulsion. In the Orient, the dominance of the man is the narcissistic reaction of the male against the unconscious power of the female. A new social super-ego in the future should be freed from such unconscious sexual symbols.

"3. *The Psychotic Orient and the Neurotic West.*

"The Oriental psychology which is a combination of the super-ego and the id can be said to be psychotic. And Western psychology, which is a combination of super-ego, ego and repressed id, is neurotic. However, the fact is more complicated, and not expressed in such simple words. The Orient suffered more deeply (the symptoms are more severe) than the West, and they have a deeper awareness of life. The fact that Oriental culture has not progressed as far as that of the West in material civilization seems to be related to the desire to return to the womb. One of the characteristic thoughts of the Oriental is self-renunciation, the condition of attaining the Higher Self—in other words, to die—in nature or in society. It also means the existence of an imaginary Greater Mother. Self-renunciation starts with the maternal idea and is transferred to the whole world, being abstracted into a philosophical concept. Self-renunciation has two effects: one is to satisfy the fantasy of the Great Mother by believing in Amida; the other is to satisfy it by relying on oneself. Amida is necessary to the salvation of people who cannot believe in themselves. In Buddhism there exists a fantasy which prevents narcissism and makes it possible for a transference. On the other hand, the Buddhists emphasize that their gospel is the cure for all disease. I do not believe that Buddhism is merely the expression of the unconscious desire of Orientals; rather, it is a treatment of unconscious desire.

"The West's unconscious desire is expressed beautifully in Christianity. The symbol of the people, i.e., Christ, was the child of Mary, but not physically related to God. (In fact, he was the child of Mary and God, but this relationship is completely repressed in the people's minds.) He was the child of the Virgin Mary only, according to Christian teaching. Here we see the repression of mother-fixation and the Oedipus complex. As a result of the repression of Oedipal father-hate and the mother-fixation for Mary, there is a worship of God. In such a psychological mechanism, all life-effort is affected by the idea of redemption from original sin. Therefore the West is very active and anxious. But no matter how active and anxious they are, the original sin remains. This is the reason that Christianity is hypocritical. The ego wants to please God (i.e., the super-ego) and distorts reality to retain the id (i.e., original sin). The active attitude of the West, based on such a psychological mechanism, is hypocritical, but it has caused progress in Western material civilization. We can feel something insecure in Western civilization, namely, the danger of the repressed id's breaking out, and also the danger of losing the authority of God, i.e., the super-ego. On the other hand, the Oriental material culture is insufficiently developed because of the inactive attitude of Orientals, which is based on their desire to return to the womb. Therefore, Oriental material culture is not insecure. It involves primitive Asiatic security.

"Due to these differences in material culture, the Orient and the West have a different mental culture. The characteristic of the Oriental culture is a quality of symbolizing by their instinctive feeling, while the characteristic of the Western culture is to conceptualize through intellect. The former is based, psychologically, on masochism; the latter is Oedipal sadism. Therefore, the Orient is categorized as feminine, centrifugal and synthetic, and the West as masculine, peripheral and analytical. The idea of Sabi in Oriental thought has been discussed so often that it need not be mentioned. From the standpoint of unconscious psychology, it is the desire to return to the womb and death, which is naturally sublime, without any guilt-feeling. This is inactivity but a world of extreme beauty.

"As such unconscious logic of the East and West is clarified, both worlds will move closer together until they become united in mental and material culture."[272] (As previously remarked, this statement may well reflect, unconsciously, the teachings of *Kokutai No Hongi,* in which Japan is considered to be destined to devour the rest of the world. *Kokutai No Hongi* also preaches the adoption and adaptation of that which is of value and discarding the rest. Tutiya may mean the same thing; or he may have a broader international viewpoint and actually mean to discard that which is useless in *both* Eastern and Western cultures.)

Before leaving this most interesting article, it will be well to call attention to the fact that, consciously or no, Tutiya never once uses the words *Japan* or *Japanese.* This would serve two purposes: viz., to indicate in subtle fashion his belief in something larger than the insular nationalism of the Japanese national entity program, and/or to free himself to speak extremely frankly about the national mental health ("Orientals are psychotic"), including the Japanese only by implication.

Also, from a psychoanalytical standpoint, Tutiya's discussion of and interpretation of the role of religion, especially Buddhism, seems to me to be much the most realistic of any in *Seishin Bunseki.* Whether the other Japanese analysts who wrote about Buddhism actually meant the same things, but did not express their ideas as clearly, or whether they were more frustrated by the Bureau of Thought Control than the forthright Tutiya, must remain a matter for conjecture.

Five months after publication of Tutiya's article,

Kenji Ohtski produced another discussion of the femininity of the Japanese, the critical paragraph of which follows: "The racial characteristics of the Orientals are 'id-ic' and feminine, as compared with those of the Occidentals, which are 'ego-ic' and masculine. . . . Among the Orientals . . . the Japanese are relatively strong in ego and not so regressive as the Chinese, it seems to me. But the death-instinct of the Japanese is crudely aggressive and not extensively sublimated into intellectual ability. This can be explained in various ways; it is probably due to the natural effect of the peculiar family-system of the Japanese."[273]

While Tutiya was even more outspoken than Ohtski, in that he called orientals "psychotic," Ohtski has nevertheless criticized the family-system and spoken of his nation's "crudely aggressive" death instinct. But Ohtski has not been as blunt as Tutiya in his mention of the id and its role in oriental life. It would be interesting to know whether this represents merely one analyst taking a slightly different view of the subject of another's paper, or whether Ohtski's article might be construed as an endeavor to soften the effect of Tutiya's outspoken and highly western conclusions. (As editor of *Seishin Bunseki,* Ohtski was, after all, the person most directly responsible for the tone of its content; i.e., it was he who was responsible for keeping it in harmony with the national entity program.)

Even Kenji Ohtski, who so often appears to be unscientific, ingenuous, or trite, toward the entry of Japan into World War II begins to give evidence of thinking which is discordant, out of harmony with the national entity program; consider, for example, these excerpts from, "The Traits of Japanese Character and Their Cause," in the July-August, 1940, *Seishin Bunseki:*

"The weakness of the family-system is that it evaluates the person from the point of view of his position and not of his ability. In such circumstances, everyone strives for the most authoritative position. This produces childishness and bureaucratic tendencies, because the head of the family or of the race becomes the object of a father-complex, so that the rest of the group remains childish. The bureaucrat is believed to be the center of the nation-family and the people have a father-complex about him. . . . [In Japan] . . . political parties become bureaucratic because they are not accepted if they are democratic. As a result the life of the people is insecure. Bureaucrats believe in obeying top governmental officials, and refuse to take individual responsibility. I am not criticizing specific people in bureaucracies; I believe that tradition and custom and political system produce these faults. I would like to warn the nation to change the system." He goes on to describe the Japanese inferiority complex: "The inferior feeling of the Japanese is based on his childish character. I don't believe the Japanese are really inferior, but we cannot compare one country's superiority to another's. In order to correct this inferiority complex we must frankly recognize the strong and weak points of our own country as well as those of other nations. The Japanese have a tendency to generalize everything; that is, if there are good points in other countries, everything seems good. They have respected Britain up to now, but they will respect Germany if she conquers in this war. It isn't good to evaluate a country from the standpoint of its military strength. We must develop a critical attitude toward Germans, particularly in our unconscious minds. If a person evaluates correctly, he will never have inferior feelings, even in the face of any nation or people in the world. If we don't have any pathological inferiority complex, we don't hesitate when we meet any person in a high position."

Ohtski in this flash of insight was indubitably aware of the non-discriminatory and totalistic nature of Japanese copying.

In these passages Ohtski also implies the falseness of *mimpi*, the inferiority-complex phenomena in *ko, chu, giri, enryo.* He gives recognition to the justifiability of *ninjo*, but he warns against *ninjo* taking the form of strivings toward high bureaucratic positions. All of this is relatively subtle; but in the following article, so striking in its departure from the norm as to have amounted in its expression to a risk of the author's life, Ohtski clearly criticizes not only fickle thoughts, but the very Bureau of Thought Control itself. Only in the final paragraph, where Ohtski fails to commit himself as to a cure for the evils of thought control, does the article suggest that he is inhibited by fear of the governmental authorities.

But the most startling of all is the "Re-Education of Japanese National Traits," which Ohtski produced a year later, only about eight months before Pearl Harbor. Probably the only thing that prevented the author's incarceration by the authorities of the Bureau of Thought Control was the inconclusive final paragraph; yet, even so, considering the 60,000 of his compatriots arrested for similar transgressions, Ohtski's outspokenness cannot but be admired:

"Re-Education of Japanese National Traits
by Kenji Ohtski

"1. *Defects of Japanese Character.*
"Last December at a large meeting of about seven

hundred people of the so-called intellectual class, Dr. Abe talked about Japanese 'trivialism,' and regretted that in such a national crisis Japanese people are still looking for little faults in each other. I agreed with him completely, but he did not make any effort to find out the psychological cause of this trait.

"I pointed out two defects of Japanese character in my book 'Cosmopolitanism and the Japanese.' One is 'the tendency to escape into pleasure in hard work,' and the other is 'blind obedience to authority.' As was mentioned in the last journal, the Japanese cannot win their struggle for existence in the world without correcting these two defects.

"Today I am going to dicuss two other defects, namely, the ingratiating tendency and trivialism.

"2. *Japanese Ingratiating Tendency and Its Psychological Cause.*

"The Japanese in general are not faithful to the thoughts which they believe in. Of course, one's thoughts are changed with conditions, and with the growth of his inner life. However, in many cases one changes from one thought to another because conditions in the outside world have been changed, and not because his inner life needs to change. Many leaders and thinkers change their statements from one to another, but they do not progress at all. It is a more important problem for present-day Japan than her having a few Communists, because it means that the Japanese have weak intelligence and weak personality (conscience, or super-ego).

"If anyone once proclaims his opinion or his thought, it is done at the risk of his life. At present many people are changing thoughts in which they have long believed only because those thoughts are considered to be dangerous at the present time. Why don't they keep silence, if they are not allowed to speak, instead of loudly expressing almost reverse opinions? Such facts are really shameful.

"Everybody has some responsibility in this fault, because we are too forgiving of such sins in each other. In the past, think how all journalists agreed with Communism; how professors and instructors connived with the students who yelled Communism's songs every morning at school, when Marxism was so popular! Those people didn't have adequate insight to criticize popular ideas at that time, and accepted everything.

"In a newspaper of January 21st, I found an article about the American politician, Kennedy. He expressed without any hesitation his own ideas against the participation of America in the World War. The country which has such brave politicians cannot be despised.

"In our country there is no politician, scholar, or thinker who is brave enough to express his own opinion of any condition. Then, what is the cause of the ingratiating tendency? Psychologically, it is felt that the Japanese does not establish his individuality, in other words his super-ego is very weak. I think that a critical attitude may be understood as a masculine attribute, psychologically. Therefore, it means that the Japanese is lacking in masculine attributes; that is, Japanese character is feminine in the good and also in the bad sense.

"3. *Japanese Trivialism and Its Cause.*

"The Japanese are so concerned about trifles that they forget the main, important thing. Politicians and thinkers nervously pay too much attention to the details of their speeches and are afraid of expressing their opinions frankly. This might be a reason why we have very few eloquent speakers. Mr. Nosei Abe wrote in his impression of one of the large meetings which he attended: 'I felt keenly that we have no eloquent speakers. In such an important meeting they read their papers, instead of speaking. They might be afraid to be blamed for little mistakes, but it is much better to have powerful passionate and grand speech even with little mistakes.'

"It is true that the Japanese are castrating the masculine spirit in each other, of which we have so little by nature, and yet they think that they are doing something good. Trivialism is encouraged by a situation where such an attitude exists. I believe that it is promoted by the bureaucratic tendency which is widespread and deeply rooted in the Japanese character. Bureaucratism is a system in which position is more powerful than the person's own ability. As long as he has an important position, even though he is not capable, his words and his orders are considered to be very important and cannot be refused. This fact may explain not only the Japanese' ingratiating attitude, but also their trivialism, because when anyone wants to trap a person in a high position, he can best do so by pointing out his little faults.

"All government universities are bureaucratic, and their professors are bureaucrats. Therefore, there is no freedom (originality) of learning and independence of thoughts. I am afraid Japanese trivialism will spoil the spirit and originality of learning. Then, how can we correct these two defects of character? It is a very serious problem, and I am not free to express my opinion frankly. It is very regrettable to find that we Japanese still cannot get rid of the past when bureaucrats were worshipped. I do hope you may find the answer in what I've written here."[274]

Sansom quotes Sir Charles Eliot's article in the 1911 *Encyclopedia Britannica* ("Asia, History"): " 'Asiatics

have not the same sentiment of independence and freedom as Europeans. Individuals are thought of as members of a family, state or religion, rather than as entities
with a destiny and rights of their own. This leads to
autocracy in politics, fatalism in religion and conservatism in both.' "[275] It is apparent from the papers by
Ohtski and Tutiya quoted above that this is obvious to
some Japanese, as well as to an occidental. A final
example from the July, 1950, *Seishin Bunseki* will serve
to indicate how clearly some Japanese analytic writers
see their people today. (We have at hand no examples
of the author's writings prior to the war, so that we
cannot categorize him as one of the brave and outspoken
among his profession; but it is likely that if he were too
fearful to be outspoken, he was nevertheless observing
objectively all that was going on about him.) With the
hind-sight of a member of a defeated nation, but with a
clarity that suggests a sharp analytical insight and an
objective intelligence, Keiji Kurosawa presents "Abnormal Morality During the Pacific Ocean War":

"After World War II, the immorality of the Japanese nation, particularly of the young people, became very
pronounced. The origin of this condition was not only
the social confusion after the war; it resulted also from
an education which despised the intellect and its critical
ability. During the war, the nation and the people were
educated by propaganda. To criticize was to be an
enemy.

"Action decided everything. The whole nation was
in one mind. Therefore they could not do anything
without orders from the authority After the war they
lost their self-respect, and all laws lost their authority.
Morals based on the ability of self-control cannot be
directed by others. To control and direct oneself is the

highest intellectual activity. As a result of denying criticism, the Japanese people lost their intellectual ability and could not understand other people's standard of behavior. Therefore when restrictions were removed, the Japanese behaved like animals.

"This situation in the Japanese nation caused cruelty during the war. The education of the soldiers was wrong. In military education, everything was controlled in the name of the Emperor, and all the responsibility for behavior was given to the Emperor. The value and rights of the individual were not recognized. The most excellent soldier was considered to be a machine with no individual will. For people who are educated in this way and do not appreciate their own personality, the idea of individualism has no significance.

"The aggressive desire of soldiers was directed toward prisoners and the people in the occupied countries during the war. He could avoid the pain of his conscience by feeling that his action was a part of group action.

"I heard of one soldier who said the woman who was crying because her house was burned down resembled his mother, and he felt so sorry for her. Another soldier saw his father's face in a Chinese farmer when he was fighting in China. Such humanitarian feelings belong only to people with a higher sensitivity toward others. However, I am very sorry to say there were few such people among the Japanese soldiers.

"The natives in Indonesia do not show any expression of gratefulness when they are given something by the soldiers. The natives were of different class from the rich even before the war. There was no intercourse between these classes; therefore it is easily understood that there can be no feeling of gratefulness where people have no social relationship. In Shanghai, also, the rich and poor people live in completely different social planes. They have no common problems to cause them to sympathize with each other. Under such conditions, people cannot have a feeling of identification, and they don't have common morals to bind them to the rest of society. This relationship is the same as between soldiers and natives in occupied places, as well as between soldiers and prisoners. There is only the relationship of superior and inferior.

"The Japanese once believed that all the world should serve Japan. That was a result of their infantile narcissistic logic. Such a primitive thought is amazing. But it was very important from the standpoint of race. When I said to a friend that if the Japanese didn't raise their moral standard they would be despised by the Chinese, he accused me of being unpatriotic. After the war, I said to one of our officers that the Japanese would have to learn about democracy from the Chinese. Even the farmer in China does not interfere with others. He knows the difference between himself and others. The officer became very angry, and said that the Japanese cannot be inferior to the Chinese.

"The idea of the Japanese being a chosen race is the basis of feudalism, and it prevents the identification of one person with another and destroys morality. . . ."[276]

Yet even in the post-war writings there are examples of traditional Japanese thinking. In "Public Mind and Private Mind: A Psychological Analysis of a Mibushi Judge," by Machiro Mori, [277] the author shows himself to be an "unreconstructed" Japanese national. Mori tells us that the judge went to a condemned murderer and urged him to appeal the decision. "He said, 'I come to you not as a judge, but as a parent. Perhaps I will be criticized and lose my judgeship, but I should like to help you as a human being.' This [newspaper] report gave an impression that the judge was very warm-hearted. However, once the decision was made by the jury and the judge delivered the sentence, even though he did not agree with it, his behavior was not proper. I believe he confused the public and the private minds. I do not say that a judge cannot have an opinion opposed to the death sentence; an individual can have any opinion. But, from the standpoint of psychoanalysis, the judge's super-ego, which was opposed to the death sentence, conquered his ego, which should have been faithful to his profession; this is not a healthy state of mind. The conquering of the super-ego by the ego is beautiful in poetry, but in reality such a life is not healthy. Only when ego coincides with super-ego and id can social life be perfect. Perhaps the character of the judge was too weak, so that he could not endure his guilt-feelings in having given a death sentence. To be a judge is to practice according to the content of the law. For a correct judgment, a healthy mind is necessary. In this instance, the judge's psychotic character appeared because his super-ego was pathologically strong and his ego was pathologically weak. . . ."

The significance of this article is its evidence that the writer has not been able to give up his old nationalistic, authoritarianistic belief in *giri*: the judge did not do what was expected of him in his role as judge. Moreover, the writer regards the judge as psychotic because he evidenced kindness and humanitarianism compatible with western attitudes, but individualistic and liberal, and hence out of keeping with the typical Japanese attitudes.

One other post-war article leaves some doubt as to the personal attitudes of the author. It is conceivable that in writing "Political Psychology and Psychoanalysis," Kikuo Nakamura is giving expression to his own views. But considering the apparently didactic intent already mentioned in many of the post-war journals, one questions whether perhaps some Occupation authority had not merely given him the assignment of writing on democratic concepts; so that, in doing *giri* to his superiors, Nakamura merely performed *jicho,* and wrote "that which was expected of him." I leave the reader the task of deciding Nakamura's motivation when he wrote: "Political psychology was established to open the way to a new understanding of politics. Also, the demand of the present age has stimulated and developed politics. 'Politics' is a description of a political system, just as anatomy in medicine describes a dead body. For instance, formerly only the election system itself was studied; no one was interested in the analysis of the human beings who carried on the election. In the idea of democracy, the individual is considered to be a person who has no limitation from outside. A congressional system is formed on the premise of ideal human beings being equal. However, all people are different from each other. If one observed the psychology of voters, it is apparent that some of them vote not through rational decision, but simply because a name is easy to write, or relatives ask him to vote that way, or sometimes because the candidate's name is the same as his own. Therefore, if one followed only the ideal form, the practice of politics is not good. Here we see the importance of the dynamic study of human beings."[278] (The remainder of the article makes a plea for more searching investigation of the psycho-dynamics of politics and for the application of psychoanalytic thinking in an effort to understand the psychological workings of individual politicians. Nakamura does not, however, discuss what he considers to be the psycho-dynamics of democratic political methods.) To me it seems as if Nakamura is here carrying water on both shoulders.

Thus we see that both the quality and the content of Japanese analytic literature has been strongly influenced by the ideology of the national entity program, and by the history of Japan through the ages. We have seen that a few daring Japanese analysts occasionally have been aware of the Japanese lack of individuality. There have been a few daring departures from nationalistic thinking, a few apparently sincere attempts at original thinking in the purely analytical fields; but that, by and large, there have been few indications of great desire to escape the bonds of *Kokutai No Hongi* and the Bureau of Thought Control, or even of the orthodox Freudian approach to psychoanalysis, excepting where the latter had to be syncretized to be made acceptable under the former dictates. And we know that for at least some analysts, the old concepts of the Japanese processing are still the acceptable ones.

15

THE GOALS OF JAPANESE PSYCHOANALYSIS

WE have learned in the foregoing chapters something of the standards of conduct and patterns
of behavior of the Japanese people. We have
also learned from Japanese history and from *Kokutai
No Hongi* of the aims, attitudes and ideologies of the
successive Japanese governments. The impress of such
a history, such a culture, such a political philosophy as
the Japanese' upon a human being could scarcely have
produced any sort of person other than the so-called
"typical" Japanese; and an aggregate of such persons
results in a governmental behavior precisely the same
as the behavior of the persons making up that government. These things being true, any movement taking
root in Japan whose aims run contrary to the clear-cut
patterns which I have outlined must necessarily have a
devastating effect upon the people and the nation, or
else must itself undergo a radical change. With these
facts in mind, we arrive at last at an answer to my original question: "What are the goals of Japanese psychoanalysis?"

Dr. Muramatsu, who, it will be remembered, is a psychiatrist, says of psychoanalyst Kosawa: "Dr. Kosawa
seems bravely to lead patients 'individualistically' and

seems sometimes to cause trouble among their families [by his psychoanalytic approach]. . . . I have known one such case treated by him."[279] Muramatsu implies by this that because of the trouble occasioned in the family of the patient being psychoanalyzed, Kosawa must be altering his patient's attitude and developing individualistic trends in him. These observations might be explained in another way. For instance, the difficulty in adjusting to *ko*—and hence in adjusting to *giri*—may have originated the need for psychoanalysis in the first place. Indubitably, the patient was already a source of disturbance to the family before starting his analysis. Constant contact with the "authoritarian" Kosawa would heighten the conflict between *ninjo* and the deeply ingrained, but not completely structured, *oya bun-ko bun* personality patterns. As a result, the patient could be even more disturbing to his family than he had been before analysis, the conflict being exaggerated by the presence of Kosawa.

Kosawa himself, in the article on Oedipus and Azase already referred to, quotes some material from a Japanese analysand who, as he approached the successful (by Japanese standards) conclusion of his treatment said, "During my vacation my mother told me on one occasion that I was now pleasing my father better again." This, of course, means that the analysand was again performing *ko* toward his father. Kosawa, in reviewing the changes in the patient's personality, says, "His psychic state is now as harmonious a one as can ever be reached by human beings." But this does not mean that he is developing individualism; he may be feeling more comfortable because he no longer assails his super-ego (emperor) with his individual strivings. What Kosawa actually describes here is an individual who is now performing *giri* in accordance with the national entity program.

It is quite impossible to see how Dr. Kosawa, or any other analyst, could have practiced western-style psychoanalysis in a nation where between 1932 and 1945, 60,000 people were arrested for "improper thoughts"—a situation which actually obtained during the existence of the Bureau of Thought Control, under Ito Enkichi. There was strict adherence during this period, in all areas of Japanese life, to the "Way." There is doubtless more than passing significance in the fact that pictures of group meetings of analysts which appear in *Seishin Bunseki* show a considerable smattering of military uniforms, and that a leading member of the Tokyo Institute for Psychoanalysis was Prince Iwakura (some of whose articles were quoted in Chapter 14).* It would hardly be possible for either the analysts or their patients to survive under such a regime, if the analysis were conducted according to occidental standards.

A system so foreign to the national entity program as western psychoanalysis—stressing as it does the importance of adult stability, maturity and especially individualism—would have to be drastically overhauled to render it compatible with Japanese political requirements. We might say that it must be "predigested" in order to render the system harmonious (*musubi*) with *giri*. My contention that this is in fact what has happened is supported by a recent letter from Dr. Marui, in answer to my specific question about adjusting *ninjo* to *giri*. Dr. Marui replied: "Through analysis of the ego, representing the trends of instinct (*ninjo*), as well as of super-ego (containing the tendency of *giri*), we arrive, I think, at a compromise between the two." (It would appear that Dr. Marui does not, as Muramatsu says Kosawa does, "lead patients bravely 'individualistically.' ")

Syncretizing psychoanalysis in the interests of the Japanese national program is the natural and inevitable result of its basic clash with the national entity. Such syncretization is imperative in the breakdown of the ideas contained in occidental psychoanalysis so that they may be converted into their opposites. Muramatsu writes, "Thus a victor may sometimes be considered as a new boss who has a real obligation to look after his weaker followers. . . . In an old popular story, a giant attacked a boy on the Gojo bridge in Kyoto to rob him of his sword, but as soon as the giant discovered that the boy was much stronger than he, he decided to become the boy's faithful follower."[280] *Japan's Prospect* recognizes this situation: "Their eager adoption of foreign ideas . . . conspicuously manifests a quality that psychoanalysts would call ambivalent. They adopt while emotionally they repudiate; they admire the foreigner while they hate him."[281]

In all of this, another duality or dichotomy is encountered: although the individuals of Japan are disindividualized and swallowed up by the Japanese national entity, these individuals constitute the nation and are a part of the entity, which in turn devours and assimilates important items of foreign information.

European analysts, at the time of the beginning of Japanese psychoanalysis, were preoccupied with biological orientations.* One Viennese analyst informed me within the last decade that the cultural matrix is not of too great importance; that oral passivity and sadism, anal gratification, anal sadism and conformity, genital configurations, the Oedipus and castration complexes will, because of the unfurling of the biological patterns, arrive on schedule despite the circumstances of cultural pressures or lack thereof.

Although Freud often expressed the importance of the mother to the infant, still, within the same paragraph in the following quotation he undoes his cultural orientation:

"A child's first erotic object is the mother's breast that feeds him, and love in its beginnings attaches itself to the satisfaction of the need for food. To start with, the child certainly makes no distinction between the breast and his own body; when the breast has to be separated from his body and shifted to the 'outside' because he so often finds it absent, it carries with it, now that it is an *'object,'* part of the original narcissistic cathexis. This first object subsequently becomes completed into the whole person of the child's mother, who not only feeds him but also looks after him and thus arouses in him many other physical sensations pleasant and unpleasant. By her care of the child's body she becomes his first seducer. In these two relations lies the root of a mother's importance, unique, without parallel, laid down unalterably for a whole lifetime, as the first and strongest love-object and as the prototype of all later love-relations—for both sexes." Yet Freud immediately reverses himself in the next sentence: "The phylogenetic foundation has so much the upper hand in all this over accidental personal experience that it makes no difference whether a child has really sucked at the breast or has been brought up on the bottle and never enjoyed the tenderness of a mother's care."[282]

It would be not unnatural for the casual thinker to expect that, since World War II, under the American Occupation, Japanese psychoanalysis might have undergone some changes. However, in light of what has been said in previous chapters about the basic immutability of the Japanese and their propensity for identification with the enemy, the degree and kind of change are bound to be somewhat superficial. We know, for example, that at the insistence of the American Military Government in 1946, a new Japanese constitution was drawn up. In the same year, the Japanese Imperial Cabinet published an "Exposition of the New Constitution," some of which is quoted in the appendix to *Kokutai No Hongi*. One passage from the "Exposition" clearly indicates that the Japanese, in accepting the constitution, have once again merely gone through the motions of change—have assimilated and sublimated it in such a way that they have actually neutralized the attempt of the Americans to alter their national entity. For example, "Particularly in the House of Peers law scholars banded themselves together to ask the Government if the national entity had not undergone any change, but the Government stood by their belief that what had suffered a change was the form of government and not the national entity. These differences of view will probably remain in the future as a scholastic problem regarding the interpretation of the New Constitution."[283] If such attitudes exist within the governmental brackets, we may also expect them among Japanese scientists.

Muramatsu, as I have noted, has suggested an increase in eclectic thinking among Japanese psychiatrists in recent years, but there is little evidence, so far as I can discover, that psychoanalysts have greatly changed in the amount of respect in which they hold all things Freudian. And even if there were a considerable breaking-away from Freudianism, this could hardly be laid to identification with the American conquerors, as American psychoanalytic thinking is still heavily influenced by Freud.

Before *Kokutai No Hongi* there was apparently an unconscious syncretization in Japanese psychoanalysis. Some of this is still evident; but there also seems to be a somewhat more subtle, intellectual, and even conscious syncretization. This we may assume to be the principal effect of the American Occupation on Japanese psychoanalysis.

I was immediately struck, upon receiving the copy of reprints from all the post-war issues of *Seishin Bunseki* (from which I have quoted in Chapter 14), by the fact that the table of contents was printed in English; it had been in German before the war. Furthermore, the Romanization of Japanese names now follows another system, apparently Hepburn. The name "Ohtski" is now spelled "Ohtsuki," which is, in fact, the way he has signed his communications to me (all of them post-war). "Ohtski" was a Japanese Romanization form and may also have been German; while "Ohtsuki" is the spelling which would customarily be used by Americans. This is possibly significant, since English is the language of the occupying forces in Japan, and Hepburn was an American. On the face of it, it would appear that the Japanese psychoanalysts may have swung from a dominance of Austro-German influences to an identification with the victorious Americans.

An interesting sidelight upon the acceptance by Japanese psychoanalysts of the traditional Japanese culture patterns is seen in an example of the "caste-system" at work among them. Ever since I first talked with Dr. Kosawa in Japan, I had felt that there was a lack of harmony between the Tokyo and Sendai psychoanalytic societies. But because of the difficulties in interrogating the Japanese which Textor so aptly described, and which I have elsewhere noted from my own experience, I was never able to ascertain the exact nature of the rift which I suspected. I thought at first that it might represent a perpetuation of some factional dispute over dogma which was copied by such Japanese analysands as Yabe and Marui from their occidental training analysts. But a recent letter from Dr. Ernest Jones throws another light on the matter. He writes: "I could never get the Tokyo and Sendai Societies onto friendly terms with each other. The main cause of the cleavage was that the former was not strictly medical,* while the latter was; but perhaps there was, as well, a little pique at a provincial Society having been started before that at the capital." Thus we see not only the caste distinction drawn between lay and medical analysts, but perhaps an indication of what Tokyo analysts might feel was an "abortive" beginning of a psychoanalytic society in Sendai. The Tokyo group might have felt that through its location at the capital it could be considered tacitly approved by the government; i.e., the Tokyo group might have considered themselves the "official" and hence the only legitimate society, under the nationalistic regime. (Such a status would tend to make up for the fact of their being "inferior" due to a lack of medical membership.) As far as I can ascertain, this schism, which had pre-war origins, has never healed.

As mentioned previously, I have submitted a number of questions about their practices to my Japanese psychoanalytic correspondents. One response is of particular interest here as an indication of the unconscious syncretization still to be seen in Japanese psychoanalysis. To the query, "Do you know of any new methods or techniques used by Japanese analysts which might be employed to advantage by American analysts?" I received negative replies from all but Mr. Ohtski, who wrote: "I use . . . moxa-therapy (a stimulus therapy). Moxa-therapy is a classical Japanese medical method. I think it is a milder form of shock therapy." Since moxa-therapy consists of the burning of the soft, downy substance from the leaves of certain plants on the patient's skin, it appears highly unlikely that American analysts would consider this technique something they wished to borrow from the Japanese. But the point of interest here is that the technique is, as Ohtski says, "a classical Japanese medical method." It has, in fact, been in use in the Orient for centuries. Thus we have a clear example of the perpetuation of a very ancient eastern method, and syncretization of this method, with western psychoanalysis, which is little more than half a century old. Observe, too, that Ohtski speaks of it as "a mild form of shock-therapy." Shock-therapy is considered in the Occident as a part of psychiatric, rather than of psychoanalytic treatment; it is never used in psychoanalysis.

Dr. Kosawa, in reply to the questions as to new methods, said that he knew of none, but offered instead the statement that he had "drawn certain principles from my patients [evidently meaning cultural principles]" which he listed as follows: "(1) The Japanese personality construct corresponds to the personality construct of the individual's mother. (2) The mother's personality construct is masochistic, due to the family-system in Japan, and it is complex and religious. This situation is equal to the relations between the child's mouth and the mother's breasts. Because of the close oral relationship with the mother, her masochism leaves his mind uninjured, even though the mother may employ corporal punishment. (3) The Japanese child develops a violent identification, through which body-ego develops strongly. Later the ego declines and the child becomes neurotic. (4) The Emperor-system of Japan involves a foster-child fantasy, and therein is sublimated the hatred for his parents which is developed in the mind of the three or four-year old. (5) We must think of the influence of Buddhism on the Japanese personality."

Clearly, Kosawa recognizes the impact of the Japanese cultural pressures upon the character of the Japanese people. His observation on the importance of the oral relationship is perceptive and wholly in line with my own thinking in reference to the relatively low insanity figures in Japan (see Chapter 5). It is also in accord with the first section of the quotation from Freud presented above. However, to interpret Kosawa's meaning in Number 5 ("the influence of Buddhism"), we must again consider the various Buddhist principles set forth in Chapter 14; and even then we cannot tell from what Kosawa says here whether he regards adherence to Buddhism as being helpful or harmful in the formation of Japanese character or merely, as Tutiya has suggested (Chapter 14), a natural concomitant of the psychology of the Japanese.

Considerably before Tutiya's article came to my attention, I had begun to suspect, from the writings of other Japanese analysts, and from what I had learned of Buddhism and other cultural aspects of Japanese life, that the significance of the id was highly important to complete understanding of the Japanese, and also in understanding the aims of Japanese psychoanalysis. The id, according to Freudian concepts, represents the reservoir of all the phylogenetic contributions to the ontogeny. The id is conceived by the Freudian orthodoxy as being subconscious or sub-ego; and it is certainly conceivable that, although they are not identical, what is posited about the unconscious as being timeless can also be posited about the id. Therefore, any system of psychology that restricts development to the pre-ego stage of mentation must certainly destroy the individualistic and appropriately spontaneous responses of the mature mind.

Although all the unconscious is not id, still, this best fulfills the coevality requirements of the Japanese: there is no past, no present, no future; everything is one—heaven, earth, emperor and people.* This, too, I feel, is the situation of the infant at birth. There is no world outside himself except the mutualistic relationship with the mother. This is akin to the primitive participation idea as expressed in the concepts of the earliest primitive identification with the present and with the world around him; that is, the animistic or earliest phase of the development of mankind. Note that there is a similarity between the human being in infancy and this non-participating epoch of the primitive. As has been described in Kahler's *Man the Measure,* there is no differentiation of man from the world around him (i.e., from his animism), until he has recognized that there was a yesterday: "None of us is completely aware of the amount of protection that consciousness affords. A life without consciousness is naked and meagre. It is wholly exposed and always at the mercy of the unknown and the unexpected. It is a life in the present with no past and no future. But this present is quite different from our present that is lapped in memory and anticipation, that is only a ripple in a vast sea of conscious, half-conscious, subconscious experiences, plans and ideas. Our present is a minute transition from past to future, a continuous flux in the broad current of a known intentional life. But the present of the animal is an overwhelming, all-comprising present, cupped in darkness, a present where there is no consciousness of either birth or death. It is a present so stable, so immobile that it is all but identical with permanence, with eternity."[284]

Probably the only point in common between Japanese and western psychoanalysis is the timelessness of the unconscious. Sansom records several attempts by Christians to syncretize their religion with the philosophies and cultures of the Orient. For example, in 1606, in India, Father de Nobile, "After some years of intense study and discussion . . . produced a work in Sanskrit that, it appears, presented a syncretic plan designed to reconcile on a high plane the Brahmanistic and Christian philosophies. This experiment failed, for though he persuaded some Brahmans to receive baptism, he found himself obliged, in order to gain general acceptance of his thesis, to give way on many subsidiary points of doctrine and ceremony."[285] Again, "In 1880 Professor Chamberlain (an Englishman who held a chair of Japanese at Tokyo University) essayed a rendering of some of the Psalms and read a paper on the subject to the Asiatic Society of Japan. He used a poetical language akin to that of the longer poems in the great anthology called *Manyoshu*—a considerable tour de force for a foreigner."[286] Sansom comments upon such efforts: "Attempts from outside to alter a system of thought sometimes produces a reaction that strengthens rather than moderates that which it is proposed to change." In a footnote to this statement he adds: "This is true . . . of other than religious traditions. Foreign artistic influences sometimes bring about an intensification of a national tradition, and, in modern times at least, foreign political doctrines tend to produce a traditionalist reaction in countries to which they are recommended."[287] I predict that psychoanalysis (by western definition) will be a failure in the same sense that Christianity has been a failure in Japan. While it will no doubt function for many years to come in its oriental guise, and while there will probably also be some men who will adhere as closely as possible to western psychoanalytic ideology and methodology, the culture of Japan, I feel certain, will not in the near future permit other than isolated examples of anything closely resembling occidental psychoanalysis and the Japanese political, spiritual and cultural programs are such that each system would have to give too much ground for there ever to be a satisfactory wedding of the Japanese and western psychoanalytic movements.

Let us recall the prescribed life-pattern of an individual in Japan before the war, a pattern hoary with the passage of the centuries: At birth he became nothing at all (*mimpi*). From infancy the Japanese child, especially the male, was taught and even forced to practice *ko* toward his father. Every Japanese had to preserve a carefully prescribed pattern of respect toward members of any higher caste than his own—toward emperor, guild, employer; i.e., he was expected to perform *jicho*, or that which was expected of him. And he had, at all times, to perform *giri*; i.e., he had to show a sense of obligation toward family, society, and/or individuals.

I am fully aware that the American Occupation officials have endeavored, through revision of the educational system, the constitution, and by other methods, to wipe out the more flagrantly undemocratic of the Japanese culture patterns. "The United States Initial Post-Surrender Policy for Japan," completed August, 1945, ". . . was designed . . . to 'bring about the eventual establishment of a peaceful and responsible government' in Japan which would conform as closely as may be to principles of democratic self-government.' " One of the means of accomplishing these objectives was to be ". . . encouraging the Japanese to desire 'individual liberties,' respect 'fundamental human rights,' and form 'democratic and representative organizations.' "[288] On March 27, 1947, in the "Policy for the Revision of the Japanese Educational System," approved by the Far Eastern Commission, we read: "Emphasis should be placed on the dignity and worth of the individual, on independent thought and initiative, and on developing a spirit of inquiry. The inter-dependent character of international life should be stressed. . . . Special emphasis should also be placed on the teaching of the sanctity of the pledged word in all human relations, whether between individuals or nations."[289] I realize that some of the disindividualizing practices have indeed been dropped or at least made less rigid since the Occupation. But I am not so naive as to believe that a few years of benevolent "democratic authoritarianism" can have erased all that was Japanese. Robert Ward, of the University of Michigan Center for Japanese Study, in an address before the University of Michigan Club of Pontiac, Michigan reminded his audience that there was ample reason to doubt that the people in outlying rural sections of Japan and many of the residents in the smaller cities have changed their thoughts or even their ways. Dr. Koizumi confirms this statement. Furthermore, I believe that I have uncovered sufficient evidence in Japanese analytic literature to indicate that a large number of even the more sophisticated Japanese give only lip service to the democratic ways to which they are submitting—that there still remain in Japan many of the type whom Textor has called the "Old Guard." Therefore, it seems probable to me that the life-pattern outlined above is still, beneath the surface, essentially the same today as always in Japan.

I postulate that this sameness over the ages is part and parcel of the concept of coevality, and that the coevality idea has been, and still is, an integral part of the belief not only of the mass of Japanese, but of Japanese psychoanalysts as well. A few, like Tutiya, seem to be more sophisticated in their understanding of the concept, and to recognize that Japanese life is governed chiefly by the id and that the entire life of a Japanese is directed toward a return to the womb.

The Japanese psychoanalyst, faced with the problem of curing a mentally ill person, must first of all diagnose him as "ill" because he does not adhere to the rigidly prescribed culture patterns I have outlined. The "cure" upon which the analyst then embarks constitutes the opposite of a cure by western standards. Instead of endeavoring, as do occidental psychoanalysts, to free the individual from his inner thongs, the Japanese analyst actually tightens those thongs. Moreover, by the very fact of the analyst's encouraging the patient to believe in the coevality concept, he forces him backward into the status of primitive mankind, where, as we have said, animism reigns. In essence, the effect is to encourage those regressive tendencies that lead the patient to revert to an embryonic state. The goals of western psychoanalysis are growth, maturation, and expansiveness; the goals of Japanese psychoanalysis are the opposite.

* * *

As has already been indicated, no study of Japanese psychoanalysis would be complete unless it stressed the importance of the contributions of the late Yaekichi Yabe, Kenji Ohtski, Heisaku Kosawa and Kiyoyasu

Marui. A great deal has already been implied as to the position held by Yabe in the history of the Japanese psychoanalytic movement, and Ohtski's philosophical orientation has been evaluated in preceding chapters. However, while Kosawa and Marui have received some mention, they merit added discussion here because of certain special features of their psychoanalytical activities.

The Introduction to Psychoanalysis, or *The ABC of Psychoanalysis,* by Kiyoyasu Marui was published in Japan in 1928. In the preface Marui states that because of the war the book became unavailable. It was printed again in 1949. A copy of the book sent to me by Marui in late 1951 is probably the 1949 revision of the 1928 edition.

Marui starts his topic with a brief discussion of three different schools of psychoanalysis: the Freudian, the Adlerian, and the Jungian. After a short commentary on these well known schools, Marui states that the remainder of the book is based upon Freudian concepts. However, in Chapter 8, translators Makio Murayama and Dr. Hide Shohara discovered that Marui documented the Freudian text with conclusions that were distinctly his own and represented his adaptation of the original Freud. Many of the remarks from Chapter 8 were gleaned from Marui's own studies on Japanese patients. The "I" used in this chapter frequently refers to "I, Marui," and not to "I, Freud."

In this chapter titled, "The Structure and Theory of Personality," Marui, the foremost contemporary Japanese psychoanalyst, supplies the reader with many of his own points of view. It is the opinion of Murayama and Shohara, after several hours study of "The Introduction to Psychoanalysis," that Kiyoyasu Marui is a died-in-the-wool old guard Japanese who converts Freudian dogma into Japanese clichés.

On March 6, 1952, I received a communication from Dr. Kosawa which seems to indicate that he shares with Ohtski a belief in the close relationship and compatibility of the Buddhist Nirvana theology with Japanese psychoanalysis. Kosawa had earlier indicated this relationship and involved psychoanalysis in his religious beliefs. (It might be remarked here that Buddhism lends itself to this type of utilization more readily than does Christianity.)

In the Kosawa communication just mentioned, and more than likely supported by him, he re-states the Japanese national and Japanese religious operational position in "Symbols of National Character."

"All mankind has by nature a vehement and abiding love for its native land. This is particularly true of the Japanese. The emperor symbolizes the native land, and the people enjoy an everlasting life as members of a great family circle, surrounded by the picturesque and noble mountains, the limpid rivers, the severe and genial landscape. They stand ever ready to welcome strangers with sincerity and love. From such a world arose the symbols of the national character of the Japanese.

"The grandness of Mount Fuji and the splendor of the cherry blossoms are today the characteristic symbols of the Japanese nation, just as many centuries ago a great classic scholar described the essence of the Japanese spirit as the fragrance of the cherry blossoms bathed in the light of the rising sun.

"Throughout our history we Japanese have been taught to love all peoples and to love nature. We have recognized the responsibility incumbent upon us to minister to the happiness of mankind and to the advancement of civilization throughout the world. We know that, to best demonstrate the ideals manifested in our history, we must awaken anew a true national consciousness. We know how immeasurably influential will be the perspective of history in inspiring the peoples of the world."

These symbols reduced to their proper meaning expose again the totalitarianism of Japan. Japan is a living, breathing entity, a oneness personified by the emperor. All people belong to a great family circle, with the Mikado as the titular head; the Mikado in essence becomes the family. (The extended meaning of family [*ie*] in the Japanese sense has been explained in these pages.)

Cherry blossoms and Japan are inseparable. As Kosawa points out "the essence of the Japanese spirit is as the fragrance of the cherry blossoms." One of my translators (Murayama) commenting on the symbolic significance of cherry blossoms recalled an old quotation: "Hana-wa sakura-gi, nito-wa bushi." ("Amongst flowers the highest, most esteemed is the cherry, and among men the *samurai*.") The nationalistic significance of the *samurai* has already been amply discussed in these pages, and from this quotation it cannot be disputed that the cherry blossom is equated with the feudal *samurai*.

The Mount Fuji symbolism (referred to by Kosawa) according to Murayama includes such ideas as: "Mount Fuji is the great personality whose head is above the clouds and looks down over the landscape. No earthquake, no storm, nor any of the elements disturb Mount Fuji." Mount Fuji is a symbol of permanence, and as Fuji is big, a man must have that sense of tranquility or equanimity in the same measure.

The last two sentences of the symbols of national

character quoted above seem innocuous enough in their present setting, but these words also could paraphrase just as well the more ominous intent of the Japanese jingoists.

At long last, the difficulty in understanding the Japanese psychology and the Japanese brand of psychoanalysis is resolved. The Japanese nation is not considered by the Japanese to be an aggregate of separate, distinct, and different individuals. Japan is thought to be a homogeneous entity. Perhaps this could best be understood by thinking of Japan itself as being a super-individual. No majority of Japanese could alter this position. They could not alter the form nor the type of government. Because of its implications for the future, this type of thinking is ominous, and perhaps more of of us should be aware of it. We should think about the fact that the Japanese government is not constituted as an instrument to serve the Japanese people. Instead the Japanese people are considered instruments to serve the Japanese government. The popular rights of the Japanese people (*minken*) are subordinated to the nationalistic institution (*kokken*) epitomized in the regality of the emperor.

By way of contrast it might be said that Thomas Jefferson and his colleagues caused to be set up a constitution for the United States of America that could be altered at any time, provided that a majority of eligible Americans utilized the proper machinery for making the change. Armed with this knowledge about the United States, and with the knowledge about the nature of Japan, it is possible to solve the enigma of their psychoanalytic pronouncement. As it has been emphasized before, Japan is an entity, a lone or single individual, an animate entity, its abstract anthropomorphism being identical with the person of the emperor. This information, gleaned irrefutably from their psychoanalytic productions, provides us with a least common denominator. It is thus possible to consider the topographical stratifications of the psyche (originally schematized by Freud) from the Japanese point of view. Keeping the Japanese ethnocentricity in mind, it even makes sense.

In their frame of reference, or better, in the framework of this least common denominator, the occidental individual is analogous to Japan conceptualized as an individual (Kami-god). This permits the syncretization of the idea of the Freudian id. The amorphous id, like Japan, is without boundaries and is timeless. The id fits the coevality concept, the concept that Japan, having no beginning or end, is coeval with heaven, earth, and the Mikado. It follows and is easily comprehensible that the Japanese identity the superego with the unlimited power and person of the emperor. This thought is not too much different from many of the Christian assumptions of a punishing God. In the adaptation accomplished by the Japanese psychoanalysts, the conscious ego becomes synonymous with an awareness of the cardinal principles of the national entity of Japan.

All of this sounds very good and even to some extent convincing, but it must not be forgotten that the adaptation of Freudian psychoanalysis to fit the prerequisites of the cardinal principles of the national entity of Japan is a super abstraction that extends beyond the tangible limits of reality.

ACKNOWLEDGMENTS

In the preparation of this book I have been most fortunate in the generous help and interest accorded me by a large number of friends and colleagues. I am deeply grateful for the open-handed manner in which these people have offered their encouragement and advice, and for the freedom I have felt to turn to them for their valued judgments whenever necessary.

The original idea for the subject matter came to me through talks with Dr. Lionel Blitzsten, of Chicago, who has himself made several trips to Japan. To Dr. Blitzsten belongs recognition for my realization of the importance of an understanding of Japanese psychoanalysis.

Special thanks are due the following people for help rendered through personal consultation and correspondence: Mr. Clark Gregory, of the Legal Section, Far East Command, who supplied me with a great deal of information which would have been impossible to obtain without his assistance; Mr. Shinji Arai, of Tokyo, who made some investigations on my behalf; Mr. A. J. Levin, of Franklin, Michigan, whose help has been invaluable and varied, both in his suggestions regarding the form of the manuscript, which he painstakingly read at various stages, and in his calling my attention to source material, as well as generously permitting me to quote from some of his own writings-in-process; Dr. Heisaku Kosawa, of the Kosawa Psychoanalytical Hospital in Tokyo, who has been liberal with his time in an

219

effort to acquaint me with the psychoanalytic movement in Japan. (Dr. Kosawa also allowed me to use some thirty issues of *Seishin Bunseki,* the *Tokyo Journal of Psychoanalysis,* which he is presenting to the Menninger Foundation for its permanent collection. Only a half dozen copies of this publication have previously been available in this country, even in the Library of Congress.) Dr. Tsuneo Muramatsu extended me many courtesies during my visits to the Orient, and has also furnished me with considerable information through correspondence. Mr. George P. Murdock, Professor of Anthropology, Yale University, and Dr. Ashley Montagu, Professor of Anthropology, Rutgers University, both supplied me with helpful information in personal communications. I am most grateful to Mr. T. Frank Mayer-Oakes, Assistant Professor of History, Wayne University, Detroit, who has read and discussed the manuscript and greatly enlarged my knowledge of the Japanese.

I am equally grateful, for translations from many copies of *Seishin Bunseki,* to Mr. Anthony Yasutake, of Royal Oak, Michigan, and to Dr. Kiyomi Koizumi, graduate of Tokyo Women's Medical College and now holder of a scholarship in physiological chemistry (awarded by the Medical Branch of the Presbyterian Board of Foreign Missions) at Wayne University College of Medicine. Dr. Koizumi has also given me information regarding the teaching of psychology and psychoanalysis in Japan. Dr. Fritz Redl, Professor of Social Work, School of Public Affairs and Social Work, Wayne University, furnished me with a translation of an article in Esperanto in the journal, and Mr. John Winzen, of Detroit, was most helpful in rendering into English a number of articles in German in the same publication. I am indebted to Dr. Mary Kosai, graduate of Tokyo Women's Medical College, who is engaged in post-graduate study at Wayne University College of Medicine, who translated a number of articles in Japanese in *Psychiatria et Neurologia Japonica*. Makio Murayama, research biochemist at Harper Hospital, Detroit, Michigan, translated into English several chapters of Kiyoyasu Marui's volume on psychoanalysis and compared Marui's viewpoint with the ideas set down in *Kokutai No Hongi, the Cardinal Principles of the National Entity of Japan*. Michael Watanabe, Physics Department, Wayne University, translated for me several articles from various issues of the *Seishin Bunseki*.

Mr. Yasutake has called my attention to several Japanese culture-patterns, knowledge of which has assisted me in preparation of this book. Miss Roxane Lambie, who was stationed in Japan with the American Red Cross after World War II, has also added helpful comments from her own observations. Miss Vehanoush Zakarian, of the Veterans' Administration in Detroit, directed my attention to the Nalbandian poem which I have quoted in Chapter 1. Dr. Charles Barker, of the staff of Pontiac State Hospital, Pontiac, Michigan, provided me with the statistics on schizophrenia which appear in Chapter 5.

I am grateful to the Surgeon General of the United States Navy, who expedited my first visit to the Orient in 1945. It was the Surgeon General of the United States Army under whose command I made my second trip in 1949, as psychiatric consultant for the Medical Section, Far East Command.

Special thanks are due my son James, who spent many hours in the public library checking reference material for me. I am also deeply indebted to the staffs of the Baldwin Public Library, Birmingham, Michigan, the Detroit Public Library, Wayne University Library, the *Detroit News* Library, and the Library of Congress who gave unstintingly of their time, skillfully ferreting out obscure information for me.

Dr. Theodore J. G. Locher, Professor of History at the University of Leiden, The Netherlands, currently Netherlands Exchange Professor of History at the University of Michigan, and Dr. John Hall, instructor in history at the University of Michigan, were most helpful in investigating some little-known facts about the American-Japanese Kanagawa Treaty for use in Chapter 10.

Muramatsu's "Background Report" appears substantially in *World Tension,* under the title of "Japan." I wish to acknowledge Dr. George W. Kisker's permission to quote extensively.

The laborious job of typing the manuscript was accomplished by Mrs. Robert C. Pettit, Miss Ann Williams, William Martmer, and Miss Lambie. My wife typed many pages of translation from Mr. Winzen's dictation. I am indebted to Mrs. Meo Rank for her critical proof reading and for her many valuable suggestions that improved the manuscript.

A mimeographed copy of the manuscript was sent to each of twenty-five experts representing a variety of disciplines. Many of the responses of these experts have been incorporated in the final draft of the manuscript. I am especially indebted to Edward Glover, Ernest Jones, Robert E. Ward, Geza Roheim, Weston LaBarre, J. R. Rees, Frank Fremont-Smith, Jarl Wagner Smitt, and J. C. Carothers for their well considered and painstaking criticisms.

J.C.M.

References for Chapter 1

AMERICAN INDIVIDUALISM, JAPANESE CONFORMITY, AND PSYCHOANALYSIS

* Page 1—Songs of liberty are usually contained within rigid verse-structures. The poet confines himself to previously defined channels for expression of his hopes. The poetic framework is strictly designed with meter, accent, and number of lines severely regulated. The English sonnet is composed of 14 lines. In Japan, the *hokku* and the *waka* are considered permissible outlets for inventiveness, originality or individual strivings. Even though the last two are considered expressions of free enterprise, they still indicate Japanese restraint: the *hokku* is regularly composed of 17 syllables and the *waka* of 31. A poetic plea for liberty is delivered in a straight-jacket. (See Tsuneo Muramatsu, "Japan: Some Psychological Perspectives," *Background Report,* 12, October, 1949.)

1 M. C. Nalbandian, "Liberty," *The Poetry of Freedom,* edited by William Rose Benét and Norman Cousins, translated by Alice Stone Blackwell (New York: Random House, 1945), pp. 779-780. (Accompanying note: "Mr. Nalbandian was born in Russian Armenia. Exiled and died of lung disease contracted in prison. In Czarist Russia this poem, printed around the margin of Nalbandian's proscribed portrait, was circulated secretly.")

2 James Clark Moloney, M.D., and Laurence Rockelein, "A New Interpretation of Hamlet," *International Journal of Psychoanalysis,* XXX, Part II (1949).

* Page 2—Italics mine, J.C.M.

** Page 2—*In einem gesellschaftlichen Verhaftnis*—"In a society relationship between individuals."

*** Page 2—*In einem gemeinschaftlichen Verhaftnis*—"In a community relationship between individuals."

3 Tsuneo Muramatsu, M.D., "Japan: Some Psychological Perspectives," *Background Report* (Oct., 1949), p. 3.

4 Holly Whyte, "The Class of '49," *Fortune* (June, 1949).

5 George P. Murdock, Professor of Anthropology, Yale University. Personal communication.

6 Bruno Bettelheim and Emmy Sylvester, "Delinquency and Morality," *The Psychoanalytic Study of the Child,* V (New York: International

University Press, Inc., 1950), pp. 329-342.

* Page 4—Not to be confused with the *psychiatric* aim, which is to effect an adjustment between the individual and his environment, manipulating the environment or urging the individual toward an environment in which he can feel comfortable. The *psychoanalyst*, on the other hand, attempts to free the individual from his inner thongs, allowing him to become a mature adult, capable of adjusting to any reasonable environment.

* Page 5—Weston LaBarre, in "Some Observations on Character Structure in the Orient," (*Psychiatry*, Vol. VIII, No. 3) remarks that the anthropologist who has spent some time in a foreign culture finds, upon returning home, that his own culture seems strange to him.

7   Muramatsu, op. cit., p. 2.

8   Ibid., p. 2.

9   Ibid., pp. 2-3.

10   Ibid., p. 3.

11   John C. Pelzel, "Some Social Factors Bearing Upon Japanese Population." *American Sociological Review*, XV, No. 1, (Feb., 1950), p. 20.

12   Ibid., p. 22.

13   Ibid., pp. 22-23.

14   Ibid., p. 22.

15   Ibid., p. 23.

16   Dr. Ph. Fr. Von Siebold, *Manners and Customs of the Japanese* (London: John Murray, 1841), p. 217.

17   Ibid., p. 130.

18   Charles Peter Thunberg, M.D., *Travels in Europe, Africa, Asia, Etc.* III, (London: F. & C. Rivington, 1796), p. 267.

19   Von Siebold, op. cit., p. 172.

20   G. B. Sansom, *The Western World of Japan* (New York: Alfred A. Knopf, 1950), p. 228.

21   Townsend Harris, *The Complete Journal of Townsend Harris* (Garden City, New York: Doubleday, Doran & Co., 1930), pp. 352-353.

22   Nyozekan Hasegawa, *Japanese National Character*, Board of Tourist Industry, Japanese Government Railways (1942), p. 29.

23   Robert King Hall (ed.) *Kokutai No Hongi* (*Cardinal Principles of the National Entity of Japan*), translated by John Owen Gountlett (Cambridge, Mass.: Harvard University Press, 1949), p. 65.

24   Talcott Parsons, "Population and Social Structure," *Japan's Prospect* (Cambridge, Mass.: Harvard University Press, 1946), p. 95.

25   Muramatsu, op. cit., p. 19.

26   Douglas G. Haring, "The Challenge of Japanese Ideology," *Japan's Prospect* (Cambridge, Mass.: Harvard University Press, 1946), p. 261.

27   Seiji G. Hishida, Ph.D., *The International Position of Japan as a Great Power* (New York: Columbia University Press, 1905), p. 131.

28   Hall, op. cit., p. 81.

29   Ibid., p. 93.

* Page 13—Usually Romanized *kō*, and borrowed from a Chinese ideograph meaning piety toward ancestors as well as living parents. The

REFERENCES

Japanese usage means "filial piety."

** Page 13—Prior to 1867 *chu* meant loyalty toward a military lord (*daimyo*).

30 Ruth Benedict, *The Chrysanthemum and the Sword* (Boston: Houghton Mifflin, 1946), p. 220.

31 Inazo Nitobe, *Bushido: The Soul of Japan* (New York: Putnam, 1905), p. 4.

32 Weston LaBarre, "Some Observations on the Character Structure in the Orient," *Psychiatry*, IX, No. 4, (Nov., 1946), pp. 375-395.

33 Muramatsu, op. cit., p. 4.

34 Fred N. Kerlinger, "Decision Making in Japan," *Social Forces*, XXX, No. 1, pp. 36-41.

References for Chapter 2

CHILD TRAINING AND JAPANESE CONFORMITY

35 Von Siebold, op. cit., p. 176.
36 Geofrey Gorer, "Themes in Japanese Culture," *Transactions of the New York Academy of Science*, V (1943), pp. 106-124.
37 Benedict, op. cit., p. 259.
38 Mildred Sikkema, "Observations of Japanese Early Training," *Psychiatry: Journal of the Biology and the Pathology of Interpersonal Relations*, X (1947), pp. 423-432.
 * Page 18—Sikkema made her studies on Hawaiian Orientals. Many of her subjects were Okinawans (those who have "iro" in their names), and Okinawans do not believe in bowel training.
39 Lecomte du Nouy, *Human Destiny* (New York: Longmans, Green & Co., 1947), pp. 209-210.
40 Thunberg, op. cit., p. 124.
41 Ibid., p. 252f.
42 Dorothy Menpes (ed. and trans.), Mortimer Menpes, *Japan: A Record in Colour* (London: Charles Black, 1905), pp. 140-141.
43 Lafcadio Hearn, *A Japanese Miscellany* (Boston: Little, Brown, and Co., 1901), p. 152.
44 Sansom, op. cit., p. 362 and elsewhere.
45 Francis Ottiwell Adams, *The History of Japan* (London: Henry S. King & Co., 1875), II, p. 324.
46 Joseph H. Longford, *The Story of Old Japan* (New York; Longmans, Green & Co., 1910), pp. 372-373.

References for Chapter 3

CONFORMITY AND RAGE IN THE JAPANESE MALE

47 John Dollard, Leonard W. Doob, Neal E. Miller, O. H. Mowrer, Robert R. Sears, *Frustration and Aggression* (New Haven, Conn.: Yale University Press, Institute of Human Relations, 1939), p. 1.
48 Jules H. Masserman, M.D., *Principles of Dynamic Psychiatry* (Philadelphia: W. B. Saunders Co., 1946), pp. 220-221.
49 Rempei Sassa, M.D., *Psychiatria et Neurologia Japonica*, XLII, 8 (Aug., 1938). Translated by Dr. Mary Kosai.
50 "A Study of Hostility in Allergic Children," *American Journal of Ortho-psychiatry*, XX (July, 1950), pp. 506-519.
51 Edwin O. Reischauer, *The United States and Japan* (Cambridge, Mass.: Harvard University Press, 1950), p. 117.
52 Ryuji Nakamura, M.D., "Suicide and Psychopathy," *Psychiatria et Neurologia Japonica*, XLIV, 7, (July, 1940).
53 The Right Hon. Sir Ernest Satow, *A Diplomat in Japan* (London: J. B. Lippincott Co., 1927), pp. 345-346.
54 Benedict, op. cit., p. 264.
* Page 30—From a personal communication from Clark Gregory, Legal Section, Far Eastern Command, who heard of these practices while attending the war crimes trials of Japanese conducted at Manila. See also A. Frank Reel, *The Case of General Yamashita* (Chicago: University of Chicago Press, 1949).

References for Chapter 4

CONFORMITY AND RAGE IN THE JAPANESE FEMALE

55 Dr. Ryugi Nakamura, "Suicide and Psychopathology," *Psychiatria et Neurologia Japonica*, XLIV, No. 7, (July, 1940). Translated by Dr. Mary Kosai.

56 Sidney L. Gulick, *Working Women of Japan* (New York: Missionary Education Movement of the United States and Canada, 1915), p. 15, quoting Alice M. Bacon, *Japanese Girls and Women*, (Boston: Houghton Mifflin, 1891), pp. 260-261.

* Page 33—At the time when the poem was written, the great tragedy would have been the absence of males to carry on the family line. In later periods of Japanese history, however, it became a matter of actual humiliation to produce no sons.

57 W. G. Aston, *A History of Japanese Literature* (London: William Heineman, 1896), p. 113.

58 Von Siebold, op. cit., p. 171.

59 Cornelia Spencer, *Understanding the Japanese* (New York: Aladdin Books, 1949), p. 168.

60 John Embree, *Suye Mura, A Japanese Village* (Chicago: University of Chicago Press, 1939), p. 81.

61 Adams, op. cit., p. 334.

* Page 38—Such writers as Sudo Nansui, mentioned by Yanaga as a political novelist, also concerned themselves with murder mysteries, frequently using female killers as their protagonists. (See Sansom, p. 417, *et ante.*)

62 James Clark Moloney, M.D., "Planned Infancy and the Paranoid Block to Human Progress," *The American Imago*, VII, No. 3, (1941).

References for Chapter 5

JAPANESE CONFORMITY AND INSANITY

63 Col. Henry A. Cotton and Col. Franklin G. Ebaugh, "Japanese Neuropsychiatry," *American Journal of Psychiatry*, CIII, No. 3, (Nov., 1946), pp. 342-348.

64 Milton M. Berger, "Japanese Military Psychiatry in Korea," *American Journal of Psychiatry*, CIII, No. 2, (Sept., 1946), pp. 214-216.

* Page 37—A private communication from the Department of Health of the Republic of Eire points, by way of contrast, to a similarly insignificant number of criminally insane, but perhaps one of the highest incidences of insanity in the world—666.9 mental patients per 100,000 population, as of December 31, 1949.

65 Leopold Bellak, *Dementia Praecox* (New York: Grune and Stratton, 1948), p. xiii.

66 Cotton and Ebaugh, loc. cit.

67 James Clark Moloney, M.D., "The Cornelian Corner and Its Rationale," *Problems of Early Infancy*. Transactions of the First Conference Josiah Macy, Jr. Foundation, (March 3-4, 1947), p. 20.

68 Douglas Haring. "Aspects of Personal Character in Japan," *Far Eastern Quarterly*, VI, No. 1, (Nov., 1946), p. 12.

69 James Clark Moloney, M.D., *Journal of Pastoral Care*, IV, Nos. 1-2.

70 Dr. Ph. Fr. Von Siebold, op. cit., p. 174.

71 Ibid., p. 174.

72 Rene A. Spitz, "Autoeroticism," *The Psychoanalytic Study of the Child*, III-IV (1949), p. 111.

73 James Clark Moloney, M.D., "How To Cherish The Infant and Free The Mother," *Mental Hygiene Bulletin*, VIII, No. 2, (1950), pp. 9-10.

* Page 45—See J. C. Moloney, M.D., *The Magic Cloak* (Wakefield, Mass.: Montrose Press, 1949), Chapter IV.

** Page 45—James Clark Moloney, M.D., *The Battle for Mental Health* (New York: The Philosophical Library, 1951), pp. 80-82.

74 James Clark Moloney, M.D., "Some Simple Cultural Factors in the Etiology of Schizophrenia," *Child Development*, XXII, No. 3, Sept., 1951).

References for Chapter 6

PSYCHO-DYNAMICS OF JAPANESE HATE DISPERSAL

75 A. J. Levin, "The Oedipus Myth in History and Psychiatry," *Psychiatry*, II, No. 3, (August, 1948), pp. 292-293.

76 Frederick Wertham, *Dark Legend* (New York: Book Find Club, by arrangements with Duell, Sloan and Pearce, 1941), p. 24.

77 Heisaku Kosawa, "Two Types of Guilt Consciousness—Oedipus and Azase," *Tokyo Journal of Psychoanalysis* (March-April, 1935).

78 Ibid. (More will be said later of this article and its implications).

79 Muramatsu, op. cit., p. 4.

80 Hall, op. cit., p. 99.

81 Nyozekan Hasegawa, op. cit., pp. 62-63.

 * Page 57—More will be said of the duality patterns in subsequent pages. See also G. B. Sansom, *The Western World and Japan* (New York: Alfred A. Knopf, 1950), p. 174, 338 and elsewhere.

82 Geza Roheim, "The Psychology of Patriotism," *The American Imago*, VII, No. 1, (March, 1950), p. 3.

83 Ibid., quoting Sandor Petofi.

84 Ibid., p. 7.

85 *Ko Ji Ki*, "Records of Ancient Matters," by Basil Hall, 2nd Ed. annotation by W. C. Aston (J. L. Thomson & Co., Kobe, 1932), published about 900 (written by a group of scholars from Korea); Compiled by Oli-no-Yasumaro from oral sources in the 5th year of the Wado Era of Empress Gemmyo (712 A.D.). Until *Ko Ji Ki* was written by the scholars there was a sinistry which handed down oral chanting—done for over 700 years. Yasumaro was asked to direct Korean writers who wrote down the chanting—as in the "Begots" in Old Testament.

86 *Nipon O Dai Itsi Ran* or *Annals of the Emperors of Japan*, translated by Isaac Titsingh, reviewed & corrected by M. J. Klaproth (London: Parbury, Allen & Co., 1834).

87 James Murdock, *A History of Japan*, I (London: Kegan, Paul Trench, Trubner & Co., Ltd., 1926), pp. 51-52, and elsewhere.

88 Hall, op. cit., pp. 75-76.

89 Kenji Ohtski, "Womanliness of the Japanese Spirit," *Seishin Bunseki* (July-August, 1940).

90 Sibylle K. Escalona, "An Appraisal of Some Psychological Factors in

REFERENCES

Relation to Rooming-In and Self-Demand Schedules," *Transactions of the First Conference on the Problems of Early Infancy,* Josiah Macy, Jr. Foundation, New York, 1947.

* Page 60—Anyone in a superior role, as for example an analyst, is considered a father-substitute: *oya bun,* in the position of father; *oya kato,* on the side of the father; *oya gokoro,* with the heart of the father. (See Muramatsu.)

** Page 60—Kwambaku: an official aide through whom knowledge of all proceedings of State came to the emperor; the highest official position, taking precedence even over the Chancellor of the Empire. (Prince Ito's *Commentaries on the Constitution,* p. 88.)

*** Page 60—Shikken: the chief executive of the Shogun during the Kamakura Period (1192-1333), often translated as regent. Their influence soon eclipsed that of the Shogun (Webster).

91 Sir Rutherford Alcock, K.C.B., *The Capital of the Tycoons: A Narrative of a Three Years' Residence in Japan,* I (London: Longman, Green, Longman, Roberts & Green, 1863), p. 228.

92 Hall, op. cit., p. 23.

93 Moloney and Rockelein, op. cit., p. 15.

94 E. Lucas Bridges, *Uttermost Part of the Earth* (New York: E. P. Dutton & Co., Inc., 1950), p. 426. Weston LaBarre points out that: "the Ona story may be one of their etiological myths and not necessarily fact," (personal communication).

95 Sir Rutherford Alcock, K.C.B., op. cit., pp. 125-126.

96 Augusta M. Campbell Davidson, M.A., *Present-Day Japan* (London: T. Fisher Unwin, 1907), pp. 286-287.

97 J. F. Embree, op. cit., p. 201.

References for Chapter 7

THE EXTRA-NATIONAL DISPERSAL OF JAPANESE HATE

* Page 67—Sansom supplies one of the most thoughtful presentations of this matter. (Op. cit., pp. 210-211.)

98 Benedict, op. cit., p. 76.

99 Muramatsu, op. cit., p. 7.

100 Chitoshi Yanaga, *Japan Since Perry* (New York: McGraw-Hill, 1949), p. 169.

101 Adams, op. cit., p. 115. (See also Sansom, op. cit., p. 307.)

* Page 69—Commenting on the Satsuma Rebellion, Schwartz writes: "The strangest aspect of the affair, to a foreign mind, is that Saigo and his followers could thus take up arms against the national government, while at the same time they were making the loudest professions of loyalty to the emperor." (Schwartz, Henry B., *In Togo's Country;* Cincinnati: Jennings & Graham, 1908, p. 31.) Along with the matter of dispersal of hate, we see here the ambivalence so characteristic of the Japanese—an ambivalence whose origins may be found in the *Ara-mitama—Niji-mitama myth.* Probably, too, Saigo still made the distinction of Tokugawa days, when the emperor, with his god-like significance, was wholly separated from the administrative government. Thus Saigo's ambivalence would not be so difficult to account for, nor illogical; he was merely operating according to a no longer active spiritual and political concept.

102 Capt. Wassily Golownin, *Memoirs of a Captivity in Japan During the Years* 1811, 1812, *and* 1813, III (London: Henry Colburn & Co., 1824), p. 95.

* Page 71—The events of today have proved that the Chinese have lived up to the prophecy which Golownin made in 1824.

103 Ibid., II, pp. 32-35.

104 Charles Eliot, *Japanese Buddhism* (London: Edward Arnold & Co., 1935), pp. 199-200.

105 Ibid., p. 200.

106 Ibid., p. 200.

107 Ibid., p. 200.

108 Hall, op. cit., p. 24.

109 D. T. Suzuki, *Zen Buddhism and Its Influence on Japanese Culture*

REFERENCES

(Kyoto: Eastern Buddhist Society, Otani Buddhist College, 1938), p. 9.

110 Ibid., pp. 11-12.

111 C. Eliot, op. cit., p. 285.

112 Ibid., p. 286.

113 Ibid., p. 287.

114 Ibid., pp. 285-398.

115 Ibid., p. 397.

116 Ibid., p. 410.

117 J. Embree, op. cit., p. 230.

118 David Murray, *The Story of Japan* (New York: Putnam, 1894), pp. 184-187.

* Page 77—"Xavier's reports on his visit to Japan were enthusiastic. 'These,' he said, 'are the best people so far discovered, and it seems to me that among unbelievers no people can be found to excel them.' " (Sansom, op. cit., p. 115.)

119 Ibid., pp. 172-176.

120 Ibid., pp. 178-179.

** Page 77—This figure is far in excess of the estimate of Sansom, who puts the number at 150,000, mostly in western Japan, with some 10,000 in Kyoto and nearby provinces. (Sansom, op. cit., p. 127.)

121 Ibid., p. 187.

* Page 78—Sansom, too, gives recognition to this fact: "The Jesuits in Elizabethan England and in Japan were feared as agents of a temporal power that threatened national security by fomenting dissension within the realm." (Sansom, op. cit., p. 130.)

** Page 78—Sansom has a good deal to say on this point, indicating not only an ideological, but a cultural and even political and economic threat. (See Sansom, op. cit., pp. 118, 120, 121, 122, 128.)

122 Hall, op. cit., p. 22.

123 D. Murray, op. cit., pp. 202-204.

124 Ibid., p. 204.

125 Ibid., p. 204.

126 Ibid., pp. 204-205.

127 Ibid., p. 205.

* Page 79—Sansom, op. cit., p. 131.

128 Ibid., p. 241.

* Page 80—According to Sansom, the Bungo lords *sought* Jesuit aid, not the reverse. (Sansom op. cit., pp. 123-124.)

129 Ibid., p. 242.

130 Sansom, op. cit., pp. 122-123.

131 Murray, op. cit., p. 242.

** Page 80—Sansom indicates that the Church gradually came to understand such a move: ". . . the Jesuits found that for most men to adopt an alien faith was to abandon their own culture, because a culture is composed of many elements, and when one is destroyed, the whole structure disintegrates." (Sansom, op. cit., p. 118.)

132 Ibid., p. 243.

*** Page 80—The Japanese showed a fanatical eagerness for martyrdom,

REFERENCES

according to Sansom (op. cit., p. 129 and elsewhere).

133 Ibid., p. 244.
134 Ibid., pp. 246-247.
135 Ibid., p. 247.
136 Ibid., p. 247.
137 Ibid., p. 248.
138 Sansom, op. cit., p. 132.
139 Ibid., p. 176.
  * Page 82—This curious sort of reverse-action logic will become increasingly understandable as a part of the Japanese habit of syncretization described in subsequent pages, especially in Chapter 13.
140 Ibid., p. 176.
141 Ibid., pp. 129-130.
142 D. Murray, op. cit., p. 254.
143 Engelbertus Kaempfer, M. D., *The History of Japan* (London: Thomas Woodward, 1727), Book IV, p. 318.
144 Sansom, op. cit., p. 172.
145 D. Murray, op. cit., p. 265.
146 Ibid., pp. 262-265.
147 Ibid., p. 266.
148 Ibid., p. 268.
149 Lin Yutang (ed.), *The Wisdom of China and India* (New York: Random House, 1942), p. 580.
150 Golownin, op. cit., II, p. 136.
151 Alexander Michie, *The Englishman in China*, II (Edinburgh and London: William Blackwood & Sons, 1900), pp. 55-57.
152 Payson Treat, *The Early Diplomatic Relations Between the United States and Japan,* 1853-1865 (Baltimore: The Johns Hopkins Press, 1917), pp. 99-101.
153 John W. Foster, *American Diplomacy in the Orient* (New York: Houghton-Mifflin, 1903), p. 344.
154 Hall, op. cit., p. 35.
155 Sansom, op. cit., pp. 231-232.
156 Shigenobu Okuma, *Fifty Years of New Japan,* I (London: Smith, Elder & Co., 1910), p. 199.
157 Chitoshi Yanaga, *Japan Since Perry* (New York: McGraw-Hill Book Co., 1949), p. 132.

References for Chapter 8

THE ACADEMIC AND LEGAL STATUS OF
JAPANESE PSYCHOANALYSIS

158 Yanaga, op. cit., p. 577.
* Page 96—Anthony Yasutake, of Royal Oak, Michigan, has informed me as follows concerning the ancient Japanese custom of refraining from stepping on the shadow of a person from a higher class: according to this custom, it was disrespectful for a person from one social class to step on the shadow of a person from a social class above his. The lowest class, composed of farmers, merchants, and *eta* (literally, a "Person with four legs," the name given to slaves whom the Japanese had brought in from Korea) could be slain for violation of this tradition. This custom was abolished in 1869 by the Meiji government in its charter oath. Article IV of this oath stated in effect that: "All the absurd usages of former times should be disregarded, and the impartiality and justice displayed in the workings of nature be adopted as the basis of action."

References for Chapter 9

DO THE JAPANESE INTEGRATE, OR MERELY COPY WESTERN PSYCHOANALYSIS?

* Page 99—See also Hermann M. Spitzer, "Psychoanalytic Approaches to the Japanese Character," *Psychoanalysis and the Social Sciences,* edited by Geza Roheim (New York: International Universities Press, 1947), p. 131f.
159 Murray, op. cit., pp. 170-171.
160 William Elliot Griffis, *The Japanese Nation in Evolution* (New York: Thomas Y. Crowell & Co., 1907), pp. 245-246.
161 Thunberg, op. cit., pp. 39-40.
162 Inazo Nitobe, *Intercourse Between the United States and Japan* (Baltimore: Johns Hopkins Press, 1891), p. 62.
163 Treat, op. cit., pp. 50-52.
164 Townsend Harris, *The Complete Journal of Townsend Harris* (New York: Doubleday, Doran & Co., Inc., 1930), pp. 309-310.
164a Ibid., pp. 528-529.
165 Ibid., p. 529, quoting L. Adams Beck, "Unbroken Ways in South Japan," *Asia,* (April, 1923), p. 272.

References for Chapter 10

THE AMERICAN BLUEPRINT COPIED BY JAPANESE IMPERIALISTS

* Page 103—See also Herman M. Spitzer, "Psychoanalytic Approaches to the Japanese Character," *Psychoanalysis and the Social Sciences,* edited by Geza Roheim (New York: International Universities Press, 1947), pp. 131f.

166 James D. Richardson, *A Compilation of the Messages and Papers of the Presidents,* V, published by Authority of Congress, 1897.

167 Murray, op. cit., pp. 316-317.

168 Herbert H. Gowen, *An Outline History of Japan* (New York: D. Appleton & Sons, 1927), p. 294.

169 Ibid., pp. 294-295.

170 David S. Muzzey, *A History of Our Country* (Boston: Muzzey, Ginn & Co., 1945 ed.), p. 350.

171 Charles and Mary Beard, *Basic History of the United States* (Philadelphia: The Blakiston Co., 1944), p. 337.

172 Yanaga, op. cit., pp. 25-26.

173 Ibid., p. 15.

174 Ibid., p. 15.

175 Ibid., pp. 16-17.

* Page 107—For the conventional American attitude on shipwrecked sailors, see John W. Foster, *American Diplomacy in the Orient* (Boston: Houghton, Mifflin, 1903), pp. 144-145.

176 Yanaga, op. cit., p. 18.

177 Ibid., p. 18.

** Page 107—See also Francis L. Hawks, *Narrative of the Expedition of an American Squadron to the China Seas and Japan* (New York: D. Appleton & Co., 1856), pp. 297-298.

178 Claud E. Fuess, *Daniel Webster,* II (New York: Little, Brown & Co., 1930), p. 24.

179 James D. Richardson, op. cit., p. 78.

180 Ibid., p. 168.

181 Yanaga, op. cit., p. 17.

182 C. W. Stewart, *Early American Visitors to Japan,* referring to Proceedings U. S. Naval Inst., Vol. XXXI (1905) pp. 953-998, and Vol. XXXVII (1911) pp. 249-255, and Senate Ex. Doc. No. 59, 32nd Congress, 1st Session, pp. 2-63.

183 Thunberg, IV, p. 63.
184 Ibid., III, pp. 71-72.
185 Golownin, op. cit., pp. 15-16.
  •   Page 110—Gowen writes: "The old fable of the shell-fish which, re-
     tiring for safety within the shelter ot its shell, woke up to find itself
     upon the fishmonger's stall, labelled 1 *sen,* kept recurring more and
     more to the official mind at Yedo."—*Five Foreigners in Japan* (New
     York: Fleming H. Revell Co., 1936), p. 190.
186 Yanaga, op. cit., p. 16.
187 32nd Congress, 1st Session, Senate Ex. Doc. No. 59, pp. 78-79.
188 T. Harris, op. cit., p. 340.
  •   Page 111—There was, as a matter of fact, no good reason why either
     of these men should have been so confused. Both drew their informa-
     tion from Aaron Haight Palmer, who—whatever else may be said
     of him of a less favorable nature—at least fully understood the work-
     ings of the Japanese government and the protocol necessary to achieve
     the desired ends. For details and the development of this whole chap-
     ter of American-Japanese history, consult A. H. Palmer, *Documents
     and Facts Illustrating the Origin of the Mission to Japan* (Washing-
     ton, D. C.: Henry Polkinhorn, 1857), pp. 5-20.
189 T. Harris, op. cit., Appendix VI, pp. 575-576.
190 Ibid., pp. 451-452.
191 Ibid., pp. 485-486.
192 Ibid., pp. 485-486.
193 Ibid., p. 554.
194 Ibid., p. 316.
195 Ibid., p. 312.
196 Gowen, op. cit., pp. 306-307.
  •   Page 113—Personal communication from Dr. T. J. G. Locher.
197 P. Treat, op. cit., p. 73.
198 William E. Griffis, *Millard Fillmore: Constructive Statesman, Defender
     of the Constitution, President of the United States* (Ithaca, N. Y.:
     Andrus and Church, 1915), p. 103.
199 Sansom, op. cit., p. 142.
200 Ibid., p. 143.
201 Ibid., p. 145.

References for Chapter 11

JAPANESE IDENTIFICATION WITH THE ENEMY

* Page 116—Defined by Jules Massermann as "Wishful adoption, mainly unconscious, of the personality characteristics or identity of another individual, generally one possessing advantages which the subject envies and desires." *Principles of Psychiatry* (Philadelphia: W. B. Saunders, 1946), p. 281.

** Page 116—And to be sure, this would apply to the Japanese, who include the fear of the father among the "four fearful things in the world," along with earthquake, thunder, and fire.—Muramatsu, *Background Report*, p. 8, quoting Bertram Schaffner, *Fatherland, A Study of Authoritarianism in the German Family*.

202 J. H. Gubbins, *The Progress of Japan* 1853-1871 (Oxford: Clarendon Press, 1911), p. 159.

203 H. Gowen, op. cit., quoting Tyler Bennett, *Americans in Eastern Asia* Ch. XXI (New York: D. Appleton & Co., 1927), pp. 310-311.

204 Henry B. Schwartz, op. cit., pp. 136-137.

205 Marshall T. Newman and Ransom L. Eng, "The Ryukyu People: A Biological Appraisal," *American Journal of Physical Anthropology*, N. S., Vol. No. 2, (June, 1947), p. 120.

206 William L. Langer, (ed.), *An Encyclopedia of World History* (Boston: Houghton, Mifflin Co., 1948), p. 891.

207 John W. Foster, op. cit., p. 378.

208 Yanaga, op. cit., p. 429.

209 Foster, op. cit., p. 382.

210 F. L. Hawks, 33rd Cong., 2nd Sess., S. Ex. Doc. 79, as quoted by Payson Treat, *Early Diplomatic Relations Between the United States and Japan* 1853-1865 (Baltimore: Johns Hopkins Press, 1917), pp. 143-144.

* Page 122—In fairness it should be noted that there were other American lessons to be utilized by the Japanese, not all of which were learned. For example, "In June, 1879 [the Emperor Meiji received former President Ulysses S. Grant in audience] Grant said that a government based on the people, whether it be a republic or a monarchy, was the strongest and that a popularly elected assembly should eventually be established in Japan. However, he emphasized

that once a popular assembly was established it could never be taken away from the people; therefore, caution must be exercised in avoiding the confusion that would arise from its premature establishment. Slow and gradual progress toward a constitutional government was advisable. . . ." Chitoshi Yanaga, *Japan Since Perry,* p. 166 The influence of Okuma and others in the government was so heavily overbalanced in favor of the British and later of Ito, who favored the German form of government, that the cautions and advice of Grant went for nought.

211 H. Gowen, op. cit., pp. 300-301.
212 Yanaga, op. cit., p. 110.
213 J. D. Richardson, op. cit., p. 168.
  • Page 124—In 1846, the Japanese required Biddle to leave Tokyo Bay, serving him with a curt note: "We are aware that our customs are in this respect [i.e., refusal to permit foreigners to visit, or even set foot on land in Japan] different from those of some other nations, but every nation has a right to manage its own affairs in its own way." —Herbert H. Gowen, op. cit., p. 194. Observe the similarity of both this Japanese note that actually preceded the Fillmore message to Congress (1852), and the Japanese note to Cordell Hull to Fillmore's message to Congress.
214 R. Benedict, op. cit., p. 44.
215 Hall, op. cit., Appendix p. 195.
216 Ibid., p. 195.

References for Chapter 12

THE PSYCHOANALYTIC MOVEMENT IN JAPAN

217 Robert B. Textor, *Failure in Japan, with Keystones for a Positive Policy* (New York: The John Day Co., 1951), p. 34.

* Page 128—It was in 1941, evidently soon after Ohtski wrote his history of the Japanese psychoanalytic movement, that the Japanese government ordered suspension of publication of *Seishin Bunseki,* the reason given being the paper shortage. A communication to me of January, 1952 proudly announced resumption of publication.

* Page 129—A letter from Dr. Glover states: "I cannot recall with any accuracy how long Prof. Yabe was in analysis with me: It was, if I remember rightly, limited by his stay here [London] to not less than six months and not more than nine. It was, so far as I can remember, a simple and straightforward analysis. Prof. Yabe had a good deal of insight and a simple and sympathetic personality."

** Page 129—Dr. Kiyoyasu Marui differed with Ohtski on the matter of the analysis of Japanese analysts outside the country. He wrote to me that there were three so analyzed, and, interpreting my question about whether the "first analysts in Japan" were analyzed as being, as I meant, the first several (plural) replied in the affirmative. Ohtski apparently thought I meant the first one (singular). There is a strange discrepancy, too, between Ohtski's article on the history of psychoanalysis and his letter quoted above: In the article he does not credit Yabe with being the first analyst in Japan, as he does in his letter.

*** Page 129—More will be said later of the importance of Japanese customs.

**** Page 129—Although not mentioned here, Yabe received his .didactic training under Dr. Ernest Jones while being analyzed by Glover.

* Page 130—This "weakness of character" statement, if made in the United States, might lead to a libel suit. But in this caption it might mean a difficulty in translation, or that Yabe was too Japanese, too addicted to *mimpi* and *giri,* to become an individualist.

* Page 134—The post-war issues will be discussed subsequently.

* Page 135—My translator, Dr. Koizumi, informs me that many members of these societies, even though they may be contributors to *Seishin Bunseki* or other journals, are not analysts or even psychiatrists or doctors. Prince Iwakura is one of these lay members.

241

References for Chapter 13

THE KEY TO THE UNDERSTANDING OF JAPANESE PSYCHOANALYSIS

218 Muramatsu, *Background Report,* op. cit., pp. 2-12.

219 See Chapter I.

220 *Nibon Shakai No Shiteki Kyomei,* (An Historical Study of Japanese Society). Edited by the Rekishigaku Kenkyukai (The Historical Science Society), Tokyo: Iwanami Shoten, 1949, v, p. 340. Reviewed in the *Far Eastern Quarterly,* Vol. XI, No. 1, Nov., 1951, by John Whitney Hall, p. 103.

 * Page 140—This word had to be coined because there was no word for popular rights in the Japanese language up until shortly after the Meiji Restoration. (See Sansom, op. cit., p. 312.)

221 Nobutaka Ike, *The Beginnings of Political Democracy in Japan* (Baltimore: The Johns Hopkins Press, 1905), p. 202.

222 Hall, op. cit., p. 65.

 * Page 142—Footnote, Hall, p. 170, reads: "The first Emperor, so called, was a warrior; hence, what almost amounts to a play on his name."

223 Hall, op. cit., p. 170.

224 Ibid., p. 176.

225 J. Murdoch, op. cit., p. 193.

226 Capt. F. Brinkley, *A History of the Japanese People* (New York: Encyclopedia Britannica, 1915), p. 193. See also Basil Hall Chamberlain, *Things Japanese* (London: John Murray, 1905), p. 421.

227 Hall, op. cit., p. 175.

228 Yoshida Kumaji, Member, Research Section, Natl. Spirit Cultural Research Institute (NSCRI); Kihira Masami, Member of the NSCRI; Watsuji Tetsuro, Professor, Tokyo Imperial University; Inoue Takamaro, Member of the NSCRI; Sakuda Soichi, Professor, Kyoto Imperial University; Kuroita Katsumi, Professor Emeritus, Tokyo Imperial University; Ohtsuka Takematsu, Official compiler of materials for the History of the Reformation; Hisamatsu Sen-ichi, Professor, Tokyo Imperial University; Yamada Yoshio, Professor, Tohoku Imperial University; Iijima Tadao, Professor, the Peers' School; Fujikake Shizuya, Professor, Tokyo Imperial University; Miyaji Naokazu, Official in charge of historical researches; Kono Shozo, President, Kokugakuin University; Ui Hakuju, Professor, Tokyo Imperial University.

REFERENCES

229 Chief of the Bureau of Thought Control of the Ministry of Education. Hall, p. 7.

230 Hall, op. cit., pp. 156-157.

231 Ibid., p. 178.

* Page 145—Italics mine. JCM.

232 Hall, op. cit., p. 179.

233 Ibid., p. 183.

234 Ibid., pp. 156-157.

* Page 147—Italics mine. JCM.

235 Hall, op. cit., pp. 181-182.

236 Ibid., p. 175.

237 A. J. Levin, *Oedipus and Samson and the Rejected Hero-Child*, MS in process, quoting Bronislaw Malinowski, *Myth in Primitive Psychology* (London: Kegan Paul, Trench, Trubner & Co., Ltd., 1926), pp. 123-124 and elsewhere.

238 Footnote in Sir Edward Reed, *Japan: Its History, Traditions and Religions*, I (London: John Murray, 1880), p. 29.

239 J. Murdoch, III, op. cit., p. 476.

240 Ibid., p. 344.

241 Ibid., p. 344.

242 Edwin O. Reischauer, *Japan, Past and Present* (New York: Alfred A. Knopf, 1951), pp. 126-127.

243 Ibid., p. 127.

244 Ibid., p. 127.

245 Robert B. Textor, op. cit., p. 17.

* Page 150—See also G. B. Sansom, op. cit., pp. 320-322, 387-388, 934.

246 Textor, op. cit., p. 15 quoting John M. Maki, *Japanese Militarism* (New York: Alfred A. Knopf, 1945), p. 156.

References for Chapter 14

EXAMPLES AND INTERPRETATIONS OF JAPANESE PSYCHOANALYTIC WRITINGS

* Page 154—Mr. Mayer-Oakes informs me that Japanese analysts, by virtue of their exalted educational position, would probably have been considered by the government, and have considered themselves, leaders in the nations. Thus they and their journals would probably not have been subjected directly to scrutiny by the Bureau; but *giri* would have required them to govern their own thinking and writing by the concepts of the national entity program.

247 Sigeaki Tukazaki, "The Psychological Point of View of Illness," *Seishin Bunseki* (May-June, 1940), translated by Fritz Redl, Ph.D.

248 Kenji Ohtski, "Character Defects of the Japanese and Their Cause," *Seishin Bunseki* (March-April, 1941), translated by Anthony Yasutake.

249 Yaekichi Yabe, "Super-Ego, Criminality, and Religiosity," *Seishin Bunseki* (October, 1933), translated by Kiyomi Koizumi.

250 *Seishin Bunseki* (March-April, 1941).

251 Hall, op. cit., p. 179.

* Page 165—Observe that this is almost the same phrasing as Hall's definition of coevality which appeared in Chapter 13.

252 L. Adams Beck, *The Story of Oriental Philosophy* (New York: Farrar and Rinehart, 1928), pp. 345-346.

253 Charles Francis Potter, *The Story of Religion* (Garden City, N. Y.: Garden City Publishing Co., 1929), p. 175.

254 Kenji Ohtski, "The National Character of the Japanese People," *Seishin Bunseki* (July-August, 1940), translated by A. Yasutake.

* Page 167—Italics mine. J.C.M.

255 Kenji Ohtski, op. cit., (Jan.-Feb., 1941).

256 Kenji Ohtski, op. cit., "The National Character of the Japanese People." "The Emperor is the symbol of the national super-ego. . . ."

257 *Seishin Bunseki* (Nov.-Dec., 1940).

258 Heisaku Kosawa, op. cit.

259 Ibid.

260 Sigeaki Tukazaki, op. cit.

261 Kenji Ohtski, "The Relation between Disease and Health," *Seishin Bunseki* (May-June, 1940), translation by Anthony Yasutake.

262 Furosenin Shu, "Hitler's Super-Ego." *Seishin Bunseki* (Nov., 1939),

REFERENCES

translated by Anthony Yasutake.

263 Prince Tomohide Iwakura, "Self-Love and Super-Ego," *Seishin Bunseki* (July, 1934), translated by Anthony Yasutake.

264 Ibid.

265 Kenji Ohtski, "Psychoanalytic Observations on Morals," *Seishin Bunseki* (Nov.-Dec., 1936), translated by Kiyomi Koizumi.

266 Kenji Ohtski, "On the Psychology of Jealousy and Revenge," *Seishin Bunseki* (Sept.-Oct., 1936), translated by Kiyomi Koizumi.

  * Page 174—Cf. Yabe's article "Super-ego, Criminality, and Religiosity," previously quoted in this chapter, p. 164.

267 Yaekichi Yabe, "Analysis of a Sleep Phobia," *Seishin Bunseki* (May. 1934), translated by Kiyomi Koizumi.

268 Yaekichi Yabe, "Personal Impressions of Dr. Edward Glover," *Seishin Bunseki* (Dec., 1933), translated by Kiyomi Koizumi.

269 Rikitaro Takamizu, "Psychoanalysis and Character Analysis," *Seishin Bunseki* (Jan.-Feb., 1936), translated by Kiyomi Koizumi.

270 Kenji Ohtski, "Problems of Sexual Self-Indulgence," *Seishin Bunseki* (May, 1939), translated by Anthony Yasutake.

271 See Sansom, op. cit.; Murdoch, op. cit., III; Nobutaka Ike, op. cit., et al.

272 Siujitu Tutiya, "Unconscious Logic of the East and West," *Seishin Bunseki* (Jan.-Feb., 1940), translated by Kiyomi Koizumi.

273 Kenji Ohtski, "Womanliness of the Japanese Spirit," op. cit., (July-August, 1940), translated by Anthony Yasutake.

274 Kenji Ohtski, "Re-Education of Japanese National Traits," *Seishin Bunseki* (April-May, 1941), translated by Kiyomi Koizumi.

275 Sansom, op. cit., p. 28.

276 Keiji Kurosawa, "Abnormal Morality During the Pacific Ocean War," *Seishin Bunseki* (July, 1950), translated by Kiyomi Koizumi.

277 Hachiro Mori, "Public Mind and Private Mind: A Psychological Analysis of a Mibushi Judge," *Seishin Bunseki* (June, 1950), translated by Kiyomi Koizumi.

278 Kikuo Nakamura, "Political Psychology and Psychoanalysis," *Seishin Bunseki* (Nov., 1950), translated by Kiyomi Koizumi.

References for Chapter 15

THE GOALS OF JAPANESE PSYCHOANALYSIS

279 Personal communication from Tsuneo Muramatsu, July 11, 1950.

* Page 201—It is almost certain, according to Dr. Koizumi, that this prince is a descendant of another by the same name who was Junior Prime Minister and Minister of Foreign Affairs in Japan in 1871. The first Prince Iwakura was a part of the embassy responsible for modification of treaties unfair to Japan. Neither was a prince in the sense of belonging to the emperor's blood-line, but was, rather, a peer comparable to British lords.

280 Muramatsu, op. cit., p. 15.

281 Douglas G. Haring, op. cit., p. 22.

* Page 202—The influence of this thinking is reflected in an article by Dr. Marui in *Psychiatria et Neurologia Japonica*, Vol. 42, No. 10, Oct., 1938, entitled "On Neurosis." The article, written a year after the publication of *Kokutai No Hongi*, suggests the psycho-biological orientation of Adolph Meyer.

282 Sigmund Freud, *An Outline of Psychoanalysis*, authorized translation by James Strachey (New York: W. W. Norton & Co., Inc., 1949), pp. 89-90.

283 Hall, op. cit., p. 200.

* Page 206—It will be remembered that Dr. Kosawa was the only medically trained psychoanalyst in the Tokyo Society at the time of my meeting with him in Japan. He is now with the Sendai group.

* Page 209—There is little reason to feel that this concept would have been destroyed, even when overlaid with the terminology of the Occupation.

284 Erich Kahler, *Man the Measure* (New York: Pantheon Books, Inc., 1943), pp. 32-33.

285 Sansom, op. cit., p. 77.

286 Ibid., p. 474.

287 Ibid., p. 82.

288 Department of State: *Occupation of Japan: Policy and Progress*, Appendix 13, completed August, 1945, as quoted in Lawrence K. Rosinger and Associates, *The State of Asia: A Contemporary Survey* (New York: Alfred A. Knopf, 1951), p. 185.

289 Hall, op. cit., p. 44.

INDEX

247

INDEX

INDEX